First World War
and Army of Occupation
War Diary
France, Belgium and Germany

37 DIVISION
63 Infantry Brigade
York and Lancaster Regiment
10th (Service) Battalion
1 August 1916 - 28 January 1918

WO95/2529/3

The Naval & Military Press Ltd
www.nmarchive.com
Published in association with The National Archives

Published by

The Naval & Military Press Ltd

Unit 10 Ridgewood Industrial Park,

Uckfield, East Sussex,

TN22 5QE England

Tel: +44 (0) 1825 749494

www.naval-military-press.com

www.nmarchive.com

This diary has been reprinted in facsimile from the original. Any imperfections are inevitably reproduced and the quality may fall short of modern type and cartographic standards.

© Crown Copyright
Images reproduced by permission of The National Archives, London, England, 2015.

Contents

Document type	Place/Title	Date From	Date To
Heading	WO95/2529/3		
Heading	Reference WO95 2529 10th Bn York & Lancs Regt. Aug 1916-Jan 1918 Conservation Department		
Heading	39th Division 63rd Infy Bde 10th Bn York & Lancs Regt. Aug 1916-Jan 1918. From 21 Div 63 Bde Disbanded		
Miscellaneous	37th Division "Q"	31/08/1916	31/08/1916
Heading	10th (Service) Battalion York and Lancaster Regiment War Diary August-1916. Twelvth Volume.		
War Diary	Camblain L'Abbe.	01/08/1916	02/08/1916
War Diary	Trenches	06/08/1916	08/08/1916
War Diary	Estree-Cauchie	12/08/1916	12/08/1916
War Diary	Dieval	13/08/1916	22/08/1916
War Diary	Estree Cauchie	23/08/1916	30/08/1916
Miscellaneous	10th (Ser) Battn. York & Lancaster Regiment. Appx I		
Miscellaneous	Operation Orders. By Lieut-Col. J.H. Ridgway, Comdg. 10th (S) Bn. York & Lancaster Regiment. Appx II	04/08/1916	04/08/1916
Miscellaneous	Operation Orders. By Lieut-Col. J.H. Ridgway, Comdg. 10th (S) Bn. York & Lancaster Regt. Appx III	11/08/1916	11/08/1916
Miscellaneous	Operation Orders. By Lieut-Col. J.H. Ridgway, Comdg. 10th (S) Bn. York & Lancaster Regiment. Appx IV	13/08/1916	13/08/1916
Miscellaneous	Operation Orders. By Lieut-Colonel J.H. Ridgway, Comdg. 10th (S) Bn. York & Lancaster Regiment. Appx V	22/08/1916	22/08/1916
Operation(al) Order(s)	Operation Orders. No. 2 By Lieut-Colonel J.H. Ridgway, Comdg. 10th (S) Bn. York & Lancaster Regiment. Appx VI	22/08/1916	22/08/1916
Miscellaneous	10th (Ser) Battn. York & Lancaster Regiment.	31/08/1916	31/08/1916
Heading	10th (Service) Battalion York and Lancaster Regiment. War Diary. September-1916. Thirteenth Volume.		
War Diary	Estree Cauchie	01/09/1916	01/09/1916
War Diary	Bajus	04/09/1916	13/09/1916
War Diary	Fresnicourt	16/09/1916	16/09/1916
War Diary	Bois De Noulette	17/09/1916	19/09/1916
War Diary	Trenches	24/09/1916	27/09/1916
War Diary	Bois De Noulette	30/09/1916	30/09/1916
Miscellaneous	List of Appendices.		
Miscellaneous	10th (Ser) Battn. York & Lancaster Regiment. Appendix No. 1		
Operation(al) Order(s)	Operation Orders No. 77. By Lieut-Col. J.H. Ridgway, Comdg. 10th (S) Bn. York & Lancaster Regiment. Appendix No. 2	03/09/1916	03/09/1916
Operation(al) Order(s)	Operation Order No. 78. By Lieut-Col. J.H. Ridgway, Comdg. 10th (S) Bn. York & Lancaster Regiment. Appendix No. 3	15/09/1916	15/09/1916
Operation(al) Order(s)	Operation Order No. 79. By Lieut-Colonel J.H. Ridgway, Comdg. 10th (S) Bn. York & Lancaster Regiment. Appendix No. 4	16/09/1916	16/09/1916

Type	Description	Date From	Date To
Operation(al) Order(s)	Operation Order No. 80. By Lieut-Colonel J.H. Ridgway, Comdg. 10th (S) Bn. York & Lancaster Regt. Appendix No. 5	23/09/1916	23/09/1916
Operation(al) Order(s)	Operation Orders No. 81. By Lieut-Colonel J.H. Ridgway, Comdg. 10th (S) Bn. York & Lancaster Regiment. Appendix No. 6	29/09/1916	29/09/1916
Miscellaneous	Honours and Awards. Appendix No. 7		
Heading	10th Battalion York and Lancaster Regiment. War Diary. October-1916. Fourteenth Volume. 14		
War Diary	Bois De Noulette	01/10/1916	01/10/1916
War Diary	Trenches	06/10/1916	09/10/1916
War Diary	Lorette	12/10/1916	12/10/1916
War Diary	Fresnicourt	16/10/1916	16/10/1916
War Diary	Villers. Brulin	18/10/1916	18/10/1916
War Diary	Etree Wamin	20/10/1916	20/10/1916
War Diary	Amplier	21/10/1916	21/10/1916
War Diary	Terramesnil	22/10/1916	28/10/1916
Miscellaneous	List of Appendices.		
Miscellaneous	Honours & Rewards. Appendix No. 1		
Miscellaneous	10th Battn. York & Lancaster Regt. Casualties during the month of October 1916. Appx 2		
Miscellaneous	10th Battn. York & Lancaster Regiment. Appendix No. 3	30/10/1916	30/10/1916
Operation(al) Order(s)	Operation Orders No. 82. By Captain W.B. Drynan, Comdg. 10th Battn. York & Lancaster Regiment. Appendix 4	05/10/1916	05/10/1916
Operation(al) Order(s)	Operation Orders No. 83. By Captain W.B. Drynan, Comdg. 10th Battn. York & Lancaster Regiment. Appendix No. 5	08/10/1916	08/10/1916
Operation(al) Order(s)	Operation Orders No. 84. By Captain W.B. Drynan, Comdg. 10th Battn. York & Lancaster Regiment. Appendix No. 6	11/10/1916	11/10/1916
Operation(al) Order(s)	Operation Orders. No. 85. By Captain W.B. Drynan, Comdg. 10th Bn. York & Lancaster Regiment. Appendix No. 7	15/10/1916	15/10/1916
Operation(al) Order(s)	Operation Orders No. 86. By Lt-Colonel J.H. Ridgway, Comdg. 10th Battn. York & Lancaster Regt. Appendix No. 8	17/10/1916	17/10/1916
Operation(al) Order(s)	Operation Orders No. 87 By Lt-Colonel J.H. Ridgway Comdg. 10th Battn. York & Lancaster Regiment. Appendix No. 9	19/10/1916	19/10/1916
Operation(al) Order(s)	Operation Order No. 88. By Lt-Col. J.H. Ridgway, Comdg. 10th Battn. York & Lancaster Regiment. Appendix No. 10	20/10/1916	20/10/1916
Operation(al) Order(s)	Operation Order No. 89. By Lt-Colonel. J.H. Ridgway, Comdg. 10th Battn. York & Lancaster Regiment. Appendix No. 11	21/10/1916	21/10/1916
Miscellaneous	37th Division "Q"	05/12/1916	05/12/1916
Heading	10th (Service) Battalion The York And Lancaster Regiment. War Diary. November-1916. Fifteenth Volume.		
War Diary	Terramesnil	01/11/1916	08/11/1916
War Diary	Acheux Wood	12/11/1916	12/11/1916
War Diary	Trenches	14/11/1916	16/11/1916
War Diary	Hamel	20/11/1916	20/11/1916
War Diary	Englebelmer	24/11/1916	24/11/1916

War Diary	Mailly Maillet	25/11/1916	25/11/1916
War Diary	Rancheval	26/11/1916	26/11/1916
War Diary	Terramesnil	01/12/1916	01/12/1916
Miscellaneous	List of Appendices.		
Miscellaneous	10th Battn. York & Lancaster Regiment. Appendix No. 1	30/11/1916	30/11/1916
Miscellaneous	10th Battn. York & Lancaster Regiment. Appendix No. 2		
Operation(al) Order(s)	Operation Order No. 90. By Lt-Colonel J.H. Ridgway, Comdg. 10th Battn. York & Lancaster Regiment. Appx 3	02/11/1916	02/11/1916
Operation(al) Order(s)	Reference Operation Orders No. 90 of 2.11.1916. Appendix I.	02/11/1916	02/11/1916
Operation(al) Order(s)	Reference Operation Orders No. 90 of 2.11.1916. Appendix II.	02/11/1916	02/11/1916
Operation(al) Order(s)	Reference Operation Order No. 90 of 2.11.1916 Appendix III.	02/11/1916	02/11/1916
Operation(al) Order(s)	Amendment to Appendix II of Operation Orders No. 90		
Operation(al) Order(s)	Amendment to Operation Orders No. 90, dated 2.11.1916. By Lt-Colonel J.H. Ridgway, Comdg. 10th Bn. York & Lancaster Regiment.	02/11/1916	02/11/1916
Operation(al) Order(s)	Operation Orders No. 91. By Lt-Colonel J.H. Ridgway, Comdg. 10th Battn. York & Lancaster Regiment. Appendix No. 4	11/11/1916	11/11/1916
Operation(al) Order(s)	Operation Orders No. 92. By Lt-Colonel J.H. Ridgway, Comdg. 10th Bn. York & Lancaster Regt. Appendix No. 5	12/11/1916	12/11/1916
Miscellaneous	10th Battn. York & Lancaster Regiment. Appx 6	13/11/1916	13/11/1916
Miscellaneous	Extract from Battalion Orders dated 27th November 1916. Appx 7	27/11/1916	27/11/1916
Operation(al) Order(s)	Operation Orders No. 91A. By Lt-Colonel J.H. Ridgway, Comdg. 10th Bn. York & Lancaster Regiment. Appendix No. 8	23/11/1916	23/11/1916
Operation(al) Order(s)	Operation Orders No. 92A. By Lt-Colonel J.H. Ridgway, Comdg. 10th Bn. York & Lancaster Regiment. Appendix No. 9	24/11/1916	24/11/1916
Operation(al) Order(s)	Operation Orders No. 93. By Lt-Colonel J.H. Ridgway, Comdg. 10th Battn. York & Lancaster Regiment. Appendix No. 10	25/11/1916	25/11/1916
Heading	10th (Service) Battalion The York and Lancaster Regiment. War Diary. December-1916. Sixteenth Volume.		
War Diary	Terramesnil	01/12/1916	13/12/1916
War Diary	Ransart	14/12/1916	14/12/1916
War Diary	Aubrometz	15/12/1916	15/12/1916
War Diary	Fleury and Conteville	16/12/1916	16/12/1916
War Diary	Nedonchelle	17/12/1916	17/12/1916
War Diary	Busnes	18/12/1916	20/12/1916
War Diary	La Fosse	22/12/1916	31/12/1916
Miscellaneous	List of Appendices.		
Miscellaneous	10th Battn. York & Lancaster Regiment. Roll Of Officers. Appendix No. 1	30/11/1916	30/11/1916
Miscellaneous	10th Bn. York & Lancaster Regt. Appendix No. 2		
Operation(al) Order(s)	Operation Orders No. 94 By. Lt-Colonel J.H. Ridgway, Comdg. 10th Bn. York & Lancaster Regiment. Appendix No. 3	30/11/1916	30/11/1916

Miscellaneous	Battalion Orders dated 7th December 1916. Appendix No. 4	08/12/1916	08/12/1916
Operation(al) Order(s)	Operation Orders No. 95. By Lt-Colonel J.H. Ridgway, Comdg. 10th Bn. York & Lancaster Regiment. Appendix No. 5	13/12/1916	13/12/1916
Miscellaneous	Extracts from 37th Div. No. 2/168 dated 12th December 1916	12/12/1916	12/12/1916
Operation(al) Order(s)	Operations Orders No. 96. By Lt-Colonel J.H. Ridgway, Comdg. 10th Bn. York & Lancaster Regiment. Appendix No. 6	14/12/1916	14/12/1916
Operation(al) Order(s)	Operations Orders No. 97. By Lt-Colonel J.H. Ridgway, Comdg. 10th Battn. York & Lancaster Regiment. Appendix No. 7	15/12/1916	15/12/1916
Operation(al) Order(s)	Operations Orders No. 98. By Lt-Colonel J.H. Ridgway, Comdg. 10th Bn. York & Lancaster Regiment. Appendix No. 8	16/12/1916	16/12/1916
Operation(al) Order(s)	Operations Orders No. 99. By Lt-Colonel J.H. Ridgway, Comdg. 10th Bn. York & Lancaster Regiment. Appendix No. 9	17/12/1916	17/12/1916
Operation(al) Order(s)	Operations Orders No. 100. By Lt-Colonel J.H. Ridgway, Comdg. 10th Bn. York & Lancaster Regiment. Appendix No. 10	21/12/1916	21/12/1916
Heading	The 10th (Service) Battalion, The York and Lancaster Regiment. War Diary January-1917 Seventeenth Volume.		
War Diary	Zelobes	01/01/1917	01/01/1917
War Diary	Trenches	02/01/1917	03/01/1917
War Diary	Bout Deville	08/01/1917	08/01/1917
War Diary	Zelobes	15/01/1917	26/01/1917
War Diary	Le Touret	29/01/1917	31/01/1917
Miscellaneous	List of Appendix, War Diary, January 1917		
Miscellaneous	10th Batt. York & Lancaster Regiment Appx 1	31/01/1917	31/01/1917
Miscellaneous	10th Battalion York & Lancaster Regiment. Appx 2		
Operation(al) Order(s)	Operation Orders No. 101. By Lt-Colonel J.H. Ridgway, Comdg. 10th Battn. York & Lancaster Regiment. Appx 3	01/01/1917	01/01/1917
Operation(al) Order(s)	Operation Orders No. 102. By Lt-Col. J.H. Ridgway. D.S.O. Comdg. 10th Bn York & Lancs Regt. Appx 4	06/01/1917	06/01/1917
Operation(al) Order(s)	Operation Order No. 103. By Major W.B. Drynan, Comdg. 10th Bn York & Lanc. Rgt. Appx 5	28/01/1917	28/01/1917
Miscellaneous	10th Battalion York & Lancaster Regiment. Appx 6		
Miscellaneous	To. 37th. Division "Q".	28/02/1917	28/02/1917
Heading	The 10th (Service) Battalion, The York and Lancaster Regiment. War Diary. February-1917. Eighteenth Volume.		
War Diary	Essars	01/02/1917	11/02/1917
War Diary	Les. Brebis	12/02/1917	12/02/1917
War Diary	Trenches	13/02/1917	17/02/1917
War Diary	Village Line	19/02/1917	19/02/1917
War Diary	Trenches	25/02/1917	27/02/1917
Miscellaneous	List of Appendices, War Diary, January 1917		
Miscellaneous	10th Battalion York & Lancaster Regiment. Appx No. 1		
Miscellaneous	10th. Battn. York & Lancaster Regiment. Appendix No. 2	28/02/1917	28/02/1917

Operation(al) Order(s)	Operation Orders No. 105 By Major W.B. Drynan, Comdg. 10th Bn. York & Lancaster Regt. Appendix No. 3	31/01/1917	31/01/1917
Operation(al) Order(s)	Operation Orders No. 106 By Lt-Col. J.H. Ridgway, D.S.O., Comdg. 10th York & Lancaster Regt. Appendix No. 4	10/02/1917	10/02/1917
Operation(al) Order(s)	Operation Orders No. 107 By Lt-Col. J.H. Ridgway, D.S.O., Comdg. 10th Bn. York & Lancaster Regt. Appendix No. 5	17/02/1917	17/02/1917
Operation(al) Order(s)	Operation Orders No. 108 By Lt-Col. J.H. Ridgway, D.S.O., Comdg. 10th Bn. York & Lancaster Regt. Appendix No. 6	24/02/1917	24/02/1917
Operation(al) Order(s)	Operation Orders No. 109 By Lt-Col. J.H. Ridgway, D.S.O., Comdg. 10th York & Lancaster Regt. Appendix No. 7	27/02/1917	27/02/1917
Heading	The 10th (Service) Battalion, The York and Lancaster Regiment. War Diary March-1917 Eighteenth Volume		
War Diary	Trenches	01/03/1917	01/03/1917
War Diary	Mazingarbe	03/03/1917	03/03/1917
War Diary	Bethune	04/03/1917	04/03/1917
War Diary	Le Hamel	05/03/1917	05/03/1917
War Diary	St. Hilaire	06/03/1917	06/03/1917
War Diary	Valhuon	09/03/1917	09/03/1917
War Diary	Houvin-Houvigneul	10/03/1917	31/03/1917
Miscellaneous	List of Appendices.		
Miscellaneous	10th Battn York & Lancaster Regiment. Appx No. 1	29/03/1917	29/03/1917
Miscellaneous	10th Battalion York & Lancaster Regiment Appendix No 2		
Operation(al) Order(s)	Operation Orders No. 110. By Lt-Col. J.H. Ridgway, D.S.O., Comdg. 10th York & Lancaster Regt. Appx No. 3	01/03/1917	01/03/1917
Operation(al) Order(s)	Operation Orders No. 111 By Lt-Col. J.H. Ridgway, D.S.O., Comdg. 10th York & Lancaster Regt. Appendix No. 4	03/03/1917	03/03/1917
Operation(al) Order(s)	Operation Orders No. 112 By Lt-Col. J.H. Ridgway, D.S.O., Comdg. 10th York & Lancaster Regt. Appx No. 5	04/03/1917	04/03/1917
Operation(al) Order(s)	Operation Orders No. 113 By Lt.-Col. J.H. Ridgway, D.S.O., Comdg. 10th York & Lancaster Regt. Appendix No. 6	05/03/1917	05/03/1917
Operation(al) Order(s)	Operation Orders No. 114 By Lt.-Col. J.H. Ridgway, D.S.O., Comdg. 10th York & Lancaster Regt. Appendix No. 7	08/03/1917	08/03/1917
Operation(al) Order(s)	Operation Orders No. 115 By Lt.-Col. J.H. Ridgway, D.S.O., Comdg. 10th York & Lancaster Regt. Appendix No. 8	09/03/1917	09/03/1917
Heading	The 10th (Service) Battalion The York and Lancaster Regiment. War Diary. April 1917 Nineteenth Volume		
War Diary	Houvin-Houvigneul	01/04/1917	05/04/1917
War Diary	Noyellette	07/04/1917	07/04/1917
War Diary	Duisans	08/04/1917	08/04/1917
War Diary	Trenches	09/04/1917	09/04/1917
War Diary	Arras	12/04/1917	12/04/1917
War Diary	Agnez-Les Duisans	14/04/1917	14/04/1917
War Diary	Manin	15/04/1917	18/04/1917
War Diary	Gouves	19/04/1917	19/04/1917

War Diary	Trenches	20/04/1917	28/04/1917
War Diary	Manin	29/04/1917	29/04/1917
Miscellaneous	List of Appendices.		
Miscellaneous	10th Battalion York and Lancaster Regiment.		
Miscellaneous	10th Battalion York & Lancaster Regiment. Appx 2	30/04/1917	30/04/1917
Miscellaneous	10th Battalion York & Lancaster Regiment. Appx 3	13/04/1917	13/04/1917
Operation(al) Order(s)	Operation Order No. 116. By Lt-Col. J.H. Ridgway D.S.O. Comdg. 10th York & Lancs Regt. Appx 4	04/04/1917	04/04/1917
Operation(al) Order(s)	Operation Order No. 118. By Lt-Col. J.H. Ridgway D.S.O. Comdg. 10th York & Lancs Regt. Appx 5	07/04/1917	07/04/1917
Miscellaneous	Battalion moved by March Route to Agnez-Les-Duisans in early morning No. Operation Order was Published Owing urgency of move Appx 6	13/04/1917	13/04/1917
Operation(al) Order(s)	Operation Order No. 121. By Lt-Col. J.H. Ridgway D.S.O. Comdg. 10th York & Lancaster Regt. Appx 7	18/04/1917	18/04/1917
Miscellaneous	10th. York & Lancaster Regiment Instruction No. 1. Appx 8	04/04/1917	04/04/1917
Miscellaneous	10th. York & Lancaster Regiment. Instructions No. 2 Appx. 9		
Miscellaneous	Report On Operations Covering Period 9th to 12th April 1917. Appx 10	09/04/1917	09/04/1917
Operation(al) Order(s)	Operations Orders No. 124 (Provisional) By Lt. Col. J.H. Ridgway, D.S.O. Comdg. 10th York & Lancaster Regiment Appx 11	21/04/1917	21/04/1917
Operation(al) Order(s)	Operations Orders No. 125 By Lieut R.M. Wilkinson, Comdg. 10th York & Lancaster Regt. Appx 12	27/04/1917	27/04/1917
Miscellaneous	Report On Operations Covering Period from 22nd to 29th April 1917 Appx 13	22/04/1917	22/04/1917
Heading	War Diary of the 10th (Service) Battalion York and Lancaster Regiment. May 1917 Twenty first Volume.		
Heading	The 10th (F) Battalion The York and Lancaster Regiment. War Diary May 1917 Twenty first Volume		
War Diary	Manin	01/05/1917	17/05/1917
War Diary	Simencourt	18/05/1917	18/05/1917
War Diary	Achicourt	19/05/1917	25/05/1917
War Diary	Tilloy-Les Mouflaines	25/05/1917	28/05/1917
War Diary	Arras	31/05/1917	31/05/1917
Miscellaneous	List of Appendices		
Miscellaneous	10th Bn York & Lancaster Regt.	30/04/1917	30/04/1917
Miscellaneous	10th Bn York & Lancaster Regiment Nominal Roll Of Officers On Fighting Strength	31/05/1917	31/05/1917
Miscellaneous	10th Bn York & Lancaster Regiment		
Operation(al) Order(s)	Operation Orders No. 126 By Lt. Col. E.E.F. Simkins Comdg. 10th York & Lancaster Regiment	17/05/1917	17/05/1917
Operation(al) Order(s)	Operation Orders No. 127 By Lt. Col. E.E.F. Simkins Comdg. 10th York & Lancaster Regt.	18/05/1917	18/05/1917
Operation(al) Order(s)	Operation Orders No. 128 By Lt. Col. E.E.F. Simkins Comdg. 10th York & Lancaster Regt.	28/05/1917	28/05/1917
Operation(al) Order(s)	Operation Orders No. 129 By Lt. Col. E.E.F. Simkins Comdg. 10th Bn York & Lancaster Regt.	30/05/1917	30/05/1917
Heading	War Diary of the 10th Battalion York & Lancaster Regiment June 1917 Twenty Second Volume		
War Diary	Beaufort	01/06/1917	02/06/1917
War Diary	Croisette	05/06/1917	05/06/1917
War Diary	Heuchin	06/06/1917	06/06/1917
War Diary	Fruges	07/06/1917	17/06/1917

War Diary	Fruges	20/06/1917	20/06/1917
War Diary	Westrehem	22/06/1917	22/06/1917
War Diary	Thiennes	23/06/1917	23/06/1917
War Diary	Caestre	24/06/1917	24/06/1917
War Diary	Brulooze	25/06/1917	26/06/1917
War Diary	Trenches	28/06/1917	30/06/1917
Miscellaneous	List of Appendices		
Miscellaneous	10th Battalion York and Lancaster Regt Roll of Officer-June 1917		
Miscellaneous	10th Battn York and Lancaster Regt Strength-June 1917		
Miscellaneous	Honours, Awards Mention in Dispatches		
Operation(al) Order(s)	Operation Orders No. 131 By Lt. Col E.E.F. Simkins Comdg 10th York & Lancaster Regt	04/06/1917	04/06/1917
Operation(al) Order(s)	Operation Orders No. 132 By Lt. Col. E.E.F. Simkins Comdg 10th York & Lancaster Regt	05/06/1917	05/06/1917
Operation(al) Order(s)	Operation Orders No. 133 By Lt. Col. E.E.F. Simkins Comdg 10th York & Lancaster Regt	06/06/1917	06/06/1917
Operation(al) Order(s)	Operation Orders No. 134 Night Operations	20/06/1917	20/06/1917
Operation(al) Order(s)	Operation Orders No. 135 By Lt. Col. A.B. Layton Comdg 10th York & Lancaster Regt	21/06/1917	21/06/1917
Miscellaneous	After Order		
Operation(al) Order(s)	Operation Orders No. 136 By Lt. Col. A.B. Layton Comdg. 10th York & Lancaster Regt	22/06/1917	22/06/1917
Operation(al) Order(s)	Operation Orders No. 137 By Lt. Col. A.B. Layton Comdg. 10th York & Lancaster Regt.	23/06/1917	23/06/1917
Operation(al) Order(s)	Operation Orders No. 138 By Lt. Col A.B. Layton Comdg. 10th York & Lancaster Regt	24/06/1917	24/06/1917
Operation(al) Order(s)	Operation Orders No. 139 By Lt. Col A.B. Layton Comdg. 10th York & Lancaster Regt.	28/06/1917	28/06/1917
Operation(al) Order(s)	Operation Orders No. 140 By Lt. Col. A.B. Layton Comdg. 10th York & Lancaster Regt	29/06/1917	29/06/1917
Heading	10th (Service) Battalion York & Lancaster Regiment War Diary July 1917 Twenty Third Volume		
War Diary	Trenches	01/07/1917	01/07/1917
War Diary	Kemmel-Dranoutre	02/07/1917	02/07/1917
War Diary	Billeting Area	03/07/1917	03/07/1917
War Diary	Trenches	11/07/1917	18/07/1917
War Diary	Camp	19/07/1917	21/07/1917
War Diary	Trenches	25/07/1917	26/07/1917
War Diary	Camp	26/07/1917	27/07/1917
War Diary	Trenches	29/07/1917	31/07/1917
Miscellaneous	List of Appendices.		
Miscellaneous	10th Batt York & Lancaster Regt Appx No 1	31/07/1917	31/07/1917
Miscellaneous	10th York and Lancaster Regiment Appx No 2	31/07/1917	31/07/1917
Operation(al) Order(s)	Operation Order No 141 By Lt Col. A.B. Layton Comdg 10th York & Lancaster Regt Appx No. 3	02/07/1917	02/07/1917
Operation(al) Order(s)	Operation Order No 142 By Lt Col. A.B. Layton, Comdg 10th York & Lancaster Regt Appx No. 4	10/07/1917	10/07/1917
Operation(al) Order(s)	Operation Order No 143 By Lt Col. A.B. Layton. Comdg 10th York & Lancaster Regt Appx No 5	13/07/1917	13/07/1917
Operation(al) Order(s)	Operation Order No 144 By Lt. Col. A.B. Layton, Comdg 10th York & Lancaster Regt. Appx No. 6	17/07/1917	17/07/1917
Operation(al) Order(s)	Operation Order No 145 By Lt Col. A.B. Layton Comdg 10th York & Lancaster Regt Appx No. 7	19/07/1917	19/07/1917
Operation(al) Order(s)	Operation Order No 146 By Lt Col. A.B. Layton Comdg 10th York & Lancaster Regt Appx No. 8	25/07/1917	25/07/1917

Operation(al) Order(s)	Operation Order No 148 By Lt Col. A.B. Layton, Comdg 10th York & Lancaster Regt Appx No. 9	20/07/1917	20/07/1917
Operation(al) Order(s)	Operation Order No 149 By Lt Col. A.B. Layton. Comdg 10th York & Lancaster Regt Appx No. 10	29/07/1917	29/07/1917
Operation(al) Order(s)	Operation Order No 147 By Lt Col. A.B. Layton, Comdg 10th York & Lancs Regt Appx No. 11	29/07/1917	29/07/1917
Miscellaneous	10th Battalion York & Lancaster Regiment. Appx No. 12	30/07/1917	30/07/1917
Heading	War Diary of the 10th York and Lancs August 1917 Vol XXIV		
Miscellaneous	To 37th Divn. H.Q.	06/09/1917	06/09/1917
War Diary	Dranoutre	01/08/1917	01/08/1917
War Diary	Locre	03/08/1917	03/08/1917
War Diary	Rossignol	08/08/1917	08/08/1917
War Diary	Trenches	15/08/1917	19/08/1917
War Diary	Rossignol	21/08/1917	22/08/1917
War Diary	Trenches	29/08/1917	30/08/1917
Miscellaneous	10th Bn York & Lancaster Rgt.		
Miscellaneous	10th Bn York & Lancaster Regiment	31/08/1917	31/08/1917
Heading	10th Battn. York & Lancaster Regiment. War Diary September 1917. XXV Volume		
Miscellaneous	37th Division "Q"	03/10/1917	03/10/1917
War Diary	Trenches	01/09/1917	01/09/1917
War Diary	Bois Confluent	02/09/1917	03/09/1917
War Diary	Kemmel	07/09/1917	07/09/1917
War Diary	Kokereele Camp	10/09/1917	10/09/1917
War Diary	Kokereele Camp	21/09/1917	21/09/1917
War Diary	Trenches	27/09/1917	30/09/1917
Miscellaneous	10th Bn. York & Lancaster Regiment		
Miscellaneous	10th Bn. York & Lancaster Regiment.	30/09/1917	30/09/1917
Heading	War Diary of The 10th Battalion, York And Lancaster Regiment. October 1917 Twenty sixth Volume.		
War Diary	Trenches	01/10/1917	06/10/1917
War Diary	Vierstraat	08/10/1917	08/10/1917
War Diary	Trenches	10/10/1917	10/10/1917
War Diary	Mont Kokereele	14/10/1917	15/10/1917
War Diary	Meteren	21/10/1917	31/10/1917
Miscellaneous	10th York & Lancaster Regiment.		
Heading	War Diary Of The 10th Battalion York & Lancaster Regiment. November 1917. Twenty Seventh Volume.		
War Diary	St. Jean Area.	01/11/1917	01/11/1917
War Diary	Meteren	06/11/1917	06/11/1917
War Diary	Locre	09/11/1917	09/11/1917
War Diary	Bois Confluent	10/11/1917	10/11/1917
War Diary	Dezon Camp	17/11/1917	17/11/1917
War Diary	Trenches	25/11/1917	25/11/1917
Miscellaneous	10th York & Lancaster Regiment.		
Miscellaneous	10th Battalion York & Lancaster Regiment.		
Heading	10th Service Battalion York & Lancaster Regiment War Diary 31st December 1917 Vol XXVIII		
War Diary	Trenches	01/12/1917	01/12/1917
War Diary	Support	06/12/1917	06/12/1917
War Diary	Reserve	13/12/1917	13/12/1917
War Diary	Trenches	21/12/1917	21/12/1917
War Diary	Support	21/12/1917	21/12/1917
War Diary	10th York & Lancaster Regiment	31/12/1917	31/12/1917

Miscellaneous	10th Bn York & Lancaster Regt		
Heading	63rd Brigade. 37th Division. Battalion Broken Up In February 1918. 10th Battalion York & Lancaster Regiment. January 1918		
Heading	10th Battalion York & Lancaster Regiment War Diary For January 1918 Vol 29		
Miscellaneous	10th Bn. York & Lancaster Regiment.		
Miscellaneous	10th York & Lancaster Regiment		
War Diary	In The Field	01/01/1918	28/01/1918

WO 95/25249/3

REFERENCE

WO

95

2529

**10th BN YORK & LANCS REGT.
AUG 1916 – JAN 1918**

CONSERVATION DEPARTMENT

37TH DIVISION
63RD INFY BDE

10TH BN YORK & LANCS REGT.
AUG 1916 - JAN 1918.

FROM 21DIV 63BDE

DISBANDED

Subject: War Diary.

32 " 10.Y&L Vol 12

37th Division "Q".

Herewith War Diary for the month of AUGUST for the Battalion under my Command, forwarded to you in accordance with 37th Divisional Routine Orders.

signature Lieut-Colonel.
31/8/1916. Comdg. 10th (S) Bn. York & Lancaster Regt.

Aug '16
Jan '18

CONFIDENTIAL.

10th (Service) Battalion
YORK and LANCASTER Regiment.

WAR DIARY.

AUGUST - 1916.

TWELVTH VOLUME.

Army Form C. 2118

WAR DIARY or INTELLIGENCE SUMMARY

10th (Service) Battn. York & Lancaster Regt.

(Erase heading not required.)

Place	Date	Hour	Summary of Events and Information	Remarks and references to Appendices
CAMBRAIN L'ABBE.	Aug. 1st		Bn. HdQrs and 1 Coy (C) billeted in CAMBRAIN L'ABBE, and 3 Coys (A.B.&D.) bivouced in BOIS-DES-ALLEAUX. The latter 3 Coys. finding working parties for Divnl Sectr.	Appx I.
	2nd		Reinforcement of 1 O.R. arrived from Base. 2/Lieut. E.S. CHAMBERS joined Battn. from 11th (Res) Bn.	Appx I.
TRENCHES.	6th		Battn relieved 8th Lines in BERTHONVAL II Sub Sector, having on right 4th MIDDX and on left the N.F.	Appx II.
	8th		Reinforcement of 3 O.R. arrived from 26th & 34th I.B.D.	Appx I.
ESTREE-CAUCHIE	12th		Divnl. Relief. 9th Divn relieving 34th. Battn relieved in BERTHONVAL II Sub Sectn by 5th Cameron Highrs and proceeded by route march to ESTREE-CAUCHIE taking over billets for one night in this village.	Appx III.
DIEVAL.	13th		Battn proceeded by route march to DIEVAL (not billets). Drawing etc carried out in this area until 22nd inst.	Appx IV.
	22nd		Bde attached to 9th Divn. 8 Offrs and 400 Other Ranks proceeded by route march to 9th Divn. Artillery for work on communications etc.	Appx V.
ESTREE-CAUCHIE.	23rd		Remainder of Battn proceeded by route march to ESTREE-CAUCHIE taking over original billets as occupied on night 12/13th inst.	Appx VI.
	24th		The part of Battn in ESTREE-CAUCHIE carrying out cleaning of all specialists etc.	
	29th		2 O.D.Cs left to join working party with 9th Divn R.A.	
	30th		2/Lt. Douglas departed for Eng'land with reference to his transfer to R.C.A. Lieut. H.W. SHOYES. joined Battn from 15th R(? Res) Battn.	Appx I.

Mitchell
Lt. Colonel.
Comdr 10th Bn. York & Lancaster Regt.

10th (Ser) Battn. York & Lancaster Regiment.   Appx I

Casualties incurred during the month of AUGUST 1916.

Date	Regtl.No.	Rank and Name		Nature of Casualty
7/8/16.	22109	Pte. Rollinson,	G.	Wounded.
	8554	L:C. Jackson,	G.W.	Killed in Action.
8/8/16.	22157	Pte. Wells,	E.	Wounded (to duty).
10/8/16.	12/894	Pte. Cox,	F.L.	Wounded.
	21923	: Wilby,	C.	Wounded.
	22896	: Williams,	C.J.	Killed in Action.
11/8/16.	17556	Pte. Stacey,	J.W.	Wounded.
	17363	: Hargreaves,	T.	Wounded.
12/8/16.	14435	L:C. Hallsworth,	W.	Died of Wounds, which were received same morning.
13/8/16.	19715	Pte. Watson,	F.	Wounded.
	15906	: Paley,	H.P.	Wounded.
	8510	Cpl. Ball,	C.H.	Accidentally Wounded (Died of Wounds - 16/8/1916).

Sick Wastage. - AUGUST 1916.

Officers.

Capt. E.G.J. Fairnie, to Field Amb (sick) 22/8/16.

Other Ranks.

Remaining in F.A. 31/7/16.	24.	
To Field Ambulance.	50.	74.
From Field Ambulance.	34.	
Remaining in F.A. 31/8/16.	12.	46.
Total sick Wastage.		28.

Strength - AUGUST 1916.

August 1st.   Effective Strength. 26 Officers.   874 Other Ranks.
             Available Strength. 26 Officers.   828 Other Ranks.

August 31st. Effective Strength. 25 Officers.   831 Other Ranks.
              Available Strength. 22 Officers.   813 Other Ranks.

Increase.   Officers.

     2/Lt. E.S. Chambers joined from 11th (Res) Battn. 2/8/1916.
     Lieut. H.W. Sames joined from 15th (Res) Battn. 30/8/1916.

   Other Ranks.

     1 Other Rank arrived from 34 Inf. Base Depot, 1/8/1916.
     3 Other Ranks arrived from 34 Inf. Base Depot, 8/8/1916.

Decrease.   Officers.

     Major J.B.O. Trimble to 11th Bn. East Yorks R. 17/8/1916.
     2/Lt. J.A. Heald transferred to Gen List (W.O. List No. 91 dated 15/7/1916).
     2/Lt. J. Douglas to England, 29/8/16, to report to War Office (on transfer to R.G.A.).

   Other Ranks.

     Casualties 11.   To Munitions 1.   Permanent Base 5.
     Under age (To England) 1.   Sick Wastage 28.   Total 47.

OPERATION ORDERS.

Appx II

By Lieut-Col. J.H. Ridgway,
Comdg. 10th (S) Bn. York & Lancaster Regiment.
4th AUGUST 1916.

1. The Battalion will take over Trenches BERTHONVAL II on night of 6th/7th AUGUST. Companies will take over the same lines as before with exception of A. Coy., who will be in support, D. Coy. taking their place in the line.

   Battalion will parade at 7.0 p.m. (Dress: Marching Order). Move off by half Companies at 200 yards interval by the same route as taken on coming out.

   Order of March: A. D. B. and C. Companies. Lewis Gunners and Signallers will leave at 6.0 p.m. and march in small parties. Guns will be carried from junction of VILLERS au BOIS Road and track leading across Heath.

   A. Company will take over their dug-outs and then go up for rations. Ration party will go up WORTLEY AVENUE as soon as last Company of Battalion is clear of that Avenue.

   Companies will arrange to take over mining fatigues at once on arrival, so that no interruption of work takes place.

   Stores to be taken to trenches must be kept down to the smallest amount required.

   Companies will report relief complete by sending the word "HOUDAIN".

   Transport will be at Headquarters Yard to take up all stores and Rations to Ration Dump at 6.30 p.m., and will not leave here till usual time for leaving.

   All Officers' valises and kits to be left at Q.M. Stores to be at C. Company Headquarters by 5.30 p.m.

(Sd) H. Broadbent, Lieut. & Adjt.
10th (S) Bn. York and Lancaster Regiment.

OPERATION ORDERS.   Appx III

By Lieut-Col. J.H. Ridgway,
Comdg. 10th (S) Bn. York & Lancaster Regt.
11th AUGUST 1916.

1. The Battalion will be relieved in trenches on night of 12th/13th AUGUST by 5th Cameron Highlanders.

2. Guides, one per platoon, one per section Lewis Gunners and one for Bombers, will report at Battalion Headquarters at 8.0 p.m. under Lieut. Elsworth, to guide Camerons from junction of BOYAU 123 and WORTLEY Avenue. Companies will come in in the following order :-
A. D. B. C.

3. Companies will hand over all working parties to incoming Companies, explaining what are permanent. There must be no break in the mining fatigues.

4. All stores to be handed over and a receipt obtained.

5. On relief Companies will report at Battalion Headquarters, ZOUAVE Valley, and then proceed to take over billets in ESTREE CAUCHIE.

6. It is probable that the Brigade will march at 7.0 p.m. on night of 13th inst.

7. Billeting party, under 2/Lt. Samuels, will parade at 2.0 p.m. 12th inst. at Battalion Headquarters.

8. Quartermaster's Stores and Transport will move to ESTREE CAUCHIE in their own time.

9. Transport Officer will arrange transport to be at CABARET ROUGE by 10.0 p.m. to remove stores.

10. Cooks under Master Cook will parade after teas and proceed to ESTREE CAUCHIE, and prepare breakfast for Companies on arrival. Probable hour of arrival 5.0 a.m.

(Sd) H. Broadbent, Lieut. & Adjt.
10th (S) Bn. York and Lancaster Regiment.

OPERATION ORDERS.   Appx IV

By Lieut-Col. J.H. Ridgway,
Comdg. 10th (S) Bn. York & Lancaster Regiment.
13th AUGUST 1916.

1. The Battalion will march to DIEVAL tonight, moving off at 7.0 p.m.

   Dress: Marching order with steel helmets.

2. Order of March: Headquarters, D., A., B., C.

3. Transport will follow in rear of Battalion. Lewis Gun Handcarts to march with first line transport. All baggage to be loaded by 6.0 p.m. Lieut. Knowles will superintend loading.

                                    (Sd) H. Broadbent, Lieut. & Adjt.
                        10th (S) Bn. York & Lancaster   Regiment.

OPERATION ORDERS.

Appx Y

By Lieut-Colonel J.H. Ridgway,
Comdg. 10th (S) Bn. York & Lancaster Regiment.
22nd AUGUST 1916.

1. The following working parties will parade today at 2.0 p.m., under Captain Drynan, on C. Company's Parade Ground.

    1. B. Company.   2 Officers.   100 Other Ranks.

    2. A. Company.   3 Officers.   100 Other Ranks.
        D. Company.   1 Officer.   100 Other Ranks.

    3. D. Company.   1 Officer.
        C. Company.   70 Other Ranks.

    4. C. Company.   20 Other Ranks.
        Bombers.   10 Other Ranks.
        A. Company.   1 Officer.

    The above are required for work on 9th Division R.A. Communications.
           No. 1 with   50th F.A. Bde.
           No. 2 with   51st F.A. Bde.
           No. 3 with   52nd F.A. Bde.
           No. 4 with   53rd F.A. Bde.

2. The above parties will march to GOUY SERVINS and Pt. W 18 a 5.7., via BRYAS, LA COMTE, Cross Roads P 9 d 7.4, ESTREE CAUCHIE.

    Each party will be met by guides as follows:-

    Nos. 1 and 2 at Railway Crossing at W 18 a 5.7 at 9.30 p.m.
    Nos. 3 and 4 at Church at GOUY SERVINS at 8.30 p.m.

3. 2 Cookers will accompany party, one for party of 100 and one for 200 party.

    Dixies will be taken by remaining parties.

    2 Limbers wagons will go with 200 parties.
    1 Limber wagon with 100 party.
    1 Limber wagon with 70 party.
    1 Limber wagon with 30 party.

4. Dress: Marching order. Steel helmets carried.

5. O.C. Parties will find out full particulars on morning of 23rd of the work required to be done.

6. Rations will be taken for 23rd. They will be rationed by 9th Division from 24th inclusive.

                                     (Sd) H. Broadbent, Lieut. & Adjt.
                    10th (Ser) Bn. York & Lancaster Regiment.

OPERATION ORDERS. No. 2.   Appx VI

By Lieut-Colonel J.H. Ridgway,
Comdg. 10th (S) Bn. York & Lancaster Regiment.
22nd AUGUST 1916.

1. The Battalion will march tomorrow to ESTREE CAUCHIE.

    Order of march: Headquarters, remainding men of Companies will fall in on C. Company's parade ground and be formed into one Company.

    Parade at 1.0 p.m.

    Route: BRYAS, LA COMTE, Cross Roads P 9 d 8.5, GAUCHIN LEGAL, ESTREE CAUCHIE.

    Dinners tomorrow at 11.30 a.m.

2. All Officers' kits etc. to be loaded in Field at Quartermaster's Stores by 12 noon.

    Transport will accompany the Battalion, and will park at GOUY SERVINS.

3. Billeting party will assemble at Orderly Room at 9.30 a.m.

    A cyclist guide will be at Cross Roads, W 5 Central at 6.0 p.m. to wait arrival of Supply Wagons, and then to lead them to ESTREE CAUCHIE.

                                (Sd) H. Broadbent, Lieut. & Adjt.
                        10th (Ser) Battn. York & Lancaster Regiment.

10th (Ser) Battn. York & Lancaster Regiment.

Roll of Officers serving in above Battalion - 31/8/1916.

Rank.	Name.		Date of Arrival.	Present Employment.	Special Training.
Lt-Col.	Ridgway,	J.H.	1/9/14.	Commanding Offr.	
Captain	McClellan,	C.D.St.G.	5/6/16.	Sick.	
Captain	Fitts,	R.H.	11/9/15.	Company Commdr.	Grenades.
:	Airey,	C.F.	11/9/15.	Transport Offr.	
:	Drynan,	W.B.	11/9/15.	Company Commdr.	Grenades. Lewis and Vickers' Guns.
:	Fairnie,	E.G.J.	19/11/15.	Sick.	Grenades.
Lieut.	Ramsden,	J.H.	10/10/15.	Company Commdr.	Grenades.
:	Groves,	S.J.S.	17/3/16.	Town Major, Fourth Army.	
:	Elsworth,	L.A.	11/9/15.	Intelligence O.	Grenades and Sniping.
:	Broadbent,	H.	11/9/15.	Adjutant.	Grenades and Signalling.
2nd Lt.	Hall,	D.A.	25/7/16.	Company Commdr.	Grenades.
:	Nicholson,	C.A.J.	6/1/16.	Platoon Commdr.	Grenades.
:	Wilkinson,	R.M.	9/10/15.	Staff duties, 103 Inf. Bde.	Grenades.
:	Knowles,	F.E.	9/10/15.	Platoon Commdr.	Grenades. Transport.
:	Mitchell,	R.J.	19/11/15.	Lewis Gun Offr.	Grenades. Lewis & Vickers Guns. Light Trench Mortar
:	Baines,	C.	9/10/15.	Attd. R.F.C. (on prob).	
:	Quance,	A.L.	10/3/16.	Platoon Commdr.	Grenades. Physical Training and Bayonet Fighting.
:	Ayres,	F.	10/11/15.	Sick.	Grenades. Vickers and Lewis Guns.
:	Payne,	F.E.	11/10/15.	Bombing Officer.	Grenades.
:	Hawley,	D.D.	29/5/16.	Platoon Commdr.	Musketry. Lewis Guns
:	Samuels,	E.	25/1/16.	Signalling Offr.	Grenades. Sign'l'ng.
:	Hockly,	A.	15/6/16.	Platoon Commdr.	Signalling. Light Trench Mortar.
:	Chambers,	E.S.	21/7/16.	Platoon Commdr.	Range Finding. Trench Warfare.
:	Lamond,	A.L.	21/12/14.	a/Quartermaster.	Grenades. Sign'l'ng.
Lieut.	Samea,	H.W.	25/8/16.	Platoon Commdr.	
Captain	Plaister,	G.R.	11/9/15.	Medical Officer, R.A.M.C.	

31/8/1916.

Lieut-Colonel.
Comdg. 10th (S) Bn. York & Lancaster Regt.

To/
63rd Infantry Brigade.

CONFIDENTIAL.

10th (Service) Battalion
YORK and LANCASTER Regiment.

WAR DIARY.

SEPTEMBER - 1916.

THIRTEENTH VOLUME.

Army Form C. 2118.

WAR DIARY
10th (Service) Bn. York & Lancaster Regt.
INTELLIGENCE SUMMARY
(Erase heading not required.)

Instructions regarding War Diaries and Intelligence Summaries are contained in F. S. Regs., Part II and the Staff Manual respectively. Title Pages will be prepared in manuscript.

Place	Date 1916 SEPT	Hour	Summary of Events and Information	Remarks and references to Appendices
ESTREE CAUCHIE	1st		Bn in billets at ESTREE CAUCHIE, 8 Officers and 400 other Ranks attached 9th Durt R.A. as working party. Lieut W.B.S. O'BRIEN joined Battn from England.	appx. No. 1.
BATUS.	4th		Battn (less W.P) marched by route march to BATUS occupying billets.	appx. No 2
	8th		Draft of 14 other Ranks joined from 34 I.S.D.	appx. No 1.
	11th		Lieuts H.W. CARTER & R. FISHER (Staffs. R) joined from 9th Durt I.S.D.	appx. No 1
	13th		Working party rejoined Battn from 9th Durt R.A. Lieut F.H. STROTHER joined from England.	appx. No 1.
FRESNICOURT	16th		Battn proceeded by route march to billets at FRESNICOURT, staying for one night.	appx. No 3.
BOIS DE NOULETTE	17th		Battn less Q.M. Stores and transport proceeded by route march to BOIS DE NOULETTE occupying billets. Q.M. Stores and transport to COUPIGNY.	appx. No 4.
	19th		Lieuts T.E. HILL & H.A. WALNE joined Battn from England. 1 other Rank joined from A.H.T.D. ABBEVILLE.	appx. No 1.
TRENCHES.	24th		Battn proceeded by route march to trenches, relieving 8th LINCOLNS in SOUCHEZ II having on right 4th MIDDX and on left 1/12 R Infr Bde.	
	25th		Draft of 5 other Ranks joined from England via 34th I.B.D.	appx No. 5.
	29th		Lieut A.H. OAKLEY joined from England.	appx. No 1.
BOIS DE NOULETTE	30th		Battn relieved in trenches SOUCHEZ II by 8th Lincolns, and proceeded by route march to billets in BOIS DE NOULETTE.	appx. No 6.

Moxley
Lt. Col.

Comdg: 10th (Service) Bn. York & Lancaster Regt.

LIST OF APPENDICES.

	No.
Casualties - Sick Wastage - Strength.	1.
Operation Orders, No. 77.	2.
Operation Orders, No. 78.	3.
Operation Orders, No. 79.	4.
Operation Orders, No. 80.	5.
Operation Orders, No. 81.	6.
Honours and Awards.	7.

Appendix No. 1.

10th (Ser) Battn. York & Lancaster Regiment.

Casualties incurred during the month of SEPTEMBER 1916.

Date.	Regtl. No.	Rank and Name.	Nature of Casualty.
25:9:1916.	16821	Cpl. Goodhall, J.R.	Wounded.
	34125	L/C. Hetherington, T.	Wounded.
	19192	Pte. Garlick, J.	Wounded.
	21397	: Hague, J.R.	Wounded.
26:9:1916.	2781	Pte. Plimmer, C.	Wounded.
	22876	: Rushbrooke, C.	Wounded.
	21299	: Davidson, C.	Wounded.
27:9:1916.	21246	L/C. Marriot, C.	Wounded.
28:9:1916.	34169	Pte. Marson, J.	Wounded.

Sick Wastage - SEPTEMBER 1916.

Officers.

Lieut. W.B.S. O'BRIEN,
    admitted   7:9:1916.
    discharged 17:9:1916.
Capt. C.D.St.G. McCLELLAN,
    admitted 19:9:1916.

Other Ranks.

Remaining in F.A. 31:8:16	12.	
To Field Ambulance	63.	75.
From Field Ambulance	20.	
Remaining in F.A. 30:9:16	34.	54.
Total Sick Wastage.		21.

Strength - SEPTEMBER 1916.

September 1st.   Effective Strength. 25 Officers. 831 Other Ranks.
                    Available Strength. 22 Officers. 813 Other Ranks.

September 30th. Effective Strength. 30 Officers. 822 Other Ranks.
                    Available Strength. 29 Officers. 783 Other Ranks.

Increase.   Officers.

    2/Lt. W.B.S. O'BRIEN joined from England,   1:9:1916.
    2/Lt. H.A. CARTER (S.Staffs) joined from England, 11:9:1916.
    2/Lt. R. FISHER (S.Staffs) joined from England, 11:9:1916.
    2/Lt. J.M. STROTHER joined from England, 13:9:1916.
    2/Lt. J.E. HILL, joined from England, 19:9:1916.
    2/Lt. H.A. WAINE, joined from England, 19:9:1916.
    2/Lt. M.H. OAKLEY, joined from England, 27:9:1916.

Other Ranks.

    14 Other Ranks joined from 34 Infantry Base Depot 8:9:1916.
    1 Other Rank joined from A.H.T.D., ABBEVILLE, 19:9:1916.
    5 Other Ranks joined from 34 Infantry Base Depot 25:9:1916.

Decrease.   Officers.

    2/Lt. C. BAINES. Permanent employment R.F.C.
    Capt. E.G.J. FAIRNIE, To England Sick, 6:9:1916.

Other Ranks.

    Casualties   9.   To Base (under age)   1.
    Sick wastage 21.

Appendix No. 2.

OPERATION ORDERS No. 77.

By Lieut-Col. J.H. RIDGWAY,
Comdg. 10th (S) Bn. York & Lancaster Regiment.
3rd September 1916.

1. The Battalion will march to BAJUS tomorrow. Parade 2.0 p.m. in front of Orderly Room.   Dress: Marching Order.

2. Order of March: Headquarters,   A. B. C. D., Lewis Gunners.

3. All transport will follow in rear of Battalion and will be in column of route in Transport Field ready to follow on.
All wagons to be packed by 1.0 p.m.   Officers' Mess Cart will be packed by 1.30 p.m. (one box or basket per Company; remainder in baggage wagons).

4. Dinners will be at 12 noon.

5. Billets will be evacuated by all men by 1.15 p.m. and left clean ready for Commanding Officers inspection - one Officer per Company to be present at this inspection.

6. Any man falling out on march will be made a prisoner and brought up before the Commanding Officer, unless he is in possession of a note signed by Company Officer and Medical Officer.

7. Billeting party, under 2/Lt. Samuels, will parade outside Orderly Room at 10.0 a.m.   2/Lt. Samuels is appointed Town Major of BAJUS.

8. Parades for tomorrow: 7.0 a.m. Physical Drill.

(Sd) L.A. ELSWORTH, Lt. & Adjt.
10th (S) Bn. York and Lancaster Regiment.

Appendix No. 3.

OPERATION ORDERS No. 78.

By Lieut-Col. J.H. RIDGWAY,
Comdg. 10th (S) Bn. York & Lancaster Regiment.
15th September 1916.

Reference: 30B 1:40,000.

1. The Battalion will move to FRESNICOURT on morning of 16th September 1916, and take over billets there.

2. Billeting party will parade at Orderly Room at 9.0 a.m.

3. All wagons to be loaded by 8.0 a.m., under the strict supervision of 2nd Lt. Knowles. Officers' Mess Cart to be loaded by 8.45 a.m.
   Blankets will be rolled up in bundles by platoons (H.Q. Units in one roll each), labelled and loaded on wagon before breakfasts.

4. Billets to be cleaned and evacuated by 9.0 a.m. for inspection, which will be attended by one representative per Company.
   Tents will be left standing with curtains rolled.

5. Parade: 9.30 a.m.
   Dress: Marching Order.
   Order of March: Headquarters, C. D. A. B., Lewis Gunners. Head of column to pass Church at that hour. Transport will follow immediately in rear of Lewis Gun Limbers.

6. Dinners will be cooked en route.

7. Route: LA COMTE - REBREUVE - OLHAIN - FRESNICOURT.

(Sd) L.A. ELSWORTH, Lt. & Adjt.
10th (S) Bn. York and Lancaster Regiment.

Appendix No. 4.

OPERATION ORDERS. No. 79.

By Lieut-Colonel J.H. RIDGWAY,
Comdg. 10th (S) Bn. York & Lancaster Regiment.
16th September 1916.

1. The Battalion will march tomorrow at 8.30 a.m.

2. Reveille at 5.30 a.m.
   Breakfasts at 6.30 a.m.

3. All wagons to be loaded by 7.45 a.m. Blankets will be rolled and stacked at Q.M. Stores before breakfasts.

4. Dress: Marching Order.
   Order of March: Headquarters, D. A. B. C., Lewis Gunners, Transport will follow in rear of Lewis Gunners.

5. Head of Column to pass A. Company's Huts at 8.30 a.m.

6. Officers' Kits to be loaded by 7.30 a.m. Officers' Mess Cart by 7.45 a.m.

7. Huts will be vacated at 8.0 a.m. and left ready for inspection.

(Sd) L.A. ELSWORTH, Lt. & Adjt.
10th (Ser) Battn. York and Lancaster Regiment.

Appendix No. 5.   SECRET.

OPERATION ORDERS NO. 80.

By Lieut-Colonel J.H. RIDGWAY,
Comdg. 10th (S) Bn. York & Lancaster Regt.
23rd September 1916.

1. The Battalion will relieve the 8th Lincolnshire Regiment in the SOUCHEZ II Section tomorrow night.
   Fall in on Battalion Parade Ground at 6.30 p.m.
   Dress: Marching Order.
   Route: By Tram Lines through wood to Colonel's House, where guides will meet Companies.
   From edge of wood to Colonel's House, Companies will march by Platoons at three minutes' interval.
   Order of March will be issued later.

2. Lewis Gunners and Bombers will take over in the afternoon, parading at 2.30 p.m. and proceeding to trenches via AIX-NOULETTE, entering Trench at N. end of ARRAS ROAD Trench.
   These detachments will pass through AIX-NOULETTE in small parties at three minutes' interval.
   R.S.M. and Coy. S.M's. to proceed with these parties and take over Trench Stores, work in progress etc.

3. D. Company will be in reserve in dug-outs S. of NOULETTE, and will take over immediately after teas.
   This Company will be required to furnish ration parties at 8.0 p.m. at FRENCH DUMP: 1 N.C.O. and 15 Men per Company, 1 N.C.O. and 10 men for Headquarters, the whole to be under an Officer (Dress: Light Marching Order). These parties will, after delivering rations to Companies, do 2 hours work before returning to their billets. O.C. Companies to arrange beforehand what work they require them to do.
   D. Company will also detail two men to look after blankets, stores etc. left behind in BOIS-de-NOULETTE. Men to report to Orderly Room at 9.0 a.m. tomorrow.

4. Rations for D. Company will be dumped at Colonel's House, and a party detailed to pick them up from there at 8.0 p.m.

5. All blankets (except D. Company's) will be rolled in bundles and marked, and placed in a dug-out, which will be notified later. This is to be completed by noon.

6. All dixies and cooks will proceed to trenches immediately after teas, via AIX NOULETTE, entering ARRAS ROAD Trench at N. end. This party to be under the Master Cook.

7. Transport Officer will arrange for horses to move one Cocker to Q.M. Stores, and one to D. Coy's Lines; the latter will be met by a guide at Church, AIX NOULETTE, from D. Coy. and taken to its position.
   One water cart will also be required for D. Coy. at same time.

8. Companies will report to Battalion Headquarters by runner when relief is completed by sending word "RUSSIA".

9. All work in progress will be carefully taken over by Companies, and carried on with at once.

OPERATION ORDERS No. 80 - 23/9/1916.   Page 2.

10. Company Dug-out Platoons will take over the work of Sister Dug-Out Platoons of Companies and will be known by the letter of the Company they are taking over from.

   The following schedule shows the approximate position of each dug-out, and the rendezvous for the dug-out Platoons with a representative of 152 Field Coy. R.E.

Approximate position and purpose.	Position.	Letter of Platoon.	Rendezvous of each Party with R.E.
KELLET LINE, Accommodation for Infantry.	S 2 a 80.70.	W.	Junction of ASH TRENCH & KELLET LINE.
BOSCHE WALK, Accommodation for Infantry.	M 32 c 52.35.	X.	Junction of BOSCHE ALLEY & KELLET LINE.
RATION TRENCH, Battalion Dressing Station.	M 32 c 5.5.	Y.	Junction of RATION TRENCH & the STRAIGHT.

Each platoon will work 4 reliefs as under, and each relief should parade at the rendezvous indicated above 30 minutes before time of work.

Time of Work.	No. of Men of Party.	Tools.	Remarks.
6 a.m. - noon.	4.	Provided at	N.C.O. of Platoon
noon - 6.0 p.m.	4	site of	should march
6 p.m. - mdn't.	7.	work.	parties to
mdn't - 6 a.m.	4.		rendezvous.

Lieut. RUDYARD, 152 Co. R.E. will supervise all work in connection with dug-outs.

11. Telephones are not to be used for any messages whatsoever, except S.O.S. and Gas.

12. Officers' valises will be left in the same store as men's blankets; also heavy baskets. Company's Messes should go up as light as possible, and then Companies can send down to stores in day time for what extra things they require.

13. All billets will be left clean and ready for inspection by 6.0 p.m.

(Sd) L.A. ELSWORTH, Lt. & Adjt.
10th (Ser) Battn. York & Lancaster Regiment.

Appendix No. 6.   SECRET.

OPERATION ORDERS No. 81.
By Lieut-Colonel J.H. RIDGWAY,
Comdg. 10th (S) Bn. York & Lancaster Regiment.
29th September 1916.

The Battalion will be relieved tomorrow night by 8th Lincolnshire Regiment, and will take over same huts as before in BOIS-de-NOULETTE.

Relief will commence at 7.0 p.m.

Lewis Gunners will be relieved in the afternoon.

All dixies, Mess boxes, etc. may be sent down after teas, but RATION TRENCH must be clear of everybody up to FRENCH DUMP before 7.0 p.m.

Companies will hand over all stores, gum boots etc. to incoming Companies and obtain receipts. R.S.M. will hand over all Headquarters Stores.

Companies will also hand over all work in progress.

Transport Officer will bring up cookers to Wood, and also arrange to take D. Coy's Cooker and water cart to same place. Rations will be brought up to BOIS-de-NOULETTE.

Companies will detail men to take over Road Control Posts, Guards etc. Men detailed must report to O.C. 8th Lincolns at 9.30 a.m. tomorrow in BOIS-de-NOULETTE.
Distribution will be given out later.

The following working parties will be found on night of October 1st:- A. and B. Companies 50 men each, under 2 Officers from A. Company, and 1 Officer from B. Company.

Companies will be placed at the disposal of O.C. Companies for inspections, cleaning up, etc. for first two days.

Baths in Wood will be available on October 1st, commencing with A. Company at 9.0 a.m.

Companies finding fatigues for 253 Tunnelling Coy. R.E. will find these on night of relief. These men will rejoin after completion of their tour of duty.

Other parties under 152 Coy. R.E. will not be required on night of relief.

Mess cart will be at FRENCH DUMP at 8.0 p.m. to remove baskets and Orderly Room boxes.

Companies should send down 1 N.C.O. to draw blankets from store and put them in Company Huts. O.C. Lewis Gunners will find carrying parties for these.

Breakfasts on October 1st: 8.0 a.m.

(Sd) L.A. ELSWORTH, Lt. & Adjt.
10th (S) Bn. York & Lancaster Regiment.

Appendix No. 7.

HONOURS and AWARDS.

Extract from 63rd Infantry Brigade Order No. 405 of 20:9:1916.

The following Russian Decoration has been awarded:-

The Medal St. George, 3rd Class.

No. 4509 Private FRED FOX, 10th York & Lancaster Regiment.

During the operations of July 1st/3rd.

"Stretcher bearer - For gallantry and devotion to duty in showing absolute disregard to shell fire. He assisted in carrying in a wounded Officer which took several hours to do, and on nearing the Aid Post the whole party were buried by a shell. Pte. FOX extricated himself and dug out the remainder of the party and the Officer; and when any shells came over he threw himself over the Officer to protect him as much as possible. This man worked himself to a standstill".

(NOTE: St. George's Medal is 4 Classes. The first and second class are in gold and awarded to non-commissioned Officers. The third and fourth are in silver and awarded to Private Soldiers. The name of the recipient is engraved on the medal and ribbon. The third and fourth classes are approximately equivalent to the British D.C.M.).

Confidential.

10th Battalion
YORK and LANCASTER Regiment.

WAR DIARY.

OCTOBER - 1916.

FOURTEENTH VOLUME.

WAR DIARY

10th Bn York and Lancaster Regiment

INTELLIGENCE SUMMARY

Army Form C. 2118.

(Erase heading not required.)

Instructions regarding War Diaries and Intelligence Summaries are contained in F. S. Regs., Part II. and the Staff Manual respectively. Title Pages will be prepared in manuscript.

Place	Date 1916 OCT.	Hour	Summary of Events and Information	Remarks and references to Appendices
BOIS DE NOULETTE	1st		Battalion stationed in Bde Reserve, occupying Redoubts in BOIS DE NOULETTE.	
TRENCHES.	6th		Battn proceeded by route march to trenches, relieving 8th LINCOLN Regt. in SOUCHEZ II, having on right the MIDDX Regt. and on Left 10th K.O.Y.L.I. Regt.	Appx 4.
		8h	Lieut. A.R. ROBINSON joined from England.	Appx 2.
		9½h	Bde front extended. Two Coys front taken over by Battn from the 10th K.O.Y.L.I.	Appx 5.
			Lancs on left.	
	12h		Capt. R.H. FITTS wounded.	Appx 2.
LORETTE.			Battn relieved in SOUCHEZ II by SOM. L.I. and took over Bde Support Line and Defences on LORETTE SPUR. Bn HQ situated in ABLAIN	Appx 6
			ST. NAZAIRE.	
FRESNICOURT	16h	✱	10me Relief. Bn relieved in LORETTE Defences by 24th CANADIAN INFY. (2nd CAN. DIV) and proceeded by route march to FRESNICOURT	Appx 7.
			occupying Billets.	
VILLERS. BRULIN.	18h		Battn proceeded by route march to VILLERS BRULIN occupying Billets.	Appx 8
ETREE WAMIN	20h		Battn proceeded by route march to ETREE WAMIN occupying Billets	Appx 9
AMPLIER.	21st		Battn proceeded by route march to AMPLIER occupying Billets.	Appx 10.
TERRAMESNIL	22nd		Battn proceeded by route march to TERRAMESNIL occupying Billets.	Appx 11.
	28th		Two drafts of 24 and 56 Other Ranks respectively arrived from 34th Infy. Base Depot.	
		✱	Transfer to V Corps. Reserve Army.	

W. Ripley
Lt. Col.
Comdg 10th Bn York & Lancaster Regt.

List of Appendices.
_____

	Appendix No.
Honours and Awards.	1.
Casualties, Sick, and Strength.	2.
Roll of Officers - 30th October 16.	3.
Operation Orders, No. 82.	4.
Operation Orders No. 83.	5.
Operation Orders No. 84.	6.
Operation Orders No. 85.	7.
Operation Orders No. 86.	8.
Operation Orders No. 87.	9.
Operation Orders No. 88.	10.
Operation Orders No. 89.	11.

Appendix No. 1

HONOURS & REWARDS.

Copy of 63rd Brigade Routine Order No. 411 of 10th October 1916.

Military Medals have been awarded to the following by the Corps Commander under authority by His Majesty the King (M.S.H. 2260 dated 2/6/1916).

10th York & Lancaster Regiment.

No. 3881 Sergeant ROBERT SPEIGHT.

For the prompt way in which this N.C.O. collected and led his men on the night of August 13-14 1916, when the enemy blew a mine on VIMY RIDGE. This N.C.O. immediately led his men forward and seized the near lip of the crater and after repulsing certain of the enemy started to consolidate. During this time the enemy were shelling very heavily and also using machine guns. This N.C.O. showed total disregard to danger and by his promptness of action undoubtedly saved further casualties.

No. 20812 Sergeant HERBERT CLARKE.

For the prompt way in which this N.C.O. collected and led his men on the night of August 13-14 1916, when the enemy blew a mine on VIMY RIDGE on the left of his section. He immediately led his men to the crater and started consolidating in conjunction with Sergeant Speight. During this time there was heavy machine gun fire and shell fire. This N.C.O. showed a total disregard of danger and by his promptness undoubtedly saved many casualties.

10th Battn. York & Lancaster Regt.

Casualties incurred during the month of OCTOBER 1916.

Date.	No.	Rank	Name.	Nature of Casualty.
7:10:1916.	16788	Pte.	Hayes, W.	Wounded (shell shock).
8:10:1916.	19248	Pte.	Porley, S.	Wounded.
9:10:1916.	15626	Cpl.	Walker, A.	Wounded (to duty).
11:10:1916.	22087	Pte.	Atkinson, K.I.	Wounded.
12:10:1916.		Captain	FITTS, R.H.	Wounded.
	17592	Pte.	Dunbar, T.	Died of wounds.
	34077	:	Moorwood, J.	Wounded.
	17462	:	Peterson, G.	Wounded.
13:10:1916.	21895	Pte.	Broadley, W.	Wounded.

Sick Wastage - OCTOBER 1916.

Officers.

Lieut. H. BROADBENT,
    admitted 6:10:1916.
    discharged 9:10:1916.
Lieut. H.W. SAMES,
    admitted 30:10:1916.

Other Ranks.

Remaining in F'd Amb,
    30:9:1916. 34.
To F'd Amb. during
    OCTOBER. 69.   103.
From F'd Amb. during
    OCTOBER. 45.
Remaining in F'd Amb,
    30:10:1916. 5.   50.

Total Sick Wastage. 53.

Strength - OCTOBER 1916.

September 30th. Effective Strength. 30 Officers, 822 Other Ranks.
               Available Strength. 29 Officers, 783 O. Ranks.

October 30th. Effective Strength. 30 Officers, 835 O. Ranks.
              Available Strength. 28 Officers, 830 O. Ranks.

Increase. Officers.

    Lieut. A.R. ROBINSON, joined from England, 8:10:1916.

Other Ranks.

    24 O.Ranks joined from 34 I. B. Depot, 28:10:1916.
    56 O.Ranks joined from 34 I. B. Depot, 28:10:1916.

Decrease. Officers.

    Captain C.D. St. G. McClellan to England sick, 5:10:1916.

Other Ranks.

Died of Wounds 1. Wounded 5. To England (under age) 1. S.I. Wound 1. Sick wastage 53. To P.B. 2. To establishment of 21 Div. Gas School personnel 1. To Munitions 3.

Appendix No. 3.

10th Battn. York & Lancaster Regiment.

ROLL of OFFICERS - 30th October 1916.

Rank.	Name.		Date of Arrival in Country.	Present Employment.
Lt-Col.	RIDGWAY,	J.H.	1: 9:1914.	Commanding Officer.
Captain	FITTS,	R.H.	11: 9:1915.	In hospital - Wounded.
:	AIREY,	C.F.	11: 9:1915.	Company Commander.
:	DRYNAN,	W.B.	11: 9:1915.	Second in Command.
:	ELSWORTH,	L.A.	11: 9:1915.	Adjutant.
:	RAMSDEN,	J.H.	10:10:1915.	Company Commander.
Lieut.	O'BRIEN,	W.B.S.	26: 8:1916.	Platoon Commander.
:	GROVES,	S.J.S.	17: 3:1916.	Company Commander.
:	BROADBENT,	H.	11: 9:1915.	Company Commander.
:	SAMES,	H.W.	25: 8:1916.	In Field Ambulance - Sick.
:	HALL,	D.A.	25: 7:1916.	Platoon Commander.
:	ROBINSON,	A.R.	4:10:1916.	Employed at 63 Inf.Bde. H.Q.
:	WILKINSON,	R.M.	9:10:1915.	Assistant Adjutant.
:	QUANCE,	A.L.	10: 3:1916.	Platoon Commander.
2nd Lt.	NICHOLSON,	C.A.J.	6: 1:1916.	Absent without leave - 21:10:1916.
:	KNOWLES,	F.E.	9:10:1916.	Transport Officer.
:	MITCHELL,	R.J.	19:11:1915.	Platoon Commander.
:	AYRES,	F.	10:11:1915.	Lewis Gun Officer.
:	PAYNE,	F.E.	11:10:1915.	Bombing Officer.
:	HAWLEY,	D.D.	29: 5:1916.	Platoon Commander.
:	SAMUELS,	E.	25: 1:1916.	Signalling Officer.
:	HOCKLY,	A.	15: 6:1916.	Platoon Commander.
:	CHAMBERS,	E.S.	21: 7:1916.	Platoon Commander.
:	LAMOND,	A.W.	21:12:1914.	Acting Quartermaster.
:	FISHER,	R.	3: 9:1916.	Platoon Commander.
:	CARTER,	H.W.	3: 9:1916.	Platoon Commander.
:	STROTHER,	J.M.	3: 9:1916.	Platoon Commander.
:	WALNE,	H.A.	16: 9:1916.	Platoon Commander.
:	HILL,	J.E.	16:: 9:1916.	Platoon Commander.
:	OAKLEY,	M.H.	4: 9:1916.	Platoon Commander.
Captain	PLAISTER, (R.A.M.C.)	G.R.	11: 9:1915.	Medical Officer.

Appendix No. 4

Copy No.   S E C R E T

OPERATION ORDERS No. 82.
By Captain W.B. DRYNAN,
Comdg. 10th Battn. York & Lancaster Regiment.
5th October 1916.

1. The Battalion will relieve 8th Lincolnshire Regt. in the SOUCHEZ II Section tomorrow night.
   Fall in on Battalion Parade Ground at 5.30 p.m.
   Dress: Marching Order.
   Route: By Tram Lines through Wood to Colonel's House, to trenches.
   Companies will take over as follows:-
   Right Company - C. Coy.
   Centre Company - D. Coy.
   Left Company - A. Coy.
   Reserve Coy.   - B. Coy.
   From edge of Wood to Colonel's House, Companies will march by Platoons at intervals of three minutes.
   Order of March: C. A. D.

2. Lewis Gunners and Bombers will take over in the afternoon, parading at 1.30 p.m. and proceeding to trenches via AIX-NOULETTE, entering Trench at N. end of ARRAS ROAD TRENCH.
   These detachments will pass through AIX-NOULETTE in small parties at three minutes' interval.
   R.S.M. and Coy. S.M's to proceed with these parties and take over Trench Stores, work in progress, etc.

3. B. Company will be in reserve in dug-outs S. of NOULETTE, and will take over immediately after teas.
   This Company will be required to furnish ration parties at 5.0 p.m. at Colonel's House. All available men should parade under an Officer (Dress: Light Marching Order). These parties will, after delivering rations to Companies, do 2 hours work before returning to their billets. O.C. Companies will arrange beforehand what work they require them to do.

4. D. Company will provide 1 Platoon each night to do duty in KELLET RIGHT.
   Tomorrow night this Platoon will move up after the 8th Lincolnshire Regt. is clear of the Trenches.

5. The following working parties will be found as detailed below from the Platoons in Support:-

   (a) 1 N.C.O. and 14 men from B. Company to report at FRENCH DUMP at 1.0 p.m. to No. 1 Sec. 152nd Field Co. R.E.   Carrying party.

   (b) 1 N.C.O. and 23 men from D. Company to report at FRENCH DUMP at 9.0 a.m. to No. 4 Sec. 152nd Field Co. R.E.   Revetting.

6. Rations for B. Company will be dumped at Colonel's House, and a party detailed to pick them up from there at 7.0 p.m.

7. All blankets and stores which are not required for the trenches must be ready to go back to Q.M. Stores at 10.0 a.m. These will be carried to Cross Roads near R.E. Dump where the Transport will be in waiting.

8. Dixies and cooks will proceed to the trenches with their Companies.

9. The Transport Officer will arrange for horses to move one cooker to Q.M. Stores and one to B. Company's Lines. One Water Cart will go to B. Coy. at the same time.

10. Companies will report to Battalion H.Q. by Runner when Relief is completed by sending the word "THIEPVAL".

11. All work in progress will be carefully taken over by Companies, and carried on with at once.

12. Careful attention must be paid in taking over Trench Stores, as Coy. Commanders will be held responsible for any article missing.

13. If whale-oil is available, every man must rub his feet before going into trenches. All men are to change their socks daily if the trenches are wet.

14. Telephones are not to be used for any messages whatsoever, except "S.O.S." and "GAS".

15. All billets will be left clean and reay for inspection by 5.0 p.m.

16. Patrols must be sent out every night to learn all they can re enemy wire.
    This is most important.

(Sd) L.A. ELSWORTH, Capt. & Adjt.
Issued at 6 p.m. 10th Battalion York & Lancaster Regiment.

Distribution.

War Diary and File.	1 - 3.
63rd Inf. Bde.	4.
Comdg. Officer.	5.
A. Company.	6.
B. Company.	7.
C. Company.	8.
D. Company.	9.
Lewis Gun Officer.	10.
Bombing Officer.	11.
Signalling Officer.	12.
Snipers.	13.
Quartermaster.	14.
Transport Officer.	15.
Medical Officer.	16.

Appendix No. 5

SECRET
- - - - -

OPERATION ORDERS No. 83.
By Captain W.E. DRYNAN,
Comdg. 10th Battn. York & Lancaster Regiment.
8th October 1916.

1. D. Company will relieve right Company of 10th Loyal North Lancashire Regt tomorrow at 9.0 a.m. Guides to be arranged between Coy. Commanders. D. Coy. will move by MORROW TRENCH.

2. B. Company, less two platoons, will relieve B. Company 10th Loyal North Lancashire Regt. in MORROW TRENCH at 9.0 a.m. tomorrow, moving by ANGRES TRENCH and COOKER ALLEY. Guides to be arranged between Company Commanders.

3. 2 Platoons of B. Company will relieve 2 Platoons D. Company in BAJOLE LINE at 8.0 a.m.

4. A. Company will extend its right to the Listening Post of D. Coy. inclusive, at 8.0 a.m., using three platoons in front line, if necessary.

5. C. Company will extend its left to the Listening Post of B. Coy. exclusive, at 8.0 a.m., using three platoons in front line.

6. 4th Middlesex Regt. will relieve C. Company from ASH ROAD inclusive to the right at 8.0 a.m.

7. Lewis Guns right of ASH ROAD and in KELLET RIGHT will be relieved by 4th Middlesex Regt. at 8.0 a.m.

8. Lewis Guns will take over new positions by arrangements of Lewis Gun Officers.

9. Trench Stores and details of work will be taken over by B. and D. Companies from 10th Loyal North Lancashire Regt. A. Coy. will take over stores from D. Company before 8.0 a.m.

10. Companies will report relief complete by sending the word "BAPAUME".

11. B. and D. Coy Sgt-Majors will move into new trenches at least half an hour before relief to take over trench stores, etc.

12. B. and D. Coys. will carry dixies and day's rations to their new positions.

13. Companies will provide their own ration parties as follows:-

    D. Coy. & 2 Platoons B. Coy. at COLONEL'S GOUSE at 6.30 p.m. under B. Coy's Sgt-Major.
    A. C. & 2 Platoons B. Coy. at FRENCH DUMP at 6.45 p.m. under R.S.M. Likewise all sections till further orders.

14. The following working parties will be taken over by B. Coy. from the two platoons in the BAJOLE LINE:-

---

(a) 1 N.C.O. and 14 men. to report at FRENCH DUMP (No. 1 Sec. 152 Fd Co. R.E. Carrying party.

(b) 1 N.C.O. and 23 men. to report at FRENCH DUMP (No. 4 Sec. 152 Fd Co. R.E. Revetting.

(Sd) L.A. ELSWORTH, Capt. & Adjt.
Issued at 2.0 p.m.   10th Battn. York & Lancaster Regiment.

Appendix No. 6

Copy No.   SECRET

OPERATION ORDERS No. 84.
By Captain W.B. DRYNAN,
Comdg. 10th Battn. York & Lancaster Regiment.
11th October 1916.

1. The Battalion will be relieved tomorrow night by 8th Somerset Light Infantry, and will take over dug-outs in the LORETTE Defences. Relief will commence at 7.0 p.m.

2. Lewis Gunners will be relieved in the afternoon, and will move out by RATION TRENCH, FRENCH DUMP, and ARRAS ROAD TRENCH. Panniers and magazines will be deposited at FRENCH DUMP under a guard, who will see that they are put into the transport.

3. Companies will hand over all stores, gum boots, etc. to incoming Companies, and obtain receipts. R.S.M. will hand over all Headquarters Stores.
Companies will also hand over all work in progress.

4. All mess boxes, etc. must be at FRENCH DUMP by 6.0 p.m. sharp. This is most important and Companies must not be later.

5. Transport Officer will bring up necessary transport to FRENCH DUMP to remove to ABLAIN ST. NAZARRE all mess boxes and Lewis Gun magazines.

6. Officers' valises will be dumped at Battalion H.Q. Mess baskets will be brought to Companies Dumps by C.Q.M.Sgts.

7. When Companies leave the trenches for the Road, an interval of 200 yards will be kept between platoons. Connecting files will be used to keep in touch.

8. On day after relief, work in progress will be carried on.

9. Companies and Sections will carry dixies with them.

                                            (Sd) L.A. ELSWORTH, Capt. & Adjt.
Issued at 4.0 p.m.   10th Battn. York & Lancaster Regiment.

Distribution.

War Diary and File.	1 - 3.
63rd Inf. Bde.	4.
Comdg. Officer.	5.
A. Company.	6.
B. Company.	7.
C. Company.	8.
D. Company.	9.
Lewis Gun Officer.	10.
Bombing Officer.	11.
Signalling Officer.	12.
Snipers.	13.
Quartermaster.	14.
Transport Officer.	15.
Medical Officer.	16.

Appendix No. 7

Copy No.   S E C R E T

OPERATION ORDERS, No. 85.
By Captain W.B. DRYNAN,
Comdg. 10th Bn. York & Lancaster Regiment.
15th October 1916.

Reference Map: LENS 1:100,000.

1. The Battalion will be relieved tomorrow about 7.30 p.m. by the 27th Canadian Infantry, and will take over billets in FRESNICOURT.

   Route: GOUY SERVINS, PETIT SERVINS, GRAND SERVINS, FRESNICOURT.

2. One guide per platoon and Section to report to 2/Lt. HAWLEY at Battalion Orderly Room at 6.0 p.m., who will proceed with them to Road Control at first angle in road ¼ mile N.W. of ABLAIN ST. NAZAIRE.

3. Companies and Sections will march out independently to Battalion rendezvous at point in road at U in GOUY SERVINS, reporting to Assistant Adjutant on arrival.

4. Lewis Gun Detachments will report on relief to Lewis Gun Officer at Battalion H.Q.

5. A limber will be at Battalion H.Q. to take Lewis Guns, Magazines, etc. away.

6. One N.C.O. per Company will report at Battalion H.Q. at 10.30 a.m. to 2nd Lt. SAMUELS, who will report to Town Major at FRESNICOURT by noon.

7. Relief complete will be reported by sending the word "TANKS".

8. Dug-out Platoons and 6 pioneers at present with 152nd Field Company R.E. will rejoin on 16th. 2/Lt. FISHER will report to this Company at AIX-NOULETTE at 6.0 p.m. and take charge of these men, proceeding direct to FRESNICOURT.

9. All trench stores and material will be handed over and receipts obtained.

10. Reserves of S.A.A., Grenades, etc. to be handed over with statements shewing the exact quantities, and receipts obtained.

11. Signed copies of all Stores handed over to be sent to Battalion H.Q. by midday after Relief.

12. Officers' valises, mess kit, and dixies to be at Battalion H.Q. by 6.0 p.m.

                                                        (Sd) L.A. ELSWORTH, Capt. & Adjt.
Issued at 7.30 p.m.   10th Bn. York & Lancaster Regiment.

Distribution.

War Diary and File	1 – 3.	Lewis Gun Officer	10.
63rd Inf. Bde.	4.	Bombing Officer.	11.
Comdg. Officer.	5.	Signalling Officer.	12.
A. Company.	6.	Snipers.	13.
B. Company.	7.	Quartermaster.	14.
C. Company.	8.	Transport Officer.	15.
D. Company.	9.	Medical Officer.	16.

Appendix No. 8

Copy No.
SECRET

OPERATION ORDERS No. 86.
By Lt-Colonel J.H. RIDGWAY,
Comdg. 10th Battn. York & Lancaster Regt.
17th October 1916.

Reference Map: FRANCE 1:100,000 (LENS 11).

1. The Battalion will march tomorrow to VILLERS-BRULIN, where they will take over billets.

    Route: GAUCHIN-LEGAL, CAUCOURT, BETHONSART.

    Order of March: Bombers, Signallers, A, B, C, D., Lewis Gunners, Transport.

    Head of Column will pass entrance to Transport Field at 10.0 a.m.

    Dress: Full Marching Order. Steel helmets will be worn.

2. Billeting party will parade at Orderly Room at 9.0 a.m., under 2nd Lt. SAMUELS.

3. All wagons to be loaded by 9.0 a.m.

    Blankets will be rolled in bundles by platoons (H.Q. units in one roll each), labelled, and loaded on wagon before breakfasts.

4. Billets to be cleaned and evacuated by 9.0 a.m. for inspection. One Officer per Company to be present.

5. Reveille: 6.30 a.m.
   Breakfast: 7.30 a.m.

6. Dinners will be cooked en route.

(Sd) L.A. ELSWORTH, Capt. & Adjt.
Issued at 4.30 p.m. 10th Battn. York & Lancaster Regiment.

Distribution.

War Diary and File.   1 - 3.
63rd Inf. Bde.   4.
Comdg. Officer.   5.
A. Company.   6.
B. Company.   7.
C. Company.   8.
D. Company.   9.
Lewis Gun Officer.   10.
Bombing Officer.   11.
Signalling Officer.   12.
Snipers.   13.
Quartermaster.   14.
Transport Officer.   15.
Medical Officer.   16.

Appendix No. 9

Copy No.

S E C R E T

OPERATION ORDERS No. 87.
By Lt-Colonel J.H. RIDGWAY,
Comdg. 10th Battn. York & Lancaster Regiment.
19th October 1916.

Reference Map: FRANCE 1:100,000 (LENS 11).

1. The Battalion will march tomorrow to ETREE WAMIN, and take over billets.

   Route: TINQUES - PENIN - LIGNEREUIL.

   The Battalion will join the remainder of the Brigade at junction of TINQUES and ST.POL-ARRAS Road at 10.0 a.m.

   Order of March: Bombers, Signallers, B. C. D. A., Lewis Gunners, Transport.

   Head of Column to pass pond at 8.45 a.m.

   Dress: Full Marching Order. Steel helmets.

2. Billeting party, under 2nd Lt. SAMUELS, will parade at Orderly Room at 8.30 a.m.

3. All wagons to be loaded by 7.45 a.m., Mess Cart by 8.0 a.m. Blankets will be rolled in bundles of tens (small units in one bundle), labelled and stacked at Q.M. Stores before breakfast.

4. Reveille: 5.30 a.m.
   Breakfast: 6.30 a.m.

   Dinners will be cooked en route.

5. Billets to be clean and evacuated by 8.0 a.m. for inspection. One Officer to be present.

6. Refilling point: 20th inst. - CHELLERS, MAIRIE, 9.0 a.m.
   21st inst. - ½ kilometre North of HOUVIN on HOUVIN & MONTS-EN-TENOIS Road, 7.0 a.m.

7. On the 21st the Battalion will march with "A" Column, under Lt-Col. BICKNELL, D.S.O.
   Starting point, Cross Roads S.W. of E in ETREE WAMIN, at 9.0 a.m. marching to HALLOY.

(Sd) L.A. ELSWORTH, Capt. & Adjt.
Issued at 8.30 p.m.   10th Battn. York & Lancaster Regiment.

Distribution.

War Diary and File.	1 - 3.	Lewis Gun Officer.	10.
63rd Inf. Bde.	4.	Bombing Officer.	11.
Comdg. Officer.	5.	Signalling Officer.	12.
A. Company.	6.	Snipers.	13.
B. Company.	7.	Quartermaster.	14.
C. Company.	8.	Transport Officer.	15.
D. Company.	9.	Medical Officer.	16.

Copy No.   Appendix No. 10

                                    S E C R E T

                    O P E R A T I O N   O R D E R S   No. 88.
                           By Lt-Col. J.H. RIDGWAY,
                       Comdg. 10th Battn. York & Lancaster Regiment.
                           20th October 1916.

1. The Battalion will march tomorrow to AMPLIER and take over
    Hutments.

    Route: BEAUDRICOURT - LUCHEUX - HALLOY.

    The Battalion will join the remainder of "A" Column at
    Cross Roads S.W. of first E in ETREE WAMIN at 9.10 a.m.

    Order of March: Bombers, Signallers, C. D. A. B., Lewis
    Gunners, Transport.

    Head of Column to pass Cross Roads due North of the M in
    WAMIN at 9.0 a.m.
    A. Company will join Battalion at Cross Roads S.W. of first
    E in ETREE WAMIN, and must be careful to keep road clear to
    allow 4th Middlesex Regt. and 8th Somerset L.I. to pass.
    They should follow immediately in rear of 8th Somerset L.I.
    Dress: Full Marching Order. Steel helmets.

2. Billeting party will parade at Orderly Room at 9.0 a.m.
    under 2nd Lt. SAMUELS, who will report to Staff Captain at
    the Church, AMPLIER, at 11.0 a.m.

3. All wagons to be loaded by 8.0 a.m., Mess Cart by 8.0 a.m.
    Blankets will be rolled in bundles of tens (small units in
    one bundle), labelled and stacked at Q.M.Stores before
    breakfast.

4. Reveille: 5.30 a.m. Breakfasts: 6.30 a.m.
    Dinners will be cooked en route.

5. Billets to be clean and evacuated by 8.0 a.m. for inspection,
    one Officer to be present.

                                        (Sd) L.A. ELSWORTH, Capt. & Adjt.
Issued at 8.15 p.m.   10th Battn. York & Lancaster Regiment.

Distribution.

                            Copy No.

War Diary and File.   1 - 3.
63rd Inf. Bde.   4.
Comdg. Officer.   5.
A. Company.   6.
B. Company.   7.
C. Company.   8.
D. Company.   9.
Lewis Gun Officer.   10.
Bombing Officer.   11.
Signalling Officer.   12.
Snipers.   13.
Quartermaster.   14.
Transport Officer.   15.
Medical Officer.   16.

Copy No.

Appendix No. 11

SECRET.

OPERATION ORDERS No. 89.

By Lt-Colonel J.H. RIDGWAY,
Comdg. 10th Battn. York & Lancaster Regiment.
21st October 1916.

1. The Battalion will march tomorrow to TERRAMESNIL, and take over billets there.

   Reveille: 6.0 a.m.
   Breakfasts: 7.0 a.m.

   Battalion Parade 9.30 a.m. (markers to report to R.S.M. at 9.15 a.m.).
   Dress: Full marching order.

2. Blankets will be stacked at Q.M. Stores before breakfast.

3. Wagons and Mess Cart to be loaded by 8.30 a.m.

4. Billeting party to parade under 2nd Lt. SAMUELS at 8.30 a.m.

Issued at 11.0 p.m.
(Sd) L.A. ELSWORTH, Capt. & Adjt.
10th Battn. York & Lancaster Regiment.

Distribution.

	Copy No.
War Diary and File.	1 - 3.
63rd Inf. Bde.	4.
Comdg. Officer.	5.
A. Company.	6.
B. Company.	7.
C. Company.	8.
D. Company.	9.
Lewis Gun Officer.	10.
Bombing Officer.	11.
Signalling Officer.	12.
Snipers.	13.
Quartermaster.	14.
Transport Officer.	15.
Medical Officer.	16.

SUBJECT: War Diary.

37th Division "Q".

Herewith War Diary of the Unit for the
month of November 1916.

5th December 1916.

Lt-Colonel.
Comdg. 10th Bn. York & Lancaster Regt.

CONFIDENTIAL.

10th (Service) Battalion
THE YORK AND LANCASTER REGIMENT.

WAR DIARY.

NOVEMBER - 1916.

FIFTEENTH VOLUME.

Army Form C. 2118.

WAR DIARY
10th Bn. York and Lancaster Regt.
INTELLIGENCE SUMMARY

(Erase heading not required.)

Instructions regarding War Diaries and Intelligence Summaries are contained in F.S. Regs., Part II. and the Staff Manual respectively. Title Pages will be prepared in manuscript.

Place	Date 1916 Nov.	Hour	Summary of Events and Information	Remarks and references Appendices
TERRAMESNIL	1st.		Battn occupying billets in TERRAMESNIL.	
	2nd		Lieut. & Q.M. A. JAMIESON joined Battalion from England.	app 1
	6th		2nd Lieut. J.F. MAGEE joined Battalion from England.	app 2
	8th		Draft of 9 other Ranks joined from 3th. Infy Base Depot.	app 2
ACHEUX WOOD	12th		Battalion proceeded by route march to ACHEUX WOOD occupying huts.	app 4
TRENCHES.	14th		Battn proceeded to line to take part in operation North of the River ANCRE, taking over a line from H.A.C. (Infy) 63rd (Naval) Divn. in the vicinity of BEAUCOURT SUR ANCRE. Reserve R.Cos and specialists, Q.M. stores and transport to 63rd Infy Brigade Reserve Depot Camp at ENGLEBELMER- MARTINSART Road.	app 3 app 5 app 6
	16th		Draft of 4 other Ranks joined from 34th Infy Base Depot.	app 7
	20th		Battn relieved in line by 1/4th South Staffs. 1116 Divisn and proceeded to reserve position in HAMEL occupying billets in cellars etc.	app 6
HAMEL				
ENGLEBELMER	24th		Battn proceeded by route march to ENGLEBELMER occupying billets. reserve detachment, Q.M. Stores joined Battn at this place.	app 8
			Draft of 3 other Ranks joined from 34th Infy Base Depot.	app 2
MAILLY MAILLET	25th		Battn proceeded by route march to MAILLY MAILLET occupying billets.	app 9
RAINCHEVAL	26th		Battn proceeded by route march to RAINCHEVAL occupying billets.	app 10
	Decr			
TERRAMESNIL	1st.		Battn proceeded by route march to TERRAMESNIL occupying billets.	

M. Rayway
Lt. Col.
Comdg 10th Bn. York & Lancaster Regt.

LIST of APPENDICES.

1. List of Officers on Strength - 30th November 1916.
2. List of CASUALTIES - SICK WASTAGE - REINFORCEMENTS during month.
3. Operation Orders No. 90.
4. Operation Orders No. 91.
5. Operation Orders No. 92.
6. Report on Operations - 13th to 22nd November 1916.
7. Commendation.
8. Operation Orders No. 91A.
9. Operation Orders No. 92A.
10. Operation Orders No. 93.

Appendix No. 1

10th Battn. York & Lancaster Regiment.

ROLL of OFFICERS on Strength – 30th November 1916.

Rank.	Name.		How Employed.
Lt-Col.	RIDGWAY,	J.H.	Commanding Officer.
Captain	AIREY,	C.F.	Sick.
"	DRYNAN,	W.B.	2nd in Command.
"	ELSWORTH,	L.A.	Adjutant.
"	BROADBENT,	H.	Company Commander.
Lieut.	HALL,	D.A.	Sick.
"	ROBINSON,	A.R.	
"	WILKINSON,	R.M.	Company Commander.
2nd Lt.	NICHOLSON,	C.A.J.	Sick.
"	KNOWLES,	F.E.	Transport Officer.
"	MITCHELL,	R.J.	
"	AYRES,	F.	Company Commander.
"	PAYNE,	F.E.	Bombing Officer.
"	HAWLEY,	D.D.	Lewis Gun Officer.
"	SAMUELS,	E.	Signalling Officer.
"	LAMOND,	A.W.	On Leave.
"	STROTHER,	J.M.	Company Commander.
"	WALNE,	H.A.	Sick.
"	HILL,	J.E.	
"	OAKLEY,	M.H.	
Lt. & Q.M.	JAMIESON,	A.	Quartermaster.
Captain	PLAISTER, (R.A.M.C.)	G.R.	Medical Officer.

Appendix No. 2

10th Battn. York & Lancaster Regiment.

CASUALTIES incurred during the month of NOVEMBER 1916.

Sickness.	In Trenches.	Working Parties, Resting, etc.
Officers.	**Officers.**	**Officers.**
Capt. J.H. RAMSDEN, admitted 2:11:1916.	Killed-in-Action.	N I L.
Lieut. D.A. HALL, admitted 9:11:1916.	2/Lt. R. FISHER (S.Staffs R.) 15:11:16.	
2/Lt. E.S. CHAMBERS, admitted 12:11:1916.	Wounded.	
2/Lt. R.J. MITCHELL, admitted 16:11:1916. discharged 22:11:1916.	Lieut. A.L. QUANCE, 14:11:16.	
Capt. C.F. AIREY, admitted 18:11:1916.	Lieut. S.J.S. GROVES, 15:11:16.	
2/Lt. H.A. WALNE, admitted 19:11:1916.	2/Lt. H.W. CARTER (S.Staffs R.) 15:11:16.	
	Lieut. W.B.S. O'BRIEN, 16:11:16.	
	2/Lt. J.F. MAGEE, 19:11:16.	
Other Ranks.	**Other Ranks.**	**Other Ranks.**
Remaining in F'd Amb. 30:10:16 5.	Killed-in-Action 26.	N I L.
To F.A. in Novr. 104. 109.	Died of Wounds. 4.	
	Missing. 2.	
From F.A. in Novr. 19.	Wounded. 164.	
Remaining in F'd Amb. 30:11:16. 18. 37.	Rejoined after treatment. 9.	
	Total Wounded. 155.	
Total Sick Wastage. 72.		

REINFORCEMENTS arriving during the month of NOVEMBER 1916.

Officers. Lt. & Q.M. A. JAMIESON joined from England. 2:11:1916.
2nd Lieut. J.F. MAGEE joined from England. 6:11:1916.

Other Ranks.
9 Other Ranks joined from 34th Inf. Base Depot, 8:11:1916.
4 Other Ranks joined from 34th Inf. Base Depot, 16:11:1916.
6 Other Ranks joined from 34th Inf. Base Depot, 18:11:1916.
3 Other Ranks joined from 34th Inf. Base Depot, 24:11:1916.

STRENGTH - NOVEMBER 1916.

October 30th.   Effective Strength. 30 Officers. 835 Other Ranks.
                Available Strength. 28 Officers. 830 Other Ranks.

November 30th. Effective Strength. 27 Officers. 596 Other Ranks.
                Available Strength. 17 Officers. 576 Other Ranks.

Decrease. **Officers.** Capt. R.H. FITTS to England Wounded, 29:10:1916.
2/Lt. A. HOCKLY to England (to report to C.R.E. NEWARK T.C.), 4:11:1916.
Lieut. H.W. SAMES to England Sick, 4:11:1916.
Capt. J.H. RAMSDEN to England Sick, 13:11:1916.
2/Lt. R. FISHER, Killed-in-Action, 15:11:1916.

Other Ranks.
Killed in Action. 26.   To Base (under age) 1.
Died of Wounds.   4.   To Railway Con. Co.
Missing.   2.   R.E.   1.
Wounded.   155.   Sick Wastage.   72.
                          Total   261.

SECRET

Copy No.

OPERATION ORDERS No. 90.
By Lt-Colonel J.H. RIDGWAY,
Comdg. 10th Battn. York & Lancaster Regiment.
2nd November 1916.

Reference Maps: 1:40,000.
1:20,000.

1. The Reserve Army is to attack North and South of the ANCRE: II Corps to the South, V Corps (ours) to the North.

2. The II Corps is to attack Northwards and form a defensive flank facing East. On reaching line of River ANCRE, it is to force a passage, capture MIRAUMONT, and all crossings over River between MIRAUMONT and BRIDGE ROAD (Q 18 b 8.3) both inclusive; the line MIRAUMONT-BEAUCOURT-sur-ANCRE between L 35 c 9.3 and a point South of BOIS d'HOLLANDE will also be captured by II Corps.

3. The V Corps, consisting of five Divisions and supported by Artillery of 8 Divisions and 40 Heavy Batteries, is to capture the BEAUREGARD DOVECOTE, and to form a defensive flank from BEAUREGARD DOVECOTE along high ground due West to a point opposite JOHN COPSE.

   Subsequent operations will be in a North Easterly direction in conjunction with II Corps.

4. The objectives allotted to each Division, boundaries, and timings are shewn on Maps already issued to Companies.

5. The 63rd Division, which is right Division of V Corps, is to attack on the front from RAILWAY ROAD to about Q 17 a 4.5, and its objective PUISIEUX RIVER TRENCH from MIRAUMONT-BEAUCOURT Road to about R 2 b 2.9.

6. The role of 37th Division is as follows:-

   112th Brigade is placed at disposal of G.O.C. 2nd Division, to capture the BEAUREGARD DOVECOTE after PUISIEUX Trench has been taken.

7. On Y Day, the 63rd Brigade will move to FORCEVILLE at an hour and date to be notified later.

   On Z Day, the 63rd Brigade will move to a place of assembly in Q 28 a-c.

8. The 111th Brigade will follow in rear of 63rd Brigade.

   The 63rd Brigade, followed by 111th Brigade, will keep in touch with rear of 63rd Division during the attack, and on the PUISIEUX RIVER TRENCH being taken, both Brigades will be prepared to advance towards MIRAUMONT, with the object of exploiting a success in a North-Easterly direction in conjunction with II Corps.

9. The Brigade when ordered to march from FORCEVILLE to place of assembly will move by track already reconnoitred, in the following order:-
10th Y. & L., 8th Lincs., 8th S.L.I., 4th Middlesex, 63rd T.M.Batt., 63rd M.G. Coy., and 152nd Co. R.E.
On arrival these Units will be in readiness to move off at a moment's notice.

10. It is proposed to move in the following formation in the open. Trenches must be avoided, and Companies kept well in hand.

```
    [ ] 200 yds. [ ] 300 yds. [ ] 200 yds. [ ]
         8th Lincolns.              10th York & Lancs.
                          200 yds.

    [ ]          [ ]          [ ]          [ ]
```

Headquarters will be in centre of Battalion.

11. Companies will move in Artillary formation in file by Platoons in the following formation:-

```
    ___ ___  'D'  ___ ___        ___ ___  'B'  ___ ___
    ___ ___  'C'  ___ ___        ___ ___  'A'  ___ ___
```

This will give about 65 yards between each Platoon.

12. 4th Middlesex and 8th S.L.I. will follow in rear of 10th Y. & L. and 8th Lincolns respectively, and at a distance of 400 yards from rear of rear Companies of 10th Y. & L. and 8th Lincs. 63rd T.M. Batt (less 2 guns) and 63rd M.G.C. will follow in rear of 4th Middlesex Regt. and 8th S.L.I.

13. 2 Stokes Mortars, 63rd T.M. Battery, will be between 2 leading Battalions and in line with their rear Companies.

14. The above formation may be found quite unsuitable to meet hostile fire, and modification may have to be made on the spot.

15. Brigade Headquarters will be in centre of the four Battalions.

16. When Brigade deploys for attack, the formation for Battalions will be as follows, but should the front to be attacked be a big one the system may be changed to 4 lines instead of 8, each Company being on a 2 Platoon front.

3.

```
       D        B                    D              B
    _____    _____                 _____          _____
         )        )
    _____)   _____)                _____          _____
         )        )
    _____)   _____)                _____
         )        )                               A. Coy.
    _____)   _____)                _____
                                        Headquarters.
    _____        )                _____
        A.       )
    ____Coy_____ )                       C. Coy.
                                  _____
      Headquarters

    _____        )
        C.       )
    ____Coy_____ )
```

The distance to be kept between lines will be from 60 to 100 yards.

17. If Companies attack on 1 Platoon front, the 2 leading Companies will detail 10 men and N.C.O. each from their 4th wave.

    If Companies attack on 2 Platoons front, the same parties will be taken from their last wave.

    These will be used as mopping up parties and should be well instructed as to their duties.

18. It is expected that great difficulty will be found in keeping communication, therefore, whenever Battalion halts for any length of time (not a temporary halt), Companies will immediately send a runner to Battalion Headquarters. These will state where Company Headquarters are by giving map reference. They must be capable of acting as guides, if necessary. This will also apply to communication between Battalion and Brigade Headquarters, except that 2 runners will be sent.

19. The following stores will be drawn and issued:-

    At FORCEVILLE.

    Picks and shovels in the proportion of 5 shovels to 1 pick.
    Sandbags: 2 per man.
    Very Lights: 300 1" and 50 1½" per Battalion.

    These will be distributed equally between Companies and a proportion to Battalion Headquarters.

    At ASSEMBLY TRENCHES, MESNIL.

    Hand Grenades: 2 per man. Bombing Squads: 80.
                            total: 2,700 per Battalion.
    Rifle Grenades: 320 No. 23s.
    Rockets: 30 (20 white and 10 green).

    These will be equally distributed between Companies and Battalion Headquarters.

    A proportion of green Very Pistol lights will also be issued, and will be used in addition to rockets for "S.O.S." only.

4.

20. Pack animals may be used to carry Lewis Guns from FORCEVILLE to place of assembly, and will then be immediately returned to Transport.

21. Watches will be synchronised from Battalion Headquarters at 1.15 p.m., 5.15 p.m., and 8.45 p.m. on Y Day, a representative from each Company to attend with his watch.

22. Packs and Great Coats will be left at FORCEVILLE at a place to be notified later.

23. The Brigade will most probably be operating in several places, and all maps issued should be kept handy for immediate use.

24. The route to be followed across country to place of assembly from FORCEVILLE will be track running from Pt. P 27 b 4.9 on the FORCEVILLE-HEDAUVILLE Road, through P 28, 29 and 30, past the Cemetery at ENGLEBELMER, Q 25a 3.7, to the ENGLEBELMER-MARTINSART Road to Pt. Q 33 c 1.0 whence a track leads to MESNIL.

25. Artillery barrages will be issued as soon as received.

26. Every Officer, N.C.O. and Man will carry 2 days rations (this including the iron ration already in possession).

27. Signallers and Runners are to carry all messages in left breast pocket. All casualties met with who are wearing the badge of Signallers or Runners must be searched for messages. Every man must be instructed how important this is.

28. Escorts to prisoners will be in proportion of 5% of prisoners. All documents should be taken off them at once, and handed over to A.P.M. or his representative, a receipt being taken.

29. No papers and documents etc. will be taken into action. All public moneys to be handed over to Captain DRYNAN.

30. Orders for Transport and Q.M.Stores will be issued as soon as received.

31. On gaining a position, men must be started digging a new trench at once about 50 yards or so in front of German Trench taken. On no account must enemy trench be occupied as he is found to shell it within a short time.

32. Snipers and observers must get to work at once when objective is reached, as many of the enemy can be accounted for at this time by close observation of our front. Patrols must be pushed out at once and dig themselves in in a Z shaped Trench. In addition to these, reconnoitring patrols must also be pushed out. These should be detailed beforehand, if possible.

33. Contact aeroplanes will carry two black bands on the lower right plane.
   On his dropping one white flare, this means he is working with us.
   When two white flares are dropped, he wants to know our position. Red flares will then be sent off by the furthest forward line, and if on an objective by the patrols that will have been pushed out.

34. The following will be issued as soon as received:-

   Communication arrangements.
   Medical arrangements.
   R.E. arrangements.
   Traffic arrangements.
   "S.O.S." Signals.

                              (Sd) J.H.RIDGWAY, Lt-Colonel.
Issued at 11.0 p.m.   Comdg. 10th Bn. York & Lancaster Regt.

Distribution.

War Diary and File.	1 - 3.
63rd Infantry Bde.	4.
Commanding Officer.	5.
2nd in Command.	6.
Adjutant.	7.
A. Company.	8.
B. Company.	9.
C. Company.	10.
D. Company.	11.
Bombing Officer.	12.
Signalling Officer.	13.
Quartermaster.	14.
Transport Officer.	15.

SECRET

APPENDIX I.

Reference OPERATION ORDERS No. 90 of 2:11:1916.

COMMUNICATIONS.

1. <u>Battalion H.Q. Visual Station.</u>

    6 Signallers and 4 Orderlies will, if possible,

    (i)   Open visual station to Brigade.

    (ii) Open lateral visual communication with Battalions on right and left.

    (iii) Watch the advance of their Companies and open visual communication with them.

    (iv) Keep a look-out for co-operation with aeroplanes, and accept and send messages, if required.

2. <u>Battalion H.Q. Telephone Detachment.</u>

    Will keep communication with Brigade by laying 3 Cables, and, if necessary, along the metals of the Railway line running through BEAUCOURT - GRANDCOURT - MIRAUMONT.

3. <u>Company Signallers.</u>

    3 Signallers are allotted to each Company.

    They will open visual communication with Battalion H.Q., and, if necessary, when an objective is reached, will run out a line.

4. <u>Battalion H.Q. Signal Station.</u>

    Battalion H.Q. Signal Station will be marked with notice boards.

    A pigeon basket containing two pigeons will accompany the Adjutant. They will be released one at a time, and only then in case of urgent necessity.

SIGNALS - GENERALLY.

Messages must be short as possible, and not contain long words; e.g. "O.C. B. Coy" might be cut down to "B. Coy". All figures should be written out.

Signallers wear blue band round right arm above the elbow. Signallers and Orderlies will carry all messages in left breast pocket, which will be left vacant except for any such messages and their pay book. Any casualty wearing either Signallers or Orderlies badge will be searched by anyone who sees them, and any message found will be either

      (i)   Delivered immediately to the addressee,
      (ii) Handed in to nearest Signal Office,
or (iii) Handed to an Officer.

This must be made known to all ranks.

Any man seeing any Signalling equipment lying about will, if possible, take the same forward and hand it to the nearest Signal Office.

Instructions for use of Code Names and Code Calls.

Unit.	Code Name.	Code Call.
63rd Brigade H.Q.	MACARONI.	BGE.
8th Lincolns.	MARMALADE.	GBE.
8th SOMERSET L.I.	MINT.	GRE.
4th Middlesex.	MATCHES.	BZE.
10th York & Lancaster.	MAPLE.	GVE.
63rd M.G. Coy.	MILK.	BQE.
63rd T.M. Batt.	MILKMAID.	GIE.

The above code names and code calls will be used within 3,000 yards of the line.

O.C. Companies will detail a suitable man or N.C.O. to keep the contact aeroplane under observation. They may also be required to furnish their Signal Station with orderlies.

It must be borne in mind the fastest rate of sending will not be more than 6 words per minute, and this must be taken into consideration when deciding whether to send a message by signal or orderly. The safest way would be to send the same message by both means.

S.O.S. SIGNAL.

The S.O.S. Signal as laid down by Reserve Army is:-

  One white rocket, one green rocket, one white rocket,
    fired in quick succession and repeated until
    Artillery fire opens.

Artillery will open fire on seeing one white and one green rocket.

If at anytime rockets are not forthcoming, Very Pistol lights may be used instead - White, green, white - repeated so long as necessary.

A proportion of green Very lights are being issued. They should be distributed and kept for S.O.S. purposes alone.

Snipers will carry rockets in sandbags. There will be two sets per Company, and two sets for H.Q.

SECRET

APPENDIX II.

Reference OPERATION ORDERS No. 90 of 2:11:1916.

Arrangements for Transport, Supplies, &c. &c.

1. Allotment of Roads and Traffic Circuits in the forward Area.

    For traffic in an easterly direction: The Road ENGLEBELMER - MESNIL - HAMEL - BEAUCOURT.

    Vehicles are forbidden to overtake and pass one another. If a breakdown occurs, the road must be cleared of the vehicle at once.

    Foot passengers and led or ridden animals will move across country and use the roads as little as possible so as to leave them free for wheeled transport.

2. Transport Generally.

    (a) Train transport (supplies) will work from refilling point to "Train wagon head" - (probably 1st Line Transport lines on 'Z' Day and MESNIL subsequently).

    (b) 1st Line Transport will work forward from "Train wagon head" to "Limber head".

    (c) Pack transport will work forward from "Limber head" to "Pack head", where they will be met by carrying parties.

    (d) The systems of limbered wagons and pack will very probably have to be worked conjointly or possible even pack entirely from "wagon head" according to circumstances.

    (e) It is hoped that sufficient animals will be placed at the disposal of Infantry Brigades to complete a maximum of 250 per Brigade.

2a. First Line Transport.

    (a) On the night Y/Z 1st Line Transport will be at FORCEVILLE.

    (b) Half the L.D. animals of each unit till be told off as pack animals, together with any extra animals that may be allotted. The remainder of the L.D. animals in the first instance will be reserved for draught, but units must be prepared to use them for pack if need be.
    The H.D. and Water cart animals will not be used for pack.

    (c) For purposes of control all 1st line transport will be pooled and will be grouped as follows:-
    (1) Pack.
    (2) Limbered wagons.
    (3) Water carts and cookers.

    (1) Pack animals will be subdivided into three reliefs under
    Lieut. PIKE, 8th Somerset Light Infantry.
    2/Lt. HODGSON, 4th Middlesex Regt.
    2/Lt. KNOWLES, 10th York & Lancaster Regt.

2.

2.
(Cont.)

(2) Limbered wagons will be under 2/Lieut. RAHBULA, 8th Lincolnshire Regiment who will be assisted by 2/Lieut. DUKES, 8th Lincolnshire Regiment.

(3) Water carts and cookers will be under 2/Lieut. HAWES, 63rd Machine Company.

The Sergeants and full Corporals of units will do duty with that section of transport which is controlled by their own Officers.

(d) The loads placed in limbered wagons must be made up in such a way as to admit transfer to pack at any moment. Pack saddles, issue or improvised, sufficient for all animals will be considered as part of the equipment of every limbered wagon, and those for the off mules of the team will be carried on the animals.
The issued pack saddles will be used in the first instance and the improvised pack saddles to make up the number required.

(e) Sufficient leaders must be allotted to the transport by units to enable one man to lead one animal, counting the maximum number of animals that could be used as pack animals.

3. Train Transport.

Baggage wagons will be returned to the Train Company at LEALVILLERS on the evening of 'Y' day after unloading regimental baggage at billets.

4. Supplies.

(a) On leaving billets on Z Day every one will have the unconsumed portion of that day's rations, the iron ration, and one extra grocery ration.

(b) There will be an extra ration of rum on Y Day so as to admit an issue being made early on Z morning before troops start and also an issue sent up for Z night.

(c) It is understood that a small supply of solidified spirit for cooking purposes will be available for fuel. Coke and charcoal will also be issued in sandbags of suitable weight for pack transport.

(d) A small issue of chewing gum will be made.

5. Water.

(a) Special care must be taken that all water bottles are full on leaving the place of assembly.

(b) There are 7,000 filled 2 gallon petrol tins in the dump at MESNIL: these will be drawn on for use.

(c) Every effort must be made to return empty petrol tins complete with stoppers in exchange for full ones.

(d) Water carts will be kept well filled.

6. Dumps.

(a) All dumps are common property.
The main dump to be used by the Brigade is the 63rd Divisional Dump at MESNIL, Q 28 c 7.8.

(b) 2/Lieut. R.G. WILLIAMS, 4th Middlesex Regt - Divisional Salvage Officer, will be in charge of this Dump.

(c) On no account is water to be drawn from dumps except for use in the forward area.

7. Baggage and Packs.

(a) Regimental baggage and Packs will be stored at FORCEVILLE. Exact location of stores will be notified later.

All blankets, kits, etc. will be clearly marked.

(b) Telescopic rifles and sights are not to be carried forward by attacking units. They may be handed to D.A.D.O.S., properly labelled, for safe custody.

(c) Great coats will be stored in FORCEVILLE. They must be securely tied together in bundles of five and will be sent up later by pack or other transport.

All ranks must be cautioned against leaving any private property in the pockets as it will not be possible to ensure that each man gets his own coat on redistribution.

8. Casualties.

Every effort must be made to acquaint Battalion Headquarters of the approximate casualties sustained by units.

9. Prisoners.

All prisoners of war will be conducted to 63rd Division Collecting Station at Q 31 b 3.6.
Escorts should normally consist of 10% of the number of prisoners.
Escorts and guard are forbidden to talk to prisoners or to give them tobacco or food, and will prevent them from conversing together.

10. Veterinary.

Veterinary Collecting Station (63rd Division) will be at ENGLEBELMER, near the Cemetery - Q 25 a 1.7.

11. Roads.

The following road is allotted to this Division:-

MESNIL - BEAUCOURT Stn - BEAUMONT HAMEL - AUCHONVILLERS - VETTERMONT - MESNIL.

Traffic to be in this direction only.

SECRET

APPENDIX III.

Reference OPERATION ORDERS No. 90 of 2:11:1916.

R. E. ARRANGEMENTS.

By arrangement, the following dumps of the 63rd Division are available for use by 37th Division:-

DUMPS.
1. ENGLEBELMER (Q 25 a 5.8).
2. FORT JACKSON (Q 16 d 2.½).
3. HAMEL (Q 23 d 5.5).

Copy No.   S E C R E T

AMENDMENT to APPENDIX II of OPERATION ORDERS No. 90.

The following must be read in conjunction with Operation Orders No. 90 dated 2:11:1916 - Arrangements for Transport, Supplies, etc. etc.

2. <u>Transport Generally.</u>   Unaltered.

2a. <u>First Line Transport.</u>
- (a) Transport will remain with Battalion in ACHEUX WOOD, till Battalion leaves this place.
  When Battalion leaves, 1st Line Transport will concentrate at LEALVILLERS, where Q.M. Stores will also be.
- (b) Unaltered.
- (c) Unaltered.
- (d) Unaltered.
- (e) Unaltered.

3. <u>Train Transport.</u>
    Unaltered for the present.   (If possible, arrangements will be made to keep baggage wagons till Battalion leaves ACHEUX WOOD).

4. <u>Supplies.</u>
- (a) Delete "On leaving Billets on Z Day" and substitute "On leaving ACHEUX WOOD".
- (b) There will be an extra ration of rum on Y Day so as to admit of an issue being made on the morning on which Battalion leaves ACHEUX WOOD, and also an issue being sent up that night.
- (c) Unaltered.
- (d) Unaltered.

5. <u>Water.</u>   Unaltered.

6. <u>Dumps.</u>   Unaltered.

7. <u>Baggage and Packs.</u>
- (a) Regimental Baggage and Packs will be stored at LEALVILLERS, and will be moved there as soon as Battalion has left ACHEUX WOOD. Exact location of Stores will be notified later.
  All blankets, kits, etc. will be clearly marked.
- (b) Unaltered.
- (c) Great Coats will be stored in ACHEUX WOOD and will be sent up to Battalion from this place.
  They must be securely tied in bundles of five.
  All ranks must be warned not to leave anything in pockets, as there is no certainty of getting same coats on redistribution.

8. <u>Casulaties.</u>   Unaltered.

9. <u>Prisoners.</u>   Unaltered.

10. <u>Veterinary.</u>   Unaltered.

11. <u>Roads.</u>   Unaltered.

Add the following:

12. <u>Drawing of tools, Grenades, etc.</u>
    Instructions as to drawing of tools, grenades, etc. will be issued later.

13. <u>Ordnance.</u>
    Brigade has arranged for an emergency supply of 1200 yards of flannelette and 30 gallons of Rifle Oil. This will be supplied from Brigade Headquarters on demand.

(Sd) L.A. ELSWORTH, Capt. & Adjt.
11.0 p.m. 11:11:1916.   10th Battn. York & Lancaster Regiment.

AMENDMENT to OPERATION ORDERS No. 90, dated 2:11:1916.
By Lt-Colonel J.H. RIDGWAY,
Comdg. 10th Bn. York & Lancaster Regiment.

1) Operation Order No. 90 dated 2:11:1916 is modified to this extent:-

   The Line to be captured on Z Day by V Corps will be the YELLOW LINE, but the following addition is made to include BEAUCOURT-sur-ANCRE - R 7a 4.3 - R 7 b 0.5 - R 7 b 3.6 to R 8 d 0.9.

   XIII Corps will form a Defensive Flank on the extreme North.

   The Intermediate Line - green - will remain the same.

2. Weather permitting, V Corps will be prepared to resume the Advance in conjunction with II Corps to the BROWN LINE on Z plus 2 days, guns and ammunition being brought forward during the interval.

3. Today is X Day. Time will be synchronised on T Day at 12.30 p.m., 4.30 p.m., and 8.30 p.m., if possible.

4. Z Day will be notified separately. Timings and Zero hour will be settled later.

5. Details regarding storage of kits, issue of bombs, tools, etc. will be issued later.

6. On the night of Y/Z, the 37th Division will be in V Corps Reserve.

(Sd) L.A. ELSWORTH, Capt. & Adjt.
Issued at 12 noon, 11:11:16. 10th Battn. York & Lancaster Regiment.

Appendix No. 4

Copy No.   S E C R E T

O P E R A T I O N   O R D E R S   No. 91.
By Lt-Colonel J.H. RIDGWAY,
Comdg. 10th Battn. York & Lancaster Regiment.
11th November 1916.

Reference: LENS 1:100,000. 57 D 1:40,000.

The Brigade will move tomorrow to LEALVILLERS and ACHEUX WOOD.

The Battalion will move tomorrow to ACHEUX WOOD, and take over billets.

Route: Northern outskirts of BEAUQUESNE - RAINCHEVAL - ARQUEVES.

Head of Column to pass Orderly Room at 8.15 a.m.

Order of March: B. D. A. C., H.Q. Coy, Lewis Gunners, Transport.

Dress: Full Marching Order. All Officers must dress as much like men as possible. Puttees will, in any case, be worn by everybody.

Billeting party, under 2/Lt. SAMUELS, will report to Town Major, ACHEUX WOOD, at 10.0 a.m.

Reveille: 5.30 a.m. Breakfasts: 6.30 a.m. Dinners will be cooked en route.

All wagons to be loaded by 7.30 a.m; Mess Cart by 7.45 a.m. Blankets to be rolled and labelled ready for loading by 7.0 a.m. (these will be stacked by Companies at Q.M. Stores at this hour).

All billets to be vacated by 7.30 a.m. and ready for inspection by that hour. The 2nd in Command will obtain a receipt from the Town Major that they are clean and tidy. One Officer per Company to attend inspection.

Lewis Gun carts will be drawn in pairs by pack animals. No packs, rifles or any other gear to be carried on these carts. A sufficient number of men to march with each pair of carts to act as brakesmen, the remainder to march in rear of carts.

All cooks will be properly dressed in marching order. The 2nd in Command will keep visiting all transport on line of march to see that these orders are enforced.

Orders re carriage of Petrol tins, improvised saddles, etc. will be issued later.

O.C. Companies and Sections will render a certificate by 6.0 p.m tomorrow, that every Officer, N.C.O. and Man on the strength of his Company or Section has been instructed in the use of the new box respirator.

(Sd) L.A. ELSWORTH, Capt. & Adjt
Issued at 12 noon.   10th Bn. York & Lancaster Regiment.

Distribution.

War Diary and File.	1 - 3.	Lewis Gun Officer.	10.
63rd Infantry Brigade.	4.	Bombing Officer.	11.
Commanding Officer.	5.	Signalling Officer.	12.
A. Company.	6.	Snipers.	13.
B. Company.	7.	Quartermaster.	14.
C. Company.	8.	Transport Officer.	15.
D. Company.	9.	Medical Officer.	16.

Copy No. Appendix No. 5

OPERATION ORDERS No. 92.
By Lt-Colonel J.H. RIDGWAY,
Comdg. 10th Bn. York & Lancaster Regt.
12th November 1916.

The Battalion will be prepared to move at ½ hours' notice at 6.0 a.m. tomorrow.

Reveille: 4.0 a.m.
Breakfast: 5.0 a.m.
Dinners will be cooked en route.

All packs, blankets and greatcoats will be stacked by Companies in a Hut which Quartermaster will set aside for this purpose, as near wooden road as possible.

Greatcoats will be tied in bundles of fives. Nothing to be left in pockets, as there is no vertainty of getting same coats back. Blankets will be rolled in bundles of tens, and securely tied and labelled.

If Battalion moves, Water Carts will also accompany Battalion, and should be ready to move at very short notice.

(Sd) L.A. ELSWORTH, Capt.& Adjt.
10th Battn. York & Lancaster Regiment.

10th Battn. York & Lancaster Regiment.   App: 6

Report on Operations — 13th to 22nd November 1916.

Reference Map: 57D 1:40,000.

November 14th.

The Battalion marched from ACHEUX WOOD at 10.0 a.m. to Camp near ENGLEBELMER (Q 31 b).

At 8.0 p.m. it was ordered into the line in front of BEAUCOURT-sur-ANCRE, which had been captured that morning by the 63rd (Naval) Division. The Battalion (less Reserve N.C.Os, Specialists, Q.M. Stores, Transport, etc.) moved via MARTINSART - MESNIL - HAMEL, and came under heavy shell fire moving up RAILWAY ROAD.

On the night 14th/15th, 2nd Lt. H.A. WALNE, C. Company, went out in charge of a patrol to examine bridge across ANCRE River in R 7 c Central. The bridge was examined and found to be made of brick and stone, and in good condition.

2nd Lt. WALNE proceeded to make strong point to cover bridge (R 7 c Central) with Lewis Gun and 20 Other Ranks. This was found difficult owing to the marshy state of the ground. The shell fire was incessant - a Lewis gun was lost, and there were 18 Other Ranks casualties. During this time, Sergeant E.S. HOWARD did very good work encouraging the men to work, and when ordered to retire assisted with the wounded.

November 15th.

Heavy bombardment of BEAUCOURT all day in the form of a barrage.

The Relief was completed at 6.0 a.m., troops of the H.A.C., the 13th R.F., and 13th K.R.R. being relieved. 8th Lincolns were situated on our left.

Battalion H.Q. was established in German dug-out at Q 18 b 9.9. running from point R 7 b 4.5 South to the Road (6.0). B. Company was in trench running from Road (6.0) to R 7 b 6.7, with C. Company in Support in trench in Village along Road running South from Cross Roads.

These trenches were only partly dug, and were carried on by us.

During the night 15th/16th, 2nd Lt. WALNE again visited bridge which was still found to be intact. Lieut. W.B.S. O'BRIEN patrolled Road running from R 7 b 0.8 to 5.9. Nothing of the enemy was seen in either case.

November 16th.

Continuous heavy bombardment.

Battalion H.Q. moved further forward to German dug-out at R 7 c 9.4.

Consolidation continued.

2nd Lt. F.E. PAYNE reconnoitred ANCRE TRENCH to a point near BOIS d'HOLLANDE, where he was prevented going further by our own barrage. He discovered damaged German heavy gun, and also many dead Germans in full marching order in QUARRY at R 8 c 1.9. He encountered no enemy.

2nd Lt. J.M. STROTHER took a patrol out from B. Company, and proceeded up road to R 1 d 5.2, then Eastwards crossing two disused trenches to about R 2 c 3.1, where he was prevented going farther by our barrage. He was fired on by Germans from PUISIEUX TRENCH, who also advanced towards him, but retired owing to our shelling. Though 2nd Lt. STROTHER was wounded in the head by a bullet soon after leaving the trench, he finished the patrol.

B. Company sent out a patrol under a N.C.O. which proceeded to about 200 yards West of BOIS d'HOLLANDE without encountering enemy. Was also fired on from PUISIEUX TRENCH while returning.

ANCRE TRENCH occupied that night by one Company 8th Somerset Light Infantry, and a post established in BOIS d'HOLLANDE by them.

Parties with Lewis Guns were sent out to make strong points at R 7 b 8.3; R 8 c 0.9 and R 7 d 8.8, under 2nd Lts. HAWLEY, PAYNE and WALNE respectively. Also two posts to the North at R 1 d 4.4 and R 1 d 8.3, under 2nd Lts. STROTHER and OAKLEY.

Patrols were also sent out to our front, and did not encounter any of the enemy, but got into communication with 8th Somerset L.I. in BOIS d'HOLLANDE.

November 17th.

Shelling was intermittent and heavy, especially on RAILWAY ROAD in BEAUCOURT and in valley.

Consolidation was carried on all day. During the night our posts in R 7 d were relieved by the 8th Lincolns and 8th Somerset L.I. Latter al so pushed out posts to make line continuous to BOIS d'HOLLANDE.

November 18th.

The attack of the 19th Division South of the River commenced at 6.10 a.m. This was supported by an attack on PUISIEUX TRENCH by the 8th Somerset L.I. and 4th Middlesex at 11.0 a.m. with this Battalion in reserve. All the Trench South of the Road was captured.

During this period the shelling was extremely heavy.

4th Middlesex Regt. relieved 8th Somerset L.I. and B. and C. Coys. 10th York & Lancaster Regt. were ordered to report to O.C. 4th Middlesex Regt. and came under his orders.

November 19th.

Consolidating. Artillery not quite so active though a heavy barrage was put on BEAUCOURT during the commencement ot the 111th Brigade attack on the left at 3.0 p.m.

November 20th.

Situation much quieter.

The Companies in the line and strong points were relieved by the 7th Bn. South Staffs. Regt. at 8.30 p.m., and spent the night 20/21st in the open at Q 29 b.

November 21st to 24th.

Billets taken over in HAMEL. Working parties and Burial parties provided.

Total Casualties.

Killed in Action	One Officer.	26 Other Ranks.
Died of Wounds.		4 Other Ranks.
Missing.		2 Other Ranks.
Wounded.	Five Officers.	164 Other Ranks.

Appx 7.

Extract from Battalion Orders dated 27th November 1916.

573. Commendation.

The Commanding Officer wishes to place on record the very fine work performed by the Battalion and Company Runners and the Stretcher Bearers during the recent Operations. It was mainly due to their devotion to duty that communication was kept up between Battalion and Company Headquarters, and Battalion and Brigade Headquarters, and the wounded evacuated during a very trying time. These men continually went backwards and forwards, on many occasions whilst the enemy had placed a barrage on the village; thus showing great courage and devotion to duty, and setting a very fine example to the other men of the Battalion.

Appendix No. 8.

Copy No.   S E C R E T

OPERATION ORDERS No. 91A.
By Lt-Colonel J.H. RIDGWAY,
Comdg. 10th Bn. York & Lancaster Regiment.
23rd November 1916.

The Brigade will march tomorrow to ENGLEBELMER. Route: MESNIL - MARTINSART.

Leading Company 10th York & Lancaster Regt. will pass Starting Point (Fork Roads, Q 23 d 4.2, Reference Map 57 D) at 8.15 a.m.

The Battalion will march by Companies at 200 yards intervals, and 500 yards between Battalions. The Machine Gun Corps will be in front of Battalion.

Order of March: H.Q., A. B. C. D. Coys.

Great coats and ground sheets will be carried strapped on the back.

Reveille: 6.30 a.m.   Sick Parade: 6.15 a.m.
Breakfasts: 6.30 a.m.
Cookers, water cart, limbers for Signallers and Lewis Guns will be loaded and ready at 7.30 a.m. This applies to Officers' Mess Cart.

Company Commanders horses will arrive at 8.0 a.m.

Company Commanders will pay particular attention to march discipline, a slow steady pace to be maintained, and on traffic being met to keep well to the right of the road. Names of any men falling out will be reported to Orderly Room immediately on arrival in billets, and will be seen by Medical Officer on arrival there.

Dinners will be cooked en route.

The party of 30 Other Ranks, under 2nd Lt. STROTHER, will rejoin their Companies tomorrow at 7.0 a.m.

Billeting party will report at ENGLEBELMER to Town Major at 8.0 a.m. Orders have been sent to Q.M. Stores re latter.

                                                                       (Sd) L.A. ELSWORTH, Capt.& Adjt
Issued at 8.30 p.m.   10th Battalion York & Lancaster Regiment.

Appendix No. 9

Copy No.   S E C R E T

OPERATION ORDERS No. 92.A
By Lt-Colonel J.H. RIDGWAY,
Comdg. 10th Bn. York & Lancaster Regiment.
24th November 1916.

The Brigade will march tomorrow and take over billets at MAILLY MAILLET.

The Battalion will follow the 8th Somerset Light Infantry, leading Company passing Starting Point (Q 19 b 4½.5) at 10.15 a.m. The Battalion will march by Companies at 200 yards interval.

Order of March: H.Q., B. C. D. A.

Packs will be carried by the men, and jerkins carried rolled on top of pack, and not worn.

Transport to follow Battalion.

Lewis Gun handcarts will be drawn by pack animals. Sufficient number of men to be detailed with each trolley to act as brakesmen. Remainder will follow in rear of Battalion.

Blankets will be rolled and tied in bundles of ten, and stacked at Q.M. Stores by 9.0 a.m. One man per Company will be left behind in charge, and will come on later.

Billeting party will report to 2/Lt. SAMUELS at Battalion H.Q. at 7.15 a.m.

Reveille: 6.45 a.m.   Breakfasts: 7.30 a.m.

All wagons will be packed and loaded by 9.0 a.m., including Officers' Mess Cart.

Sick Parade: 7.15 a.m.

Company Commanders to pay particular attention that men are properly dressed, and that the strictest march discipline is maintained.

The whole of tomorrow afternoon will be spent in cleaning up generally.

Billets will be left clean.

(Sd) L.A. ELSWORTH, Capt.& Adjt.
Issued at 10.0 p.m.   10th Battn. York & Lancaster Regiment

Distribution.

War Diary and File.	1 - 3.	Lewis Gun Officer.	10.
63rd Infantry Brigade.	4.	Bombing Officer.	11.
Commanding Officer.	5.	Signalling Officer.	12.
A. Company.	6.	Captain Drynan.	13.
B. Company.	7.	Quartermaster.	14.
C. Company.	8.	Transport Officer.	15.
D. Company.	9.	Medical Officer.	16.

Appendix No. 10.

Copy No.   S E C R E T

OPERATION ORDERS No. 93.
By Lt-Colonel J.H. RIDGWAY,
Comdg. 10th Battn. York & Lancaster Regiment.
25th November 1916.

The Brigade will march tomorrow; the 10th York & Lancaster Regiment proceeding to RAINCHEVAL.
Starting point: Road Junction, P 12 c 8.2. Head of Battalion will pass starting point at 9.30 a.m.

Order of March: H.Q., C, D, A, B., Lewis Gunners, Transport.

Route: BERTRANCOURT - LOUVENCOURT - ARQUEVES.

Dress: Full Marching Order. Steel Helmets. Jerkins carried rolled on top of packs.

200 yards distance will be kept between Companies, and 500 yards between Battalions. 10th York & Lancaster Regt. follows 8th Somerset Light Infantry.

Billeting Party, under 2/Lt. SAMUELS, will parade at Battalion Orderly Room at 9.0 a.m.

Companies will halt at 10 minutes to the hour for the usual halt. Watches will be synchronised with the Adjutant's before leaving.

The march tomorrow will be a long one, and march discipline will not be relaxed in any way.

All Companies and Sections will be out of their billets by 8.0 a.m. to make room for the 4th Middlesex Regt. and 8th Lincoln Regt., who are marching in at that hour.

Reveille: 6.0 a.m.   Breakfasts: 7.0 a.m.
Medical Officer's inspection: 6.30 a.m.

Wagons to be packed by 7.30 a.m., Officers' Mess Cart by 7.45 a.m.

Three wagons from D.A.C. will be available for blankets and any other spare kit. These will report at 6.0 a.m.

Dinners will be cooked en route. Lewis Gun Handcarts will be drawn by Pack animals.

On the 27th instant, the Battalion will march to TERRAMESNIL.

                                 (Sd) L.A. ELSWORTH, Capt. & Adjt.
Issued at 11.30 p.m.   10th Battn. York & Lancaster Regiment.

Distribution.

War Diary and File.	1 - 3.	Lewis Gun Officer.	10.
63rd Infantry Brigade.	4.	Bombing Officer.	11.
Commanding Officer.	5.	Signalling Officer.	12.
A. Company.	6.	Captain Drynan.	13.
B. Company.	7.	Quartermaster.	14.
C. Company.	8.	Transport Officer.	15.
D. Company.	9.	Medical Officer.	16.

CONFIDENTIAL.

10th (Service) Battalion
The YORK and LANCASTER Regiment.

WAR DIARY.

DECEMBER - 1916.

SIXTEENTH VOLUME.

Army Form C. 2118

WAR DIARY of 10th/13th York and or Lancaster Regiment
INTELLIGENCE SUMMARY
(Erase heading not required.)

Instructions regarding War Diaries and Intelligence Summaries are contained in F.S. Regs., Part II. and the Staff Manual respectively. Title Pages will be prepared in manuscript.

Place	Date 1916	Hour	Summary of Events and Information	Remarks and references to Appendices
TERRAMESNIL	Nov. 1st		Bn in billets at TERRAMESNIL.	
	2nd		Draft of 5 ORs arrived from 34th I.B.D.	
	4th		Lieut. J. CORBAN joined from 34th I.B.D. Major D.T. WELSH joined Battn from England.	App. 2.
	9th		Cpl Cyclist 1 Bn on first communion.	
	11th		Draft of 16 ORs arrived from 34th I.B.D.	
	13th		Draft of 2 ORs arrived from 34th I.B.D.	
			Draft of 5 ORs arrived from 34th I.B.D.	
RANSART	14th		Bn proceeded by route march to RANSART en route to First Army, taking over billets.	
AUBROMETZ	15th		Bn proceeded by route march to AUBROMETZ taking over billets. Draft of 9 ORs arrived from 34th I.B.D.	App. 2.
FLEURY and CONTEVILLE	16th		Bn proceeded by route march. H.Q. and 2 Coys to FLEURY, taking over billets, 2 Coys to CONTEVILLE taking over billets.	
NEDONCHELLE	17th		Battn proceeded by route march to NEDONCHELLE taking over billets.	
BUSNES	18th		Battn proceeded by route march to BUSNES, taking over billets.	
	20th		9 Offrs joined from England. 5 ORs arrived from 34th I.B.D.	App. 2.
LA FOSSÉ	22nd		Battn proceeded by route march to VIEILLE CHAPELLE Billeting Area. Billets taken over by Battn in LA FOSSÉ.	
			Capt. S.W. WICKS joined Bn from England. Lieut. W.C. SUMNER joined Bn from England.	
	24th		Lieut. S.R. on first communion. Capt. S. LUCAS joined Battn from 2/York Lanc. R.	App. 2.
	31st		Capt. S.W. WICKS to 9th York Lanc. R. Draft of 11 O.Rs. joined from 34th I.B.D.	

M Mulray Lt Col.
Comdg. 10th/13th York Lancaster Rgt.

LIST of APPENDICES.
----

1. List of Officers on Strength - 30th December 1916.

2. CASUALTIES - STRENGTH, December 1916.

3. Operation Order No. 94.

4. Battalion Orders, 8th December 1916, for V Corps
     Commander's Inspection.

5. Operation Orders No. 95.

6. Operation Orders No. 96.

7. Operation Orders No. 97.

8. Operation Orders No. 98.

9. Operation Orders No. 99.

10. Operation Orders No. 100.

Appendix No. 1.

10th Battn. York & Lancaster Regiment.

ROLL of OFFICERS.   30th December 1916.

Rank.	Name.		Present Employment.
Lt-Col.	RIDGWAY,	J.H.	Commanding Officer.
Major	WELSH,	D.T.	Second in Command.
Captain	DRYNAN,	W.B.	Company Commander.
"	ELSWORTH,	L.A.	Adjutant.
"	LUCAS,	S.	Sick.
"	BROADBENT,	H.	On leave.
Lieut.	ROBINSON,	A.R.	Company Commander.
"	WILKINSON,	R.M.	Company Commander.
"	KNOWLES,	F.E.	Transport Officer.
2nd Lt.	NICHOLSON,	C.A.J.	Sick.
"	MITCHELL,	R.J.	Platoon Commander.
"	AYRES,	F.	Brigade School.
"	PAYNE,	F.F.	Bombing Officer.
"	HAWLEY,	D.D.	Lewis Gun Officer.
"	SAMUELS,	E.	Signalling Officer.
"	LAMOND,	A.W.	Company Commander.
"	STROTHER,	J.M.	Intelligence Officer.
"	HILL,	J.E.	Platoon Commander.
"	OAKLEY,	M.H.	Course of Instruction.
"	CORBAN,	J.	On leave.
"	FAIRBAIRN,	J.J.W.	Platoon Commander.
"	JACKSON,	F.E.	Course of Instruction.
"	WILKS,	E.L.	Platoon Commander.
"	GAUNT,	B.W.	Platoon Commander.
"	TAYLOR,	J.B.	Platoon Commander.
"	SUMNER,	W.G.	Platoon Commander.
"	TOPPING,	E.	Platoon Commander.
"	HORSFALL,	J.R.	Platoon Commander.
"	WOODMANSEY,	K.G.	Platoon Commander.
"	LUPTON,	F.	Course of Instruction.
Lt. & Q.M.	JAMIESON,	A.	Quartermaster.
Captain.	PLAISTER, (R.A.M.C.)	G.R.	Medical Officer.

Appendix No. 2

10th Bn. York & Lancaster Regt.

CASUALTIES incurred during the month of December 1916.

Sickness.	In Trenches.	Working Parties, Resting, etc.
Officers.	**Officers.**	**Officers.**
Capt. S. LUCAS, admitted 29:12:16.	N I L.	N I L.
Other Ranks.	**Other Ranks.**	**Other Ranks.**
Total Sick Wastage - 29.	N I L.	N I L.

STRENGTH - DECEMBER 1916.

November 30th 1916. Effective Strength. 27 Officers. 654 Other Ranks.
Available Strength. 17 Officers. 578 Other Ranks.

December 30th 1916. Effective Strength. 31 Officers. 652 Other Ranks.
Available Strength. 29 Officers. 608 Other Ranks.

Increase. Officers.

Major D.T. WELSH.   Joined from England.   9:12:1916.
2/Lt. J. CORBAN. Joined from VI Corps Cyclist Bn. on
                       first Commission.   4:12:1916.

2/Lt. J.J.W. FAIRBAIRN.)
2/Lt. F.C. JACKSON.   )
2/Lt. E.L. WILKS.   )
2/Lt. B.W. GAUNT.   )
2/Lt. J.B. TAYLOR.   ) Joined from England. 20:12:1916.
2/Lt. E. TOPPING.   )
2/Lt. J.R. HORSFALL.   )
2/Lt. K.G. WOODMANSEY.)
2/Lt. F. LUPTON.   )

Capt. S.W. WICKS.   Joined from England.   22:12:1916.
2/Lt. W.G. SUMNER.   Joined from 2/Worc. R. on
                         first Commission.   22:12:1916.
Capt. S. LUCAS.   Joined from 2nd Y. & L. R. 27:12:16.

Other Ranks.   5 Other Ranks from 34 I.B.D.   2:12:1916.
              16   do.   do.   9:12:1916.
               2   do.   do.   11:12:1916.
               5   do.   do.   13:12:1916.
               9   do.   do.   15:12:1916.
               5   do.   do.   20:12:1916.

Decrease. Officers.

2/Lt. E.S. CHAMBERS.   To England. Sick.   15:12:1916.
Lieut. D.A. HALL.   To England. Sick.   18:11:1916.
Lieut. A.L. QUANCE.   To England. Wounded. 20:11:1916.
2/Lt. H.W. CARTER.   To England. Wounded. 21:11:1916.
Lieut. S.J.S. GROVES.   To England. Wounded. 22:11:1916.
Lieut. W.B.S. O'BRIEN.   To England. Wounded. 22:11:1916.
2/Lt. J.F. MAGEE.   To England. Wounded. 22:11:1916.
2/Lt. H.A. WALNE.   To England. Sick.   24:11:1916.
Capt. C.F. AIREY.   To England. Sick.   26:11:1916.
Capt. S.W. WICKS. To 9th Bn. Y. & L. Regt.   27:12:1916.

Other Ranks.   Sick Wastage. 29.   Died in Hospital 1.
           Transferred to M.G. Corps. 8.   To Base (Unfit). 3.
           To Base for Dental   To Munitions (Eng.) 1.
                     Treatment. 1   To England (Com'n) 1.
                                              Total.   44.

Copy No.   Appendix No. 3

                                                                                 S E C R E T.

OPERATION ORDERS No. 94.

By Lt-Colonel J.H. RIDGWAY,
Comdg. 10th Bn. York & Lancaster Regiment.
30th November 1916.

The Battalion will march to TERRAMESNIL tomorrow and take over billets.

Order of March: H.Q., D, A, B, C., Lewis Gunners, Transport. 200 yards interval will be kept between Companies.

Dress: Full Marching Order. Jerkins rolled on top of pack. Steel helmets on face of pack. Dismounted Officers will carry packs.

Head of Column to pass Cross Roads near Church at 9.0 a.m. Transport will join Column at Fork Roads N 5 c Central.

2/Lt. SAMUELS and billeting party will report to Town Major, TERRAMESNIL, at 8.0 a.m.

Blankets will be rolled in bundles and securely tied and handed in to Q.M. Stores by 8.0 a.m. Braziers will also be handed in at the same time.

Billets to be vacated at 8.15 a.m. and left ready for inspection, an Officer per Company to attend.

Companies will halt for ten minutes at 10 minutes to the hour. Watches to be synchronised with Adjutant's before leaving.

All wagons to be packed and loaded by 8.15 a.m. Transport Officer will arrange for a limber for Mess Baskets, etc.

Reveille: 6.0 a.m. Sick Parade: 6.30 a.m. Breakfasts: 7.0 a.m. Dinners will be cooked on arrival in TERRAMESNIL.

                                                         (Sd) L.A. ELSWORTH, Capt. & Adjt.
Issued at 3.0 p.m.   10th Battn. York & Lancaster Regiment.

Distribution.   Copy.

    War Diary and File   1 - 3.
    63rd Infantry Brigade.   4.
    Commanding Officer.   5.
    A. Company.   6.
    B. Company.   7.
    C. Company.   8.
    D. Company.   9.
    Lewis Gun Officer.   10.
    Bombing Officer.   11.
    Signalling Officer.   12.
    2nd in Command.   13.
    Transport Officer.   14.
    Quartermaster.   15.
    Intelligence Officer.   16.
    Medical Officer.   17.

Appendix No. 4

Battalion Orders dated 8th December 1916.

AFTER ORDERS.
By Lt-Colonel J.H. RIDGWAY,
Comdg. 10th Bn. York & Lancaster Regiment.

The G.O.C., V Corps, will inspect Battalion tomorrow.
Full marching order. Steel helmets, Box Respirators and Gas Helmets.

Parade: 8.15 a.m. Order of March: A. B. C. D., Lewis Gunners, Transport.

5 L.G.S. wagons will be on parade, 2 Water Carts, Pack animals with loads.

Adjutant and 2 markers will report to Brigade Major at Fork Roads H 21 d 1.4 at 8.45 a.m.

Battalion will parade as strong as possible. No working parties will be found, except Town Major's Fatigue, which will be found from the same men as found it today.

Lewis Gun Carts will be drawn by Gun teams.

Stretcher Bearers will parade with stretchers under Medical Officer. Bicycles will be on parade.

2/Lt. Mitchell will take charge of Lewis Gunners vice 2/Lt. HAWLEY (on Court-Martial).
2/Lt. CORBAN will command C. Company vice 2/Lt. SAMUELS (on Court-Martial).

No rifle covers will be worn. All transport drivers, brakesmen, and pack animal men will carry rifles slung over right shoulder. Spurs and whips will be worn by all drivers. All wagons to be loaded with authorised load.

Jerkins will not be carried.

Reveille: 5.0 a.m.
Breakfasts: 6.0 a.m.
Sick Parade: 7.0 a.m.

(Sd) R.M. WILKINSON, Lieut. a/Adjt.
10th Battn. York & Lancaster Regiment.

Note. The Commanding Officer is confident that, in spite of the very short notice given by the Corps Commander, everybody will do their utmost to turn out as smartly as possible.

Appendix No. 5

Copy No.   SECRET.
                    OPERATION ORDERS. No. 95.
                    By Lt-Colonel T.H. RIDGWAY,
                       Comdg. 10th Bn. York & Lancaster Regiment.
                    13th December 1916.

The Battalion will march tomorrow to RANSART, and take over billets.
Dress: Full Marching Order. Steel Helmets. Mounted Officers will
not carry packs.
  Order of March: Headquarters, A. B. C. D., Lewis Gunners, Transport.
Head of Column to pass A. Coy. Officers' Mess at 9.0 a.m.
  Reveille: 6.0 a.m. Sick Parade: 6.30 a.m. Breakfasts: 7.0 a.m.

All blankets to be rolled in bundles of ten with jerkins inside,
securely tied and labelled. These will be stacked at Q.M. Stores by
7.30 a.m. 2 men per Company to be left with these to load them.
  All billets to be vacated and left clean for inspection by 2nd in
Command and Medical Officer at 8.15 a.m.
  2nd in Command will obtain a receipt from the Town Major that all
billets have been left clean. He will also receive and investigate
any claims that are brought in.

Dinners will be cooked enroute.
  Transport Officer will arrange for a limber in place of Mess Cart
to carry Officers' Mess baskets.
  All wagons to be loaded by 7.30 a.m. and ready to move when
Battalion moves, care being taken that there is no gap left between
tail of Battalion and Transport, as Battalion will be marching as
part of a Brigade.
  Lewis Gun Carts will be drawn by Pack Mules (2 per Mule) with
sufficient men to each pair of carts to act as brakesmen.
Remainder of men in rear of last cart.

Special attention must be paid to march discipline. Companies
closed up and proper intervals between fours.

Quartermaster will allot one wagon to each Company for blankets,
Sections placing their blankets with Companies as follows:-
        Bombers   with A. Company.
        Lewis Gunners.   with B. Company.
        Signallers & Snipers   with C. Company.
        Transport, Pioneers, etc. with D. Company.
The above order will be folloed on all marches.

No man is to fall out without a chit signed by his Company Officer.
His case will be investigated on arrival in billets, and if there is
no just cause for falling out, he will be brought up at Orderly Room.

All braziers will be handed in to Q.M. Stores by 7.0 a.m. tomorrow
for conveyance to next billet. This also refers to steam bath, if
possible. Soyer Stoves will be carried on Motor Wagons.

During halts the road must be kept clear and men must not sit or
walk about on growing crops.

Quartermaster will arrange to ration Motor Drivers from 15th incl.
This will include Petrol and Oil. They will move each day in a
convoy under 2/Lt. WILLIAMS, 4th Middlesex. The rendezvous for wagons
and that for guides at end of each day's march will be notified later.

Attached extracts from 37th Div. Memo are published for information
and guidance on all marches.

Billeting party, under 2/Lt. SAMUELS, to report to Maire, RANSART,
at 10.0 a.m. Parade at Orderly Room: 8.30 a.m.

                              (Sd) R.M.WILKINSON, Lieut a/Adjt.
Issued at 10.0 p.m.   10th Battn. York & Lancaster Regiment.

Extracts from 37th Div. No. 2/168 dated 12th December 1916.

Attention is directed to the following points which, if carefully watched, will prevent much delay in getting into billets, and receiving baggage while on the line of march during these short winter days. These points must be explained to everyone.

1. Good march discipline helps everyone, and reduces fatigue and delay on the march.

2. Billet parties must arrive at destinations early in the day, and guides must be detailed to meet incoming units well outside the billet area.

3. If a vehicle gets stuck, it is the duty of any troops in the vicinity to lend a hand to get it moving again.

4. Broken-down vehicles must be taken off the road and salvaged as soon as possible.

5. Much time is always wasted by Units failing to supply guides to show drivers of vehicles as follows, where to go on arrival (perhaps in the dark) in the billet area:-
    First Line.
    Supply.
    Baggage.
    Motor Transport.
    Those detached for special purposes.

    Such guides must meet transport well outside the billet area, or vehicles may have to be turned, and so block traffic.

6. Roads are frequently blocked by horsed vehicles closing up in large numbers, and leaving no crossing places. Distances must be kept open to allow for traffic while columns are halted.

    In the Artillery at least 500 yards between Batteries and Sections of D.A.C.

    In the Train at least 200 yards between batches of 15 vehicles.

Copy No.   Appendix No.

SECRET.

OPERATIONS ORDERS No. 96.
By Lt-Colonel J.H. RIDGWAY,
Comdg. 10th Bn. York & Lancaster Regiment.
14th December 1916.

The Battalion will march tomorrow to AUBROMETZ.

Order of March: Headquarters, B. C. D. A., Lewis Gunners, Transport. Head of Column to pass A. Company's billets at 10.0 a.m.

Reveille: 7.0 a.m. Sick Parade: 7.30 a.m. Breakfasts: 8.0 a.m.

Dinners will be cooked en route.

Blankets and jerkins to be rolled and loaded same as for today, one man per Company to travel with wagons.

All Transport to be loaded by 9.0 a.m. Mess Cart by 9.0 a.m.

Transport will drawout of Transport Field and form up between there and Battalion Headquarters, ready to follow tail of Battalion at 9.50 a.m.

Billeting party, under 2/Lt. SAMUELS, to report at Battalion H.Q. at 9.0 a.m.

Billets to be left clean and ready for inspection at 9.15 a.m. This was not the case this morning; the Commanding Officer warns all Companies and Sections that if billets are left dirty again, a party will be marched back from the next billet by an Officer, to clean up.

                                    (Sd) R.M. WILKINSON, Lieut. a/Adjt.
Issued at 12 midnight.   10th Battn. York & Lancaster Regiment.

Distribution.   Copy No.

War Diary and File.   1 - 3.
63rd Infantry Brigade.   4.
Commanding Officer.   5.
2nd In Command.   6.
Four Companies.   7 - 10.
Lewis Gun Officer.   11.
Bombing Officer.   12.
Signalling Officer.   13.
Transport Officer.   14.
Quartermaster.   15.
Intelligence Officer.   16.
Medical Officer.   17.

Appendix No. 4

Copy No.
SECRET.

OPERATION ORDERS No. 97.
By Lt-Colonel J.H. RIDGWAY,
Comdg. 10th Battn. York & Lancaster Regiment.
15th December 1916.

The Battalion will march tomorrow to MONCHY CAYEUX. a

Order of March: Headquarters, C.D.A.B., Lewis Gunners, Transport. Head of Column to pass N. end of village at 8.0 a.m.

Reveille: 5.30 a.m.   Sick Parade: 6.0 a.m.   Breakfast: 6.30 a.m.

Dinners will be cooked en route.

Blankets and jerkins to be rolled and loaded same as for today, one man per Company to travel with wagons.

All transport to be loaded by 7.0 a.m. Mess Cart by 7.15 a.m.

Transport will form up on side of road clear of metalling by 7.55 a.m.

Billets to be left clean and ready for inspection by 7.30 a.m.

In the event of only two or three Officers' Messes being found in villages, Companies will double up as follows:- A. with B., and C. with D. Lewis Gun Officer and Quartermaster with A. and B. Coys., Bombing Officer and Transport Officer with C. and D. Companies.

Billeting Party will parade at Orderly Room at 7.45 a.m.

(Sd) L.A. ELSWORTH, Capt. & Adjt.
Issued at 12.45 a.m.   10th Battn. York & Lancaster Regiment.

Distribution.	Copy No.
War Diary and File.	1 - 3.
63rd Infantry Brigade.	4.
Commanding Officer.	5.
2nd In Command.	6.
Four Companies.	7 - 10.
Lewis Gun Officer.	11.
Bombing Officer.	12.
Signalling Officer.	13.
Transport Officer.	14.
Quartermaster.	15.
Intelligence Officer.	16.
Medical Officer.	17.

a NOTE. The Battalion received further instructions on the march, and Headquarters and A. and B. Companies proceeded to FLEURY, and C. and D. Companies proceeded to CONTEVILLE.

Appendix No. 8

Copy No.

SECRET.

OPERATION ORDERS No. 98.
By Lt-Colonel J.H. RIDGWAY,
Comdg. 10th Bn. York & Lancaster Regiment.
16th December 1916.

The Battalion will march tomorrow to NEDONCHELLE.

Order of March: Headquarters, B.A., Lewis Gunners, Transport. Head of Column to pass pond near Q.M. Stores at 7.45 a.m.

Reveille: 5.15 a.m. Sick Parade: 5.45 a.m. Breakfasts: 6.15 am

Dinners will be cooked en route.

Blankets and jerkins to be rolled same as for today, one man per Company to travel with wagons.

All transport to be loaded by 6.45 a.m. Mess Cart by 7.0 a.m.

Transport will form up on side of road clear of metalling by 7.45 a.m.

Billets to be left clean and ready for inspection by 7.15 a.m.

Billeting party, under 2/Lt. SAMUELS, will parade at Orderly Room at 7.30 a.m.

C. and D. Companies will join the Battalion on the march.

(Sd) L.A. ELSWORTH, Capt. & Adjt.
10th Bn. York & Lancaster Regiment.

Issued at 11.30 p.m.

Distribution.	Copy No.
War Diary and File.	1 - 3.
63rd Infantry Brigade.	4.
Commanding Officer.	5.
2nd In Command.	6.
Four Companies.	7 - 10.
Lewis Gun Officer.	11.
Bombing Officer.	12.
Signalling Officer.	13.
Transport Officer.	14.
Quartermaster.	15.
Intelligence Officer.	16.
Medical Officer.	17.

Appendix No. 9

Copy No.   SECRET.

OPERATION ORDERS No. 99.
By Lt-Colonel J.H. RIDGWAY,
Comdg. 10th Battn. York & Lancaster Regiment.
17th December 1916.

The Battalion will march tomorrow to BUSNES and HOLLANDERIE.

Order of March(Headquarters, D. A. B. C., Lewis Gunners, Transport. Head of Column to pass Orderly Room at 9.40 a.m.

Reveille: 7.0 a.m. Sick Parade: 7.30 a.m. Breakfast: 7.45 a.m.

Dinners will be cooked en route.

Blankets and jerkins to be rolled same as for today, one man per Company to travel with wagons.

All transport to be loaded by 8.45 a.m. Mess Cart by 9.0 a.m.

Transport will form up on side of road clear of metalling by 9.35 a.m.

Billets to be left clean and ready for inspection by 8.0 a.m.

Billeting party, under 2/Lt. SAMUELS, will parade at Orderly Room at 9.0 a.m.

                                              (Sd) L.A. ELSWORTH, Capt. & Adjt.
Issued at 10.30 p.m.   10th Battn. York & Lancaster Regiment.

Distribution.   Copy No.

War Diary and File.   1 - 3.
63rd Infantry Brigade.   4.
Commanding Officer.   5.
2nd In Command.   6.
Four Companies.   7 - 10.
Lewis Gun Officer.   11.
Bombing Officer.   12.
Signalling Officer.   13.
Transport Officer.   14.
Quartermaster.   15.
Intelligence Officer.   16.
Medical Officer.   17.

Appendix No. 10

Copy No.   SECRET.

OPERATION ORDERS. No. 100.
By Lt-Colonel J.H. RIDGWAY,
Comdg. 10th Bn. York & Lancaster Regiment.
21st December 1916.

The Battalion will march tomorrow to VIELLE CHAPELLE, and take over billets.

Order of March: Headquarters, A. B. C. D., Lewis Gunners, Transport.

Starting Point: Road Junction North of m in FM East of BUSNES. Battalion will be fallen in and ready to march off with its head at Road Junction at the top of the Main Street near Baths by 9.30 a.m.

Reveille: 6.45 a.m. Sick Parade: 7.15 a.m. Breakfast: 7.30 a.m.

Dinners will be cooked en route.

Blankets and jerkins to be rolled as before, two men per Company to travel with wagons. These must be stacked by 8.0 a.m.

All transport to be loaded by 8.30 a.m. Mess Cart by 8.45 a.m.

Transport will be drawn up on road clear of metalling by 9.25 a.m.

All braziers must be returned to Q.M. Stores by 7.0 a.m.

Billets to be left clean and ready for inspection by 9.0 a.m.

Dress: Full marching order. Steel helmets will be worn.

Billeting party, under 2/Lt. SAMUELS, will parade at Q.M. Stores at 7.15 a.m. Early breakfasts will be arranged.

                                              (Sd) L.A. ELSWORTH, Capt. & Adjt.
Issued at 6.30 p.m.   10th Battn. York & Lancaster Regiment.

Distribution.   Copy.

War Diary and File.   1 - 3.
63rd Infantry Brigade.   4.
Commanding Officer.   5.
2nd In Command.   6.
Four Companies.   7 - 10.
Lewis Gun Officer.   11.
Bombing Officer.   12.
Signalling Officer.   13.
Transport Officer.   14.
Quartermaster.   15.
Intelligence Officer.   16.
Medical Officer.   17.

Confidential.

The 10th (Service) Battalion,
 The YORK and LANCASTER Regiment.

WAR DIARY.

JANUARY -- 1917.

SEVENTEENTH VOLUME.

WAR DIARY

10th Bn York & Lancaster Regt.

INTELLIGENCE SUMMARY

Army Form C. 2118.

Place	Date	Hour	Summary of Events and Information	Remarks and references to Appendices
ZELOBES.	1914 Jan. 1st.		Battn in billets at ZELOBES.	
TRENCHES	2nd		Battn proceeded by route march to trenches, relieving 13th Bn Rifle Brigade in left sub-section NEAUVE CHAPELLE.	
	3rd		Draft of 9 other ranks joined from 34th I.B.D.	
BOUT DEVILLE	8th		Battn relieved in trenches by 8th Lincolns Regt and took up position in Bde Reserve billets at BOUT DEVILLE, with Bn H.Q. at LA FOSSE.	
	9th		Draft of 8 other ranks joined from 34th I.B.D.	
	11th		Capt. E.E.J. FAIRNIE joined from England. Draft of 46 other ranks (Entrained) arrived from 34th I.B.D. These afterwards went to 63rd Inf Bde. Training Depot. (incomplete training.)	
ZELOBES	15th		Battn moved with Bde into Divnl Reserve. Billets at ZELOBES.	
	16th		Draft of 45 other Ranks joined from 34th I.B.D.	
	17th		Draft of 3 other Ranks joined from 34th I.B.D.	
	18th		1 other Rank joined from 4th T.D. ABBEYVILLE.	
	21st		2nd Lieut. D.H. DRAPER joined Battn from England.	
	24th		Draft of 80 other Ranks joined forth 34th I.B.D.	
	26th.		3 N.C.O.'s arrived from 34th I.B.D.	
LE TOURET.	29th.		Battn proceeded by route march to Le Touret, taking up left support position. FERME DE BOIS. Section Billets in Le Touret.	
	31st.		ditto	

H. Holway Lt Col.
Comdg 10th Bn York Lancs Regt.

List of Appendix, War Diary, January 1917.
---

1. Roll of Officers serving.
2. Strength.
3. Operation Order No. 101.
4. Operation Order No. 102.
5. Operation Order No. 103.
6. Honours and Awards.

---------------000ooo000---------------

10th Batt. York & Lancaster Regiment.

ROLL OF OFFICERS - 31st Jan. 1917.

Rank and Name			Present Employment.
Lt-Col.	Ridgway,	J.H.	Leave.
Major	Welsh,	D.T.	Commandant, Bde Depot.
"	Drynan,	W.B.	Commanding.
Capt.	Fairnie,	E.G.J.	Coy Comdr.
"	Elsworth,	L.A.	Adjutant.
"	Lucas,	S.	Sick.
"	Broadbent,	H.	Coy. Comdr.
Lieut.	Robinson,	A.R.	Coy Comdr.
"	Wilkinson,	R.M.	Course of Instruction.
"	Knowles,	F.E.	Platoon Comdr.
2/Lt.	Nicholson,	C.J.	Platoon Comdr.
"	Mitchell,	R.J.	Platoon Comdr.
"	Ayres,	F.	Bde School.
"	Drake,	D.H.	Bombing Officer.
"	Payne,	F.E.	Bde Bombing Officer.
"	Hawley,	D.D.	Lewis Gun Officer.
"	Samuels,	E.	Signalling Officer.
"	Lamond,	A.W.	Adjt. Bde Depot.
"	Strother,	J.M.	Leave.
"	Hill,	J.E.	Coy. Comdr.
"	Oakley,	M.H.	Platoon Comdr.
"	Corban,	J.	Asst: Adjt.
"	Fairbairn,	J.W.	Platoon Comdr.
"	Jackson,	F.C.	Platoon Comdr.
"	Wilks,	E.L.	Course of Instruction.
"	Gaunt,	B.W.	Platoon Comdr.
"	Taylor,	J.B.	Platoon Comdr.
"	Sumner,	W.G.	Bde Depot.
"	Topping,	E.	Platoon Comdr.
"	Horsfall,	J.R.	Platoon Comdr.
"	Woodmansey,	K.G.	Course of Instruction.
"	Lupton,	F.	Platoon Comdr.
Lt.Q.M.	Jamieson,	A.	Quartermaster.
Capt.	Plaister,	G.R.	R.A.M.C. Med. Offr.

appx 2

10th Battalion York & Lancaster Regiment.

Strength during month of January 1917.

30th December 1916 Officers: 31 Other Ranks: 652.

30th January 1917. Officers. 33 Other Ranks: 818.

Increase.

    Officers. Capt. E.G.J. Fairnie.   Joined from England. 9/1/1917.
             2/Lt. D.H. Drake. ditto 21/1/1917.

Other Ranks.

11	Other Ranks from	34 I.B.D.		31/12/1916.
9	do	do	do	3/1/1917.
7	do	do	do	8/1/1917.
5	do	do	do	10/1/1917.
76	do	do	do	11/1/1917.
75	do	do	do	16/1/1917.
3	do	do	do	17/1/1917.
1	do	do	do	18/1/1917.
8	do	do	do	24/1/1917.
3	do	do	do	26/1/1917.

Decrease.

CASUALTIES.

Sickness.	In Trenches.	Resting etc.
Officers Nil.	Officers Nil.	Officers Nil
Other Ranks.	Other Ranks.	Other Ranks Nil.
Total Sick wastage:- 25	Wounded:- 1	

1 To Commission.
1 To Munitions.
1 To 34 I.B.D.

Copy No.   SECRET.

OPERATION ORDERS No. 101.   app 3
By Lt-Colonel J.H. RIDGWAY,
Comdg. 10th Battn. York & Lancaster Regiment.
1st January 1917.

The Battalion will march to Trenches tomorrow and take over line, NEUVE CHAPELLE II, from 13th Bn. Rifle Brigade.

A. Company will take over left front line.
B. Company will take over right front line.
C. Company will take over left support line.
D. Company will take over right support line.

The left front Company (A. Coy) will relieve via BALUCHI Trench.
The left support Company will also use BALUCHI Trench.

A. Company will be at EUSTON Dump (M.34.a.1.8) at 9.30 a.m., where they will draw Gum Boots and put them on. Platoons will draw boots at 15 minutes' interval.

The right front Company (B. Coy) will be at EUSTON Dump at 9.40 a.m. where gum boots will be drawn, and put on. The same procedure will be adopted as with A. Coy. except that B. Company will relieve via COVERED WAY.
The right Company will also use COVERED WAY.

Left Support Company will be at EUSTON Dump at 10.30 a.m.
Right Support Company will be at EUSTON Dump at 10.40 a.m.

An interval of 15 minutes will be kept between platoons of Support Coys. so as not to congest the trench.

Headquarters will be at EUSTON Dump at 11.0 a.m. Gum boots will be available for Runners and Linesmen.

13th Bn. Rifle Brigade guides at the rate of 1 per platoon will be at EUSTON Dump at 9.15 a.m. and 10.15 a.m. respectively.

Signal Stations will be relieved with their Companies.

One guide each for Headquarters Bombers, Headquarters Lewis Gunners, H.Q. Signallers and Details will be at EUSTON Dump at 10.45 a.m.

Lewis Guns will relieve at same time as Companies.
Lewis Guns will be distributed as follows:-
                Right front Company   4 Guns.
                Left front Company   3 Guns.
                Left support Company   2 Guns.
                Reserve at PONT LOGY   1 Gun.

Regimental Aid Post will be taken over at 11.15 a.m.

The Adjutant will meet 13th R.B. Sniping Officer at Battalion Headquarters at 10.0 a.m.

R.S.M. will take over stores at MOG'S HOLE from R.S.M., 13th R.B. at 11.30 a.m. He will also obtain all information as to Ration parties, water, and cooking arrangements, and also salvage system.

All dixies will be loaded on limber and taken to ROUGE CROIX, where Coys. will arrange to carry them. Company messes should arrange to take up sufficient food for Officers to last till night time, when Mess Boxes can be sent up with rations.

All ranks before putting on Gum Boots should put on a pair of dry socks. It is hoped that arrangements will be made in the Line to dry socks daily.

Reveille: 4.45 a.m.   Breakfast: 5.30 a.m.

All blankets and Officers' valises will be rolled in bundles securely tied and labelled, and stacked in one billet per Company by 6.0 a.m. These will be collected by Transport and carted to Store, which will be found by Billeting Officer. One man per Company may be left in charge of these to load and store them. These men will come up to line with rations tomorrow night. Two front line Companies must arrange to draw Gum Boots for their men and leave them at Battalion H.Q., instructions being given to the men to collect them there.

C-Q-M-Sgts and Storemen will personally see their blankets and Officers' valises stored.

Battalion will rendezvous at 7.15 a.m. at Cross Roads, R.27.c.½.4.
Order of March: A. B. C. D. Headquarters.
Lewis Gunners and Coy. Signallers with their Companies. H.Q. Lewis Gunners and H.Q. Signallers with Headquarters.

Lewis Gunners and Coy Signallers with their Coys. H.Q. Lewis Gunners and H.Q. Signallers with Headquarters.

Mess Cart will call at Company Billets in morning as follows:- D. Coy. at 6.15.a.m. C. Coy. at 6.30.a.m., B. Coy. at 6.45.a.m., Headquarters at 7.0.a.m., A. Coy. at 7.15.a.m. to pick up small boxes to be man carried from ROUGE CROIX. After picking up A. Coy. cart will join rear of column.

On Battalion reaching CANAL de la LAWE, coys will move by half Coys, at 100 yards interval.

Issued at 4.0.p.m.

(sd) L.A. ELSWORTH, Capt. & Adj.
10th Bn York & Lancaster Regiment.

Appx. 4

OPERATION ORDERS. No. 102.
By Lt-Col. J.H. RIDGWAY. D.S.O.
Comdg. 10th Bn York & Lancs Regt.
6th January 1917.

Reference Map: 36 S.W. and RICHEBOURG.

1. **Relief.** The 8th Lincolnshire Regt. will relieve the 10th Bn. York and Lancaster Regt. in the NEUVE CHAPELLE Sector (Left Sub-Section) on the 8th January 1917.

2. **Routes.** The left front Company and the left Support Company will relieve via BALUCHI TRENCH.
The right front Company and the right Support Company will relieve via COVERED WAY.

3. **Times.** The left front Company (8th Linc. Regt.) will be at EUSTON DUMP (M.34.a.1.8.) at 9.30 a.m.
The first platoon will draw Gum Boots from the Gum Boot Store near EUSTON DUMP and put them on, remaining three platoons arriving at Gum Boot Store at intervals of 15 minutes.

The right front Company (8th Linc. Regt.) will be at EUSTON DUMP after left front Company has moved into BALUCHI.
The first platoon will draw Gum Boots from the Gum Boot Store and put them on, remaining three platoons following at 15 minutes intervals.

If the weather is fine, Gum Boots will not be supplied to Support Companies till later, when they can be drawn after Relief.

The left Support Coy. (8th Lincolns), followed by the right Support Company, will be at EUSTON DUMP at 10.40 a.m., platoons to be at 100 yards intervals.

Headquarter Details will be at EUSTON DUMP at 11.0 a.m. Gum Boots will be available for Runners and Linesmen.

4. **Guides.** Following guides will report to R.S.M., 10th Y. & L., at EUSTON POST :-
One per Platoon of A. and B. Coys., 10th Y. & L. (front line) at 9.15 a.m.
One per Platoon of C. and D. Coys., 10th Y. & L. (support line), at 10.15 a.m.
Signal Stations will be relieved with their Companies.
One guide for H.Q. Bombers.   )
One guide for H.Q. Lewis Gunners.   ) To be at
One guide for H.Q. Signallers and Details) EUSTON
One guide for party of 8th Lincolns for PONT) POST
    LOGY (This will be supplied by 10th Y. & L.) at 10.45 am.
                Snipers).

Lewis Guns will be distributed as follows :-
    Right Front Company   ... 4 guns.
    Left Front Company   ... 3 guns.
    Left Support Company   ... 2 guns.
    Reserve at PONT LOGY   ... 1 gun. (Bn. H.Q.)
Lewis Gun Teams will relieve at the same time as Companies, in whose lines gun positions are.
Reserve Gun Team will relieve with H.Q. Details.

Platoon guides will also guide Lewis Gun Teams.

The Support Companies of the relieved Battalion will remain in position until the relief of Front Line Coys. is complete. O.C. Front Line Coys will report to O.C. Support Line Companies when they are clear of F. Line. Relieved Supports will then move out.

P.T.O.

2.

5.	Aid Post.	The Regimental Aid Post, near CURZON POST (Battn. H.Q.) will be taken over at 11.15 a.m.
6.	Transport Arrangements.	All heavy Mess Boxes, Mess Stores, will be sent down to MOG'S HOLE by 6.0 p.m. 7th instant, and the M.Os Equipment will be picked up by trollies on the way down, for conveyance to Q.M. Stores. Regimental Transport will not wait at EUSTON DUMP after 7.30 p.m. for this baggage.

All dixies will be returned to Cook House by 7.45 a.m. on morning of Relief. They will then be carried down to ROUGE CROIX under Company and Section arrangements by 8.30 a.m. (Trenches to be used for this purpose).

Transport Officer will arrange for transport to move Lewis Guns, dixies, and remainder of Mess Boxes from ROUGE CROIX at 11.0 a.m.

Officers' Chargers will be at ROUGE CROIX at 12 noon. Transport Officer will also arrange a spare pony for Colonel Woods.

7.	Trench Stores, etc.	Receipts for Trench Stores handed over to relieving Battalion will be sent to Orderly Room as soon as possible after settling in billets.

Gum Boots will be taken out of Trenches and dumped by order of Coy. Commander, or an Officer detailed by him, at EUSTON DUMP, and handed over to N.C.O. in charge of store, a receipt being obtained. This receipt will accompany Coy. Commanders' Trench Store Receipt.

Trenches and Dug-outs will be left clean, tins collected, and a layer of earth placed on all latrines.

Sniping Officer, 8th Lincolns, will meet Sniping Officer 10th Y. & L. at Battn. H.Q. at 10.0 a.m.

R.S.M., 8th Lincolns, will take over all Stores at MOG'S HOLE from R.S.M. 10th Y. & L. at 11.30 a.m. R.S.M. 10th Y. & L. will explain system of salvage.

8.	Relief.	Companies will report Relief Complete by sending the word "HORN".
9.	Billeting.	2/Lt. SAMUELS will proceed at 8.0 a.m. 7th instant to reconnoitre and allot billets at BOUT DEVILLE to Coys. Coy Q.M.Sgts to meet 2/Lt. SAMUELS at H.Q. 8th Lincolns, at 10.0 a.m.

Battalion will on relief be in Brigade Reserve, and will take over billets in BOUT DEVILLE Area. Guides to meet Companies at BOUT DEVILLE at 12 noon.

Companies will march at 100 yards interval between half Coys from leaving trenches.

Quartermaster will send blankets and Officers' Valises, by Companies, to Pt. R.22.a.8.4 at 2.30 p.m. where Coys will send guides to lead them to their Headquarters.

Battalion H.Q. will be at R.21.b.6.2.

Detail of working parties for night of 8th/9th will be sent out as soon as received.

Transport and Q.M. Stores will not move from their present area.

Issued at 6.0 p.m.

(Sd) L.A. ELSWORTH, Capt. & Adjt.,
10th Battn. York & Lancaster Regiment.

OPERATION ORDER No. 103.

By Major W.B. DRYNAN,
Comdg. 10th Bn York & Lanc. Rgt.
28th January 1917.

The Battalion will relieve 6th Bedfordshire Regt in Billets, left support battalion. FERME DU BOIS Section, X 17 c 2.9, to-morrow.

Reveille: 6.30.a.m.   Breakfast: 7.30.a.m.

Order of March: Headquarters, A.B.C. and D. Coys. Lewis Gunners.

Head of column to pass starting point, R.27 c ½.4½. at 10.a.m.

Route: VIEILLE CHAPELLE-LACOUTURE-LE TOURET.

Mess boxes etc to be ready at 9.0.a.m. and will be called for. Transport Officer to arrange Mess Cart to go to D. Coy. and H.Q. Limber to A.B. and C.Coys.

Dinners to be cooked en route. One cooker for H.Q. Sections.

Blankets will be rolled in tens, and stacked outside billets at 8.30.a.m. ready for collection. Each bundle will be marked, and one man will be left in charge.

One guide per Coy. to be left behind to guide relief of 6th Beds. who will take over posts. They, with men from posts, will remain at Stores for night 29th-30th, and will report to their Coys. with rations on the 30th.

Signed lists of stores handed over will be sent to Orderly Room on the 30th.

Billets to be left clean and ready for inspection by 9.0.a.m.

Pioneers will remain at Q.M. Stores and work on Transport lines till further notice.

Working parties will be required on night of 29th January. Details later.

Movement East of CANAL DE LA LAWE by platoons at 100 yards intervals

Billeting representatives to meet 2/Lt SAMUELS at Q.M. Stores at 9.0.a.m.

(sd) L.A. ELSWORTH, Capt. & Adjt.
10th Bn York & Lancaster Regiment.

appx 6

10th Battalion York & Lancaster Regiment.

List of Honours and Awards in above Batt. Jan. 1917.

The following awards appeared in thr New Year's Honours List, January 1917.

DISTINGUISHED SERVICE ORDER.

Lt-Colonel. J.H. RIDGWAY.

MERITORIOUS SERVICE MEDAL.

No. 5354 Q.M.S. PITHERS, C.H.B.
No. 17744 Sergt. GREEN, N.

The following were mentioned in despatches.

Captain. L.A. ELSWORTH.
Lieut. R.M. WILKINSON.
Sec.Lt. J. CORBAN.

The following awards have been made for Operations on the ANCRE, November 1916.

MILITARY CROSS.

Sec.Lt. J.M. STROTHER.
Sec.Lt. D.D. HAWLEY.

MILITARY MEDAL.

No. 22485 Lce.Cpl. WILKINSON, F.

---------ooo0ooo---------

To. 37th. Division "Q".

Herewith War Diary of this Battalion, for the month ending 28th. February 1917.

28/2/1917.

[signature]
Lt. Col.,
Comdg. 10th. Bn. York & Lancaster Regt.

Confidential.

The 10th (Service) Battalion,
The YORK and LANCASTER Regiment.

WAR DIARY.

FEBRUARY - 1917.

EIGHTEENTH VOLUME.

10th Bn. York and Lancaster Regt.

INTELLIGENCE SUMMARY
(Erase heading not required.)

Place	Date 1917 Feby	Hour	Summary of Events and Information	Remarks and references to Appendices
ESSARS.	1st		Battn proceeded by route march from close billets at LE TOURET to billets in ESSARS.	
	5th		Draft of 8 O.Rs joined Battalion from 34th I.B.D.	
	6th		Draft of 92 O.Rs joined from 34th I.B.D.	
	11th		2nd Lieut. H.A. WAINE joined Battalion from England.	
LES BREBIS	12th		Battn proceeded by route march to LES BREBIS taking over billets (Division transferred to 1st Corps)	
TRENCHES.	13th		Battn proceeded by route march to Trenches, relieving 12th Royal Fusiliers in Left Sub-section., 14 BIS Section. 100S. Salient.	
	14th.		3 O.Rs killed by hostile Trench Mortar fire.	
	15th.		Capt. R. BROADBENT, O.C. "A" Coy. killed by hostile rifle fire.	
	17th.		Draft of 4 O.Rs joined from 34th I.B.D.	
VILLAGE LINE	18th/19th		Battn relieved in Trenches by 8th Lincolnshire Regt. taking over Village Line same Night. and being in support to 14 BIS Section.	
TRENCHES.	25th.		Battalion relieved in Village Line by 8th Lincolns Regt. taking over same sub section proceeded to front line Trenches, Right Coy. and as Coy. before, from 6th Lincoln Regt.	
	26th.		Draft of 4 O.Rs joined Battn from 34th I.B.D.	
	27th.		Dummy Raid carried out against enemy's line opposite Battn. front.	
			Draft of 45 O.Rs joined from 34 I.B.D.	

A. Taylor Lt. Col.
Comdg 10th Bn. York & Lanc. R.

List of Appendices, War Diary, January 1917.
----

1. Strength.
2. Roll of Officers serving.
3. Operation Order No. 105.
4. Operation Order No. 106.
5. Operation Order No. 107.
6. Operation Order No. 108.
7. Operation Order No. 108.

------------------oOo------------------

10th Battalion York & Lancaster Regiment.

STRENGTH during month of February 1917.

January 30th 1917:   Effective Strength: Offrs. 33   O.Rs. 818.
                       Available Strength: Offrs. 32   O.Rs. 778.

February 28th 1917:   Effective Strength: Offrs. 33   O.Rs. 925.
                       Available Strength: Offrs. 33   O.Rs. 875.

INCREASE.

Officers.   2/Lt H.A. WALNE, Joined from England, 11/2/1917.

Other Ranks.

8	Other Ranks	from	34 Infy	Base	Depot.		5/2/1917.
92	do	do	do	do	do	do	6/2/1917.
4	do	do	do	do	do	do	17/2/1917.
4	do	do	do	do	do	do	26/2/1917.
45	do	do	do	do	do	do	27/2/1917.

DECREASE.

Casualties.

Officers.   Capt. H. BROADBENT, Killed in Action   15/2/1917.

Other Ranks.   Killed in Action.   3.

                      Wounded in Action.   9.

To Commissions   (England)   5

To Munitions.   (England)   3

Sick Wastage.   26.

Appendix. No 2

10th. Battn. York & Lancaster Regiment.

ROLL OF OFFICERS - 28th. February 1917.

Rank and Name.		Present employment.
Lt. Col. Ridgway	J.H.	Cmdg. Officer.
Major Welsh	D.T.	2nd. in Command.
: Drynan	W.B.	Coy Comdr.
Capt. Lucas	S.	Coy Comdr.
: Fairnie	E.G.J.	Coy Comdr.
: Elsworth	L.A.	Coy Comdr.
Lieut. Robinson	A.R.	Staff Learner 37 Div.
? Wilkinson	R.M.	Platoon Comdr.
: Knowles	F.E.	Course of Instn.
2/Lt. Nicholson	C.A.J.	Platoon Comdr.
: Mitchell	R.J.	Attd. 152 Co. R.E.
: Ayres	F.	L.G. Officer
: Payne	F.E.	Platoon Comdr.
: Drake	D.H.	Bomb. Officer
: Hawley	D.D.	Platoon Comdr.
: Samuels	E.	Signalling Officer
: Lamond	A.W.	Platoon Comdr.
: Hill	L.E.	Platoon Comdr.
: Walne	H.A.	Asst. Transpt Officer
: Taylor	J.B.	Platoon Comdr.
: Strother	J.M.	Intellgce Officer
: Oakley	M.H.	
: Gaunt	B.W.	Attd. 63rd T.M.B.
: Topping	E.	Course of Instn.
: Horsfall	J.R.	Platoon Comdr.
: Wilks	E.L.	i/c Bde. Dump.
: Jackson	F.C.	Platoon Comdr.
: Fairbairn	J.J.W.	Platoon Comdr.
: Lupton	F.	Platoon Comdr.
: Woodmansey	K.G.	Platoon Comdr.
:: Corban	J.	Adjutant.
: Sumner	W.G.	Platoon Comdr.
Lt.& Q.M.Jamieson	A.	Quartermaster
Capt. Plaister	G.R.	R.A.M.C. Med. Officer.

Appendix No. 3

OPERATION ORDERS No. 105   SECRET.
By Major W.B. DRYNAN,
Comdg. 10th Bn. York & Lancaster Regt.
31st January 1917.

Battalion will be relieved by 1st Bedford Regt. and will march tomorrow to ESSARS and take over billets. Route: RUE DE BOIS.

Order of March: Platoons to march at 200 yards interval; to start immediately on relief.

Reveille: 6.30 a.m.   Sick Parade: 7.0 a.m.   Breakfast: 7.30 am.

Dinners to be cooked en route. One Cooker "A" and "B", One "C" and "D", One Headquarters.

Blankets to be rolled by 9 am, and stacked Coy billets. One man per Coy to be left behind.

Billets to be left clean and ready for inspection by 9.30 a.m.

Mess Kit, Officers' Valises, etc., to be ready at 9 am. to be called for.

Coys will report relief complete on passing Headquarters.

B. Coy will detail two guides to take relief down to posts. One Officer will be left by this Coy to bring party on to billets. Signed list of stores handed over to be sent to Battn. Headquarters on arrival in new area.

A. Coy will detail one Officer to meet party attached to D.O.T.M. at RICHEBOURG ST. VAAST Church at 2 pm and march them to the new area. This party should be shown on tomorrow's ration indent.

All Officers and other ranks of Brigade School will return to Battalion tomorrow in new area. They will appear on our ration indent dated 3rd prox. for consumption on the 7th, till which day the rations will be transferred at refilling point.

(Sd) L.A. ELSWORTH, Capt. & Adjt.
10th Bn. York & Lancaster Regiment.

Appendix No. 4

OPERATION ORDERS No.106   SECRET.
By Lt.-Col. J.H. RIDGWAY, D.S.O.,
   Comdg. 10th York & Lancaster Regt.,
        10th February 1917.

The Battalion will march on 12th February to LES BREBIS and billet there for night, and go into the line on 13th February, relieving 12th Royal Fusiliers in left sector.
   Reveille: 5.45 am. Breakfast: 6.30 am. Sick Parade: 6.15 am. Dinners cooked en route.
   Parade at 9 am. Dress: Full Marching Order, Steel Helmets, jerkins folded under pack. Order of March: Headquarters, C., D., Drums, B., A., Lewis Gunners, Transport. Head of column to pass Church, ESSARS, at 9.0 am.
   Coys will march as far as Railway Crossing E.17.d by platoons at 100 yards interval: transport in pairs. On reaching this point the Battalion will close up until NOEUX-LES-MINES is reached, when it will again open out to 200 yards between platoons and same distance between pairs of wagons.
   All blankets to be tied in bundles of 10 securely labelled, and stacked outside Q.M. Stores ready for leaving by 7.30 am. One man per Coy will be left with the blankets. Officers' valises will be loaded at Q.M. Stores by 7.45 am. Mess boxes will be ready for pickingn up by Mess Cart at 8.15 am.
   All billets to be left scrupulously clean, and ready, for inspection by 2nd in Command and Medical Officer by 8.15 am. One Officer per Company to attend.
   Billeting party under 2/Lieut. SAMBELS will parade outside Orderly Room at 8.45 am.
   Transport Officer will arrange for Lewis Gun wagons and G.S. wagons tobe brought up on evening of 11th. These will be loaded as far as possible that night. Horses and mules will return to their standings for the night.
   Companies will report arrival in billets by sending word "JOSEPH".

   On 13th February Battalion will relieve 12th Royal Fusiliers in front line.
   Reveille: 7.0.am. Breakfast: 8.0 am. Sick Parade: 7.30 am. Dinners: 11.0 am.
   Blankets and stores will be deposited by Coys at Q.M. Stores, L.35.c.7.7. by 9.30 a.m.
   Coys will march by platoons at 200 yards interval commencing with H.Q. Company at 12 noon. The remainder in following order: D., C., B., A.
   Transport Officer will arrange for wagons to take Lewis Guns, and half limber per Coy for Dixies and small Mess boxes to be at PHILOSOPHE Railway Crossing, PUITS 3, G 20 a 3.2 at 1 pm, where Coys will pick up things and carry from there.
   Coys must realise that itis a long carry, therefore only things absolutely necessary for teas should be carried up, all remainder coming up with rations that night.
   Lewis Guns will be in charge of Coy Commanders, who will take them up with their Coys. Those Coys requiring more guns to hold line than they have in their Coys, will takem guns and teams from Support Coys.
   Two guns and teams willbe included in H.Q. Company, and will go in with the Company under L.G. Officer.
   Companies in support willdo all carrying in line, detail of which will be given out later.

Guides will meet Coys at PHILOSOPHE Railway Crossing at 1 pm. in following proportion: 1 per H.Q. Coy, 1 per Platoon. Platoons to enter trenches at 5 minutes interval.

The line will be held as follows :-

        Right Company.   D.
        Left Company.   C.
        Right Support.   B.
        Left Support.   A.

Rations will be brought up nightly to CRUCIFIX DUMP, LOOS Village

All Trench Stores, Maps, Photographs, are to be very carefully taken over and receipts passed; these to be sent to Orderly Room as early as possible.

Relief complete will be reported by sending the word "WANDERER".

                                (Sd) L.A.ELSWORTH, Capt. & Adjt.,
                                10th Bn. York & Lancaster Regiment.

Appendix No. 5

OPERATION ORDERS No.107   SECRET.
By Lt.-Col. J.H. RIDGWAY, D.S.O.,
    Comdg. 10th Bn. York & Lancaster Regt.
        17th February 1917.

The Battalion will be relieved by the 8th Lincoln Regt. on the 19th inst.

1 Guide for Headquarters, 1 Guide per Coy for Lewis Guns, and 1 Guide per Platoon, will be at Headquarters, 8th Lincoln Regt. G.28.b.1.6 in NORTHERN UP Trench at 10.45 am.

Companies will come up in the following order: H.Q. Coy, Left front Company with Lewis Guns, Right Front Coy with Lewis Guns, Left Support Coy with Lewis Guns, and Right Support Coy with Lewis Guns.

Trench to be used: CHALK PIT ALLEY.

C. Coy will detail an N.C.O. to be at H.Q. 8th Lincoln Regt. at 10.45 am to take charge of all Guides and see they are handed over to the proper Coy/s they have to guide up.

Companies will send these guides to reconnoitre the route tomorrow as early as possible after receipt of these orders.

One Officer per Coy and one N.C.O per platoon will remain behind for one night to show incoming Unit the trenches.

All trench stores will be carefully handed over and receipts obtained. These lists will be forwarded to Orderly Room as soon as possible after arrival in Village lines.

All work in hand and permanent working parties will be carefully handed over.

Dug-outs will be left scrupulously clean.

On being relieved Coys will take over Village line and Gun Trench as follows :-

    C. Coy. - GUN TRENCH.
      (This Co. will always be in readiness to move if called on by O.C. 8th Lincoln Regt).
    A. Coy   - LEFT of VILLAGE LINE with 1 Platoon in NORTHERN SAP REDOUBT.
    D. Coy   - CENTRE of VILLAGE LINE with 1 Platoon in 65 METRE PT. REDOUBT.
    B. Coy   - Right of VILLAGE LINE with 1 Platoon in LOOS ROAD REDOUBT.
    Hdqrs   - NORTHERN UP at 28.b.1.6.

CHALK PIT ALLEY will be used by all Coys and Sections.

Relief complete will be reported by sending the word "HOPEFUL"

All Gumboots will be handed over by Coys and Sections and receipts signed by an Officer obtained.

Signalling Officer will arrange to send Signallers to take over H.Q. at 10.45 a.m.

Cooks with Dixies and Mess Baskets should be sent down immediately after Breakfast to new lines to prepare Dinners.

                    (Sd) L.A. ELSWORTH, Capt & Adjt.,
                        10th. Bn. York & Lancaster Regiment.

Appendix No. 6

OPERATION ORDERS. No. 108. SECRET.
By Lt. Col. J.H. RIDGWAY, D.S.O.
Comdg. 10th. Bn. York & Lancaster Regt.
24th. February 1917.

The Battalion will relieve 8th. Lincoln Regt. in front line tomorrow. Companies will take over following positions:-
A. Coy.   Left Support.
B. Coy.   Right Front.
C. Coy.   Left Front.
D. Coy.   Right Support.

Companies will leave their present line commencing at 7.30 a.m. with C. Coy, then B. Coy, then A. Coy, then Headquarters. 10 minutes interval to be kept between Platoons.

CHALK PIT ALLEY will be used by all Coys and Sections. Lewis Guns to go up with Companies.

Mess Baskets and heavy stores to be sent to R.S.M's dug-out, QUALITY STREET, by 7.0 a.m., when they will be brought up with rations.

Companies will arrange to leave a representative behind to hand over stores etc. in Village Line to 8th. Somerset Light Infantry.

All stores, and work in progress, to be carefully taken over, and receipts passed.

Dress: Marching order and Gum Boots.

If weather is thick and foggy, Companies may proceed along top of CHALK PIT ALLEY as far as GUN TRENCH in sections, with 100 yards interval between Sections.

Company Commanders must use their own discretion as to when to get into trench, care being taken that at the slightest sign of fog lifting, men get into trench at once.

The usual working parties Nos. i & iv, supplied by A and B Coys, will report as usual tomorrow, rejoining Coys in line after work. Dress: Full marching order.

Relief complete/will be reported by using B.A.B. Code.

(Sd) J. CORBAN, 2/Lt., a/Adjt.,
for O.C. 10th. Bn. York & Lancaster Regt.

Appendix No. 7

OPERATION ORDERS. No. 109.
By Lt.Col J.H. RIDGWAY, D.S.O.,
Comdg. 10th. York & Lancaster Regt.
27th. February 1917.

A Dummy Raid will be carried out tonight the 27th. instant on the front H.31.b.15.90 to H.25d.3.3.

A demonstration will be carried out at same time by the 111th. Infantry Brigade on the front H.19.d 65.60 to H.13 c 55.32.

Zero hour will be notified later.

Watches will be synchronised with Battalion H. Q. at 2.0 pm and 7.0 p.m.

Coy Commanders will arrange that only sufficient Lewis Gunners and Sentries will be left to hold front line; remainder of men will be in dug-outs by Zero minus 30 minutes. Deep dug-outs in front line may be used.

Sentries will be posted at the entrances of all dug-outs in all trenches.

All movements in trenches will cease by Zero minus 30 minutes until Hostile retaliation is over.

Therewill be a quiet period from Zero plus 7 to Zero plus 12 during which period no firing will be carried out by Artillery, Trench Mortars, Stokes or Machine guns.

As few Very lights as possible will be sent up after Zero minus 30 opposite the front H.31.b 15.90 to H.25 a 3.3.

At Zero plus 10 one Rocket breaking into golden rain will be fired from our front line by O.C. "B" Coy.

Signalling Officer will draw Rockets from Bde. Bomb Store, LOOS, tomorrow morning, and hand these to O.C. "B" Coy in afternoon.

Periscopes should be freely used opposite the front H.31 b 15.90 to H.25 a 3.3 during the whole of daylight on 27th. inst.

All Transport and Tramway or Ration parties will be clear of LOOS by 8.15 p.m. If Zero time does notadmit of ration parties being clear of trenches by then, they will remain in TOSH KEEP and TOSHALLEY till after enemy's retaliation is over.

All Platoon Officers will be with their Platoons, except Officer on duty, whowill be in front line, Coy Commanders remaining at Coy Headquarters.

After retaliation is over, Coys in frontline must keep a sharp lookout for counter raid.

Lewis Gunners and Rifle Grenadiers will co-operate freely after the quiet period on the flanks of H.31 b 15.90 to nH.25 a 3.3. These points should be carefully shewn to all Lewis Gunners and Rifle Grenadiers.

The R.S.M. will ascertain from Battalion Headquarters Zero time, before going to ration Dump.
No patrols or wiring Parties will be sent out during night.

J. CORBAN, 2/Lt., a/Adjt.,
for O.C. Comdg 10th York & Lancs Regt

Vol 19

Confidential

The 10th (Service) Battalion,
The YORK and LANCASTER Regiment.

WAR DIARY

MARCH - 1917

EIGHTEENTH VOLUME

Army Form C. 2118.

WAR DIARY of
10th York Lancaster Regiment.
INTELLIGENCE SUMMARY.

(Erase heading not required.)

Instructions regarding War Diaries and Intelligence Summaries are contained in F. S. Regs., Part II. and the Staff Manual respectively. Title pages will be prepared in manuscript.

Place	Date 1916 Month	Hour	Summary of Events and Information	Remarks and references to Appendices
Trenches.	1st.		Battalion occupying 14. Bde. Left Sub-section.	
	2nd.		Draft of 8 O.R.s joined from 34th Infy. Base Depot.	Appx 2.
MAZINGARBE.	3rd.		Battn. relieved in trenches by 2nd. Battn. Durham Light Infy. and proceeded by route march to MAZINGARBE, taking over billets.	Appx. 3.
BETHUNE	4th.		Battn. proceeded by route march to BETHUNE, billets in MONTMORENCY Barracks.	Appx. 4
LE HAMEL	5th.		Battn. proceeded by route march to LE HAMEL, billets taken over.	Appx. 5
ST. HILAIRE.	6th.		Battn. proceeded by route march to ST. HILAIRE, taking over billets.	Appx. 6
			2nd. Lieut. D.H. DRAKE proceeded to England to report to W.O. with reference to transfer to Indian Army.	
VALHUON	9th.		Battn. proceeded by route march to VALHUON, taking over billets. Transfer of Division to VI Corps. Third Army.	Appx 2 Appx 4
HOUVIN-HOUVIGNEUL	10th.		Battn. proceeded by route march to HOUVIN-HOUVIGNEUL taking over billets. Training for active operations commenced.	Appx 3
	11th.		2nd. Lieut. F. MORTON-SMITH. joined Battalion from England.	
	16th.		Draft of 114 O.R.s. joined from 34th Infy. Base Depot.	
	20th.		Capt. C.F. AIREY and Lieut. D.A. HALL joined Battalion from England.	
	24th.		Draft of 35 O.R.s. joined Battalion from 34th Infy. Base Depot.	Appx 2
	25th.		Draft of 11 O.R.s. joined Battalion from 34th Infy. Base Depot.	
	26th.		Capt. R.H. FITTS joined Battalion from England.	
	31st.		Battn. in billets HOUVIN-HOUVIGNEUL.	

Holloway Lt. Col.
Comdg. 10th York Lancaster Regt.

LIST OF APPENDICES.

1. Roll of Officers serving.
2. Strength, Casualties etc.
3. Operation Order No.110.
4. Operation Order No.111.
5. Operation Order No.112.
6. Operation Order No.113.
7. Operation Order No.114.
8. Operation Order No.115.

10th Battn York & Lancaster Regiment.

NOMINAL ROLL OF OFFICERS - 29/3/1917.

Rank & Name.		Remarks.
Lt.-Col. RIDGWAY,	J.H.	Commanding Officer.
Major WELSH,	D.T.	Second in Command.
" DRYNAN,	W.B.	Company Commander.
Captain FITTS,	R.H.	Company Commander.
" LUCAS,	S.	Company Commander.
" AIREY,	C.F.	Town Major, HOUVIN.
" FAIRNIE,	E.G.J.	Company Commander.
" ELSWORTH,	L.A.	Course of Instruction.
Lieut. HALL,	D.A.	
" ROBINSON,	A.R.	Divisional H.Q.
" WILKINSON,	R.M.	
" KNOWLES,	F.E.	Course of Instruction.
2/Lieut. MORTON-SMITH,	F.	Course of Instruction.
" Nicholson,	C.A.T.	
" MITCHELL,	R.J.	Attached 152 Co., R.E.
" AYRES,	F.	
" PAYNE,	F.E.	
" HAWLEY,	D.B.	
" SAMUELS,	E.	
" LAMOND,	A.W.	
" WALNE,	H.A.	Transport Officer.
" HILL,	J.E.	
" TAYLOR,	I.B.	
" STROTHER,	J.M.	
" OAKLEY,	M.H.	Hospital.
" HORSFALL,	J.R.	
" TOPPING,	E.	
" GAUNT,	B.W.	Attached 63rd T.M.B.
" FAIRBAIRN,	J.J.W.	
" JACKSON,	F.C.	
" LUPTON,	F.	
" WOODMANSEY,	K.G.	
" WILKS,	E.L.	
" CORBAN,	J.	Adjutant.
" SUMNER,	W.G.	
Lt. & Q.M. JAMIESON,	A.	Quartermaster.
Captain PLAISTER,	G.R.	Medical Officer.

Appendix No. 2.

10th Battalion York & Lancaster Regiment.

STRENGTH during month of March 1917.

February 28th 1917 : Fighting Strength : Officers......33
                                          Other Ranks..925

March 31st 1917   : Fighting Strength : Officers......36
                                          Other Ranks..920

INCREASE.

Officers.
  2/Lieut. Morton-Smith, F. Joined from England 15/3/17.
  Capt.   Airey,   C.F.   :   :   :   20/3/17.
  Lieut.   Hall,   D.A.   :   :   :   20/3/17.
  Capt.   Pitts,   R.H.   :   :   :   26/3/17.

Other Ranks.
  8 Other Ranks from 34 Infy Base Depot.   2/3/17.
  12   :   :   :   :   :   :   4/3/17.
  14   :   :   :   :   :   :   16/3/17.
  35   :   :   :   :   :   :   24/3/17.
  11   :   :   :   :   :   :   25/3/17.

DECREASE.

Officers.
  2/Lieut. Drake, D.H. To report to War Office.
    (Transfer to Indian Army)

Other Ranks.
  64 Sick Wastage.
   4 Wounded in Action.
   2 To Establishment of 21st Division.
   6 To Transportation Depot, BOULOGNE.
   1 To No.4 General Base Depot.
   1 To Base Depot for Dental Treatment.
   1 Classified Category II by Medical Board in
       England.
   3 To Commissions.

ooooooooooOOOOOOO((((((o))))))OOOOOOOOOooooooooo

OPERATION ORDERS No.110. Appx. No.
By Lt.-Col. J.H. RIDGWAY, D.S.O.,
Comdg. 10th York & Lancaster Regt.
1st March 1917.

Battalion will be relieved tomorrow by 2nd Durham L.I.

Companies will relieve in following order, using NORTHERN UP and RAILWAY ALLEY.

Guides as follows will report to 2/Lieut. STROTHER at PHILOSOPHE Level Crossing at 8.30 a.m. 1 per Platoon for Companies.

Guides for all Lewis Gun teams will report to Adjutant at Battn H.Q. at 9 a.m.

Relieving Coys will come up in following order: Right Front Company, Left Front Company.

Three platoons of A.Coy, Durham L.I. to relieve Left Coy, Middlesex.

1 platoon A.Coy, Durham L.I. to take over from RAILWAY ALLEY to BOYEAUX. Guide for this Platoon to be detailed by O.C. "D" Coy, 10th York & Lancs Regt.

Right Support Company. Left Support Company. Battn Headquarters.

No Coys of 10th York & Lancs will move out till whole of 2nd Durham L.I. are in front and reserve lines.

Battalion will go out through RAILWAY ALLEY.

Meat and vegetable rations will now be sent up. Men will have dinners before going out.

All Gum Boots handed in to Gum Boot Store, LOOS.

Durham L.I. Lewis Guns will arrive in LOOS tonight.

All petrol tins will be handed over to incoming Coys with other trench stores.

Coys in reserve will send guides same as front line Companies.

(Sd) J. CORBAN, 2/Lieut. & Adjt.,
10th York & Lancaster Regiment.

AFTER ORDER

Lewis Gunners, on being relieved tomorrow, will take the guns to CRUCIFIX DUMP, via RAILWAY ALLEY, RESERVE LINE and ENGLISH ALLEY, where they will be met by 2/Lieut. AYRES who will arrange to leave a guard over them.

Two limbers will be sent up on the night of the 3rd inst. to take the guns to MAZINGARBE.

OPERATION ORDERS No. 111   Appendix No. 4
By Lt.-Col. J.H. RIDGWAY, D.S.O.,
Comdg. 10th York & Lancaster Regt.,
3rd March 1917.

The Battalion will march tomorrow to BETHUNE, and go into billets for the night.

Reveille: 7.0 a.m. Breakfast: 8.0 a.m. Sick Parade: 9.0 a.m. Dinners: 11.30 a.m.

Parade 1.0 p.m. Dress: Full Marching Order, Steel Helmets, Jerkins folded under flap.

Head of Column to pass starting point at L.23.b.2.7 at 1.0 p.m. Order of March: Drums, Headquarters, A.,B.,C.,D.,Lewis Gunners, Transport. 200 yards interval between platoons; wagons in pairs.

All blankets to be securely rolled, tied and labelled, and stacked at Q.M. Stores by 10.0 a.m. Coys will leave one man each in charge. Officers' valises loaded by 10.30 a.m. Mess Cart by 12.30 p.m.

Billeting party will report to 2/Lieut. SAMUELS at Battn H.Q. at 9.30 a.m.

Platoons will halt every ten minutes to the hour for usual halt. All men not able to keep up with Battn will parade under an Officer to be detailed by O.C. "D" Coy at Battn H.Q. at 12.45 p.m., and will follow in rear of Transport at a pace equal to the slowest man. Any men who fall out from Battn en route will be collected by this Officer and brought on. Any men falling out will be given a note, signed by an Officer, giving destination of Battn. Owing to the soft state of men's feet, particular efforts will be required from Officers to maintain strict march discipline.

Owing to Battn not marching early, every effort must be made to get cleaned up, special attention being paid to shaving, brushing of clothes, greasing of boots, cleaning of rifles, packing of packs, and folding of ground sheets.

A certain amount of clothing will be issued from Q.M. Stores today, and worst cases will be fitted out with quantity available.

(Sd) J. CORBAN, 2/Lieut.& Adjt
10th York & Lancaster Regt.

OPERATION ORDERS No.112   Appx. No. 5
By Lt.-Col. J.H. RIDGWAY, D.S.O.,
Comdg. 10th York & Lancaster Regt.,
4th March 1917.

Battalion will march tomorrow to LE HAMEL. Route: CHOQUES - LE BOUDON.

Order of March: Drums, Hd.Qrs, B, C, D, A, Coys, Lewis Gunners, Transport. Battalion will be closed up.

Dress: Full Marching Order, Steel Helmets, Jerkins folded under straps of pack.

Reveille: 5.0 a.m. Breakfast: 8.0 a.m. Dinners: 11.30 a.m. Sick Parade: 7.30 a.m.

Head of Column to pass Starting Point - E.10.b.9.3 (Ref.BETHUNE Combined Sheet) at 1.0 p.m.

All blankets to be rolled and tied in bundles of 10, and stacked outside Q.M. Stores by 5.45 a.m. Officer's valises 10.30 a.m. Mess Cart 12.30 p.m. One man per Coy in charge of blankets.

Billets to be left clean and ready for inspection by 12 noon by 2nd in Command and Medical Officer. One Officer per Coy to attend.

Strictest attention to march discipline is required. Men must be kept closed up, and march on right of road, and at halts road must be kept clear. Rifles will always be slung over shoulder when marching at ease.

Billeting party, under 2/Lieut. SAMUELS, will report to Town Major, LE HAMEL, at 10.30 a.m.

On arrival in billets all Officers will remain with their Platoons till men are settled down, blankets drawn, and arrangements complete for meals. They are also responsible that water supply and latrines are pointed out to all men of their Platoons.

"A" Coy will detail an Officer to bring on men unable to march with Battalion. Fall in at Battn Hd.Qrs at 12.45 p.m. This Officer will bring on all men who may fall out from Battn en route. This will be a standing order for re-ar Coy on any march.

(Sd) J. CORBAN, 2/Lieut. & Adjt.,
10th York & Lancaster Regt.

Appendix No. 6

OPERATION ORDERS No.113
By Lt.-Col. J.H. RIDGWAY, D.S.O.,
Comdg. 10th York & Lancaster Regt.,
5th March 1917.

The Battalion will march tomorrow to ST. HILAIRE.

Parade at 10.0 a.m. Head of Column to pass fork roads, BUSNETTES (Map Ref. V.14.d.9.6; BETHUNE Combined Sheet) at 10.0 a.m. Dress: Same as today.

Order of March: Drums, Hd.Qrs, C. D. A. B., Lewis Gunners, Transport.

Reveille: 6.30 a.m. Breakfast: 7.0 a.m. Sick Parade: 7.30 a.m. Dinners will be cooked enroute.

Blankets will be stacked at Q. M. Stores by 8.0 a.m.; one man per Coy in charge.

Transport Officer will arrange for limbers to bring A. and D. Coys' blankets and Officers' valises at 8.0 a.m.

Officers' valises will be loaded by 8.45 a.m. Mess boxes by 9.15 a.m.

Billets to be left clean by 9.15 a.m. O.C. "B" Coy will arrange to visit billets of A. and D. Coys, and send in Certificate on arrival in ST. HILAIRE.

Coy Commanders will in future wear full marching order (less pack). Great-coats or Burberrys will not be worn unless men wear ground sheet.

Stricter attention is still required as to way men roll their ground sheets, and attach mess tins to packs. These are in a great many cases not correct.

Attention is drawn to Operation Orders of 3rd instant re smoking on the march. In many cases today, this order was not carried out by Platoon Officers.

The billeting party will meet 2/Lieut. SAMUELS at Battn. Hd.Qrs at 8.0 a.m.

(Sd) J. CORBAN, 2/Lieut. & Adjt.,
10th York & Lancaster Regiment.

OPERATION ORDERS No. 114   Appendix No.
By Lt.-Col. J.H. RIDGWAY, D.S.O.,
Comdg. 10th York & Lancaster Regt.,
8th March 1917.

The Battalion will march tomorrow in Brigade Group to VALHUON LE HAMEL.

Parade at 9.0 a.m. Head of Column to pass Starting Point - forked road, B.7.b.0.7 (36B, 1/40000) - at 11.0 a.m.

Dress: Full Marching Order with Steel Helmets.

Order of March: Headquarters, D. A. Drums, B. C. Lewis Gunners, Transport.

Reveille: 5.30 a.m. Sick Parade: 6.30 a.m. Breakfast: 7.0 a.m. Dinners will be cooked en route.

Blankets will be stacked at Q.M. Stores by 6.0 a.m. One man per Coy in charge. Officers' valises will be loaded by 8.0 a.m. Mess boxes by 8.15 a.m.

Billets to be left clean by 8.15 a.m.

Billeting party will meet 2/Lieut. SAMUELS at Battn Hd.Qrs at 8.0 a.m.

"C" Coy will detail an Officer to bring on men unable to march with Battn. This party will fall in at Battn Orderly Room at 8.45 a.m.

(Sd) J. CORBAN, 2/Lieut. & Adjt.,
10th York & Lancaster Regiment.

OPERATION ORDERS No. 115   Appendix No. 8.
By Lt.-Col. J.H. RIDGWAY, D.S.O.,
Comdg. 10th York & Lancaster Regt.,
9th March 1917.

The Battalion will march tomorrow in Brigade Group to HOUVIN. Route: BRYAS - OSTREVILLE - ROELLECOURT. About 10½ miles.

Head of Column to pass Starting point - Road junction N.8.c.9.8. at 8.0 a.m. (Sheet 36B. 1/40000).

Dress: Full Marching Order with Steel Helmets.

Order of March: Headquarters, A. B. Drums, C. D. Lewis Gunners, Transport.

Reveille: 5.0 a.m. Breakfast: 6.15 a.m. Dinners will be cooked en route.

Blankets will be stacked at Q.M. Stores at 6.0 a.m. One man per Coy in charge.

Officers' valises will be loaded by 7.0 a.m. Mess Boxes by 7.15 a.m.

Billets to be ready for inspection by 7.15 a.m.

Billeting party will meet 2/Lieut. SAMUELS at Bn. Orderly Room at 7.0 a.m.

Sick will be seen tomorrow one hour after arrival in Billets, except for urgent cases unable to march, who will be seen at 6.0 a.m.
The same men as today will be brought on in rear of Battn.

(Sd) J. CORBAN, 2/Lieut. & Adjt.,
10th York & Lancaster Regt.

Vol 20

CONFIDENTIAL.

63/37

The 10th (Service) Battalion

The YORK and LANCASTER Regiment.

WAR DIARY

APRIL — 1917

NINETEENTH VOLUME

WAR DIARY of
10th Bn York & Lancaster Regt.
INTELLIGENCE SUMMARY

Army Form C. 2118.

Place	Date	Hour	Summary of Events and Information	Remarks and references to Appendices
HOUDIN-HOUVIGNEUL	Oct 1917 1st		Battn billeted at HOUDIN-HOUVIGNEUL. Special Training having been carried out in view of forthcoming operations. 20 Other Ranks joined from 3rd Inf. Base Depot.	Appx. 1.
	5th.		13 O.Rs and N.C.Os joined from 3rd Inf. Base Depot. Battalion proceeded by route march to BEAUFORT. Billets taken over.	3 Appx. 4.
NOYELETTE DUISANS	7th. 8th.		Battalion proceeded by route march to NOYELETTE. Billets taken over. Battalion proceeded by route march to DUISANS, taking over billets at this place. Fighting equipment was completed and all arrangements made for going into Battle Positions the next day.	Appx. 5.
TRENCHES	9th.		Battle of ARRAS. Battalion proceeded by route march to twenty trenches in vicinity of ST. NIVERT-BLANCY. 2nd line Transport to BLANCY. Account of this Battn. but in the operations covering a period 9-12/4/1917 is attached.	Appx. 8, 9, 10.
ARRAS	12th.		This Battn. relieved soon from stand down and sent MONCHY-LE-PREUX by 14th Division. This Battalion relieved by 10th West Yorks and proceeded to ARRAS by route march. Billets in HOSPICE-DES-VIEILLARDS.	
AGNEZ-LES-DUISANS	14th.		Battalion proceeded by route march to AGNEZ-LES-DUISANS, Lieut. taken over. Lieut. H.R. EVERETT (R.A.M.C.) joined from 49th Fd. Amb. to take over duties of Medical Officer vice Capt. (PRAISTER? E.R. (R.A.M.C.) killed in action 11/4/1917.	Appx. 6.
MARIN	15th		Battn proceeded by route march to MARIN. Taking over billets.	Appx. 6.
	16th. 15th.		Re-equipping and re-fitting of Battn carried on with. Draft of 52 O.Rs. joined from 3rd Inf. Base Depot. Draft of 91 O.R. joined from 3rd Inf. Base Depot. 2/Lt W.R. ROCKNEY re-joined.	Appx. 6. Appx. 1.

WAR DIARY
10th York & Lancaster Regt.
INTELLIGENCE SUMMARY

Army Form C. 2118.

Place	Date	Hour	Summary of Events and Information	Remarks and references to Appendices
COUTURE Tincks.	19th 20th		Battalion proceeded by route march to COUTURE, billets occupied. Divisions going into line. Battalion proceeded by Motor Lorry to AGNIEZ(?) Mese (BOND PORT ARRAS) and then proceeded by route march to part of line allotted. 2/ R. SCARPE near FAMPOUX. First line transport to ROCLINCOURT Valley.	App. II.
	21st 26th		Draft of 57 other Ranks joined first line transport from 3H I.B.D. Draft of 104 other Ranks joined first line transport from 3H I.B.D. 3 Officers reinforcements joined first line transport: 2/Lt H. CAMERON, S. WILLIAMS and I. KAPLAN. Lt Col. E.E.F. SIMKINS joined to command Battn. vice Lt Col. THRIDGWAY.	App. 1. App. 1. App. 1. App. 1.
	27th		Killed in action 25/4/1917	
	28th		Battn withdrawn from line. Div. relieved by 9th (Scottish) Div. Battn arrived ROCKINCOURT Valley. Account of operations period 20-29/4/1917 is appended.	App. 13.
HARNES	29th		Battalion proceeded by Motor Bus to HARNES to re-organise and re-fit. (Billets hitherto over.)	

P.P. Simkins
Lt Col.
Comdg 10th York & Lanc R.

List of Appendices.

1. Strength.
2. Roll of Officers.
3. Honours.
4. Operation Orders No. 116 and 117.
5. Operations Orders Nos. 118 and 119.
6. Operation Order No. 120.
7. Operation Orders No. 121 and 122.
8. Battalion Instructions No. 1.
9. Battalion Instructions No. 2.
10. Report on Operations - 9-12/4/1917.
11. Operation Order No. 124.
12. Operation Order No. 125.
13. Report on Operations - 22-29/4/1917.

Appendix ...1......

10th Battalion York and Lancaster Regiment.

STRENGTH during month of APRIL 1917.

March 31st 1917 : Fighting Strength : Officers 36
                                      Other Ranks 920

April 30th 1917 : Fighting Strength : Officers 19
                                      Other Ranks 584

INCREASE.

Officers.
   Lt-Col. E.F.F. SIMKINS,   Joined to Command Bn. 27/4/17
   2/Lt. W.L. ROCKLEY, M.C. Joined from England.   16/4/17
        :   H. CAMERON,   :   :   :   26/4/17
        :   S. WILLIAMS,   :   :   :   26/4/17
        :   I. KAPLAN,   :   :   :   26/4/17

   Lieut. H.R. GRELLET, R.A.M.C. Joined from 49th F.A.
      (Does not effect Strength)   14/4/17

Other Ranks.
   42 Other Ranks joined from Base Depot,   16/4/17
   91 :   :   :   :   :   :   18/4/17
   51 :   :   :   :   :   :   21/4/17
   101 :   :   :   :   :   :   26/4/17

DECREASE.

Officers.
   2/Lt. M.H. OAKLEY, To England Sick.   30/3/17
   Capt. E.G.J. FAIRNIE, Wounded.   11/4/17
   2/Lt. C.A.J. NICHOLSON, To F.A. Wounded.   14/4/17
   Capt. G.R. PLAISTER, R.A.M.C. Killed in Action. 11/4/17
      (Does not effect Strength)
   Lt-Col. J.H. RIDGWAY, Killed in Action.   23/4/17
   Lieut. D.A. HALL,   :   :   23/4/17
   2/Lt. F. LUPTON,   :   :   23/4/17
     :   J.M. STROTHER, M.C. Killed in Action,   28/4/17
   Major W.B. DRYNAN, Wounded,   21/4/17
   2/Lt. D.D. HAWLEY, M.C. Wounded,   21/4/17
     :   E. TOPPING, Wounded, (Died of Wounds)   23/4/17
      (25/4/17)
     :   J.J.W. FAIRBAIRN, Wounded,   23/4/17
     :   J.E. HILL,   :   23/4/17
   Capt. R.H. FITTS,   :   23/4/17
   2/Lt. E. SAMUELS,   :   23/4/17
     :   F. MORTON-SMITH, Wounded,   23/4/17
     :   K.G. WOODMANSEY,   :   23/4/17

/Page 2.

DECREASE (Continued)

Officers.

Lieut.	F.E. KNOWLES,	Wounded	23/4/17
Major.	D.T. WELSH,	:	23/4/17
2/Lt.	F.C. JACKSON,	:	26/4/17
:	W.G. SUMNER,	:	28/4/17
:	F.E. PAYNE,	:	28/4/17
:	E.L. WILKS,	:	22/4/17
Capt.	S. LUCAS,	To Field Amb: Sick.	27/4/17
		(Does not effect Strength)	

Other Ranks.

72	Sick Wastage.
1	To Authorised Establishment of R.F.C. (Draughtsman)
1	To Commission.
37	Killed in Action.
391	Wounded in Action.
119	Reported Missing in Action.

---------oooooooooOOOOOOOOOooooooooo---------

Appx. 2.

10th Battalion York & Lancaster Regiment.

NOMINAL ROLL of OFFICERS -- APRIL 30th 1917.

Lt-Col.	SIMKINS	E.E.F.	Commanding Officer.
Capt.	AIREY	C.F.	Town Major, HOUVIN.
"	LUCAS	S.	Sick.
"	ELSWORTH	L.A.	
Lieut.	ROBINSON	A.R.	
"	WILKINSON	R.M.	
2/Lt.	MITCHELL	R.J.	Att'd 152 Co. R.E.
"	AYRES	F.	
"	LAMOND	A.W.	
"	WALNE	H.A.	
"	TAYLOR	J.B.	Sick.
"	GAUNT	B.W.	Att'd 63rd T.M.B.
"	HORSFALL	J.R.	
"	CORBAN	J.	
"	ROCKLEY	W.L.	
"	KAPLAN	I.	
"	WILLIAMS	S.	
"	CAMERON	H.	

Lieut & Q.M. JAMIESON   A.

Lieut. GRELLET   H.R.   R.A.M.C.

———oooooo(((((O)))))oooooo———

APPX. 3

10th Battalion York & Lancaster Regiment.

Extract from Battalion Orders dated 13th April 1917.

126 HONOURS. With reference to the King's Birthday Honours Gazette, the C.O.C. I Corps has awarded the MILITARY MEDAL to the under-mentioned:-

    4548 Pte. CURRELL W.   York & Lancaster Regiment.

His name will appear in the London Gazette in due course.

                                     (sd) J. CORBAN. Lieut. & Adjt.
                                   10th York & Lancaster Regiment.

SECRET   Appx....4....

OPERATION ORDER No. 116.

By Lt-Col. J.H. RIDGWAY D.S.O.
Comdg. 10th York & Lancs Regt.
4th April 1917.

The Battalion will march to-morrow to BEAUFORT.
Order of March: H.Q. Drums, A., B., C., D., Lewis Guns and Transport.
Dress: Full marching order, box respirators.
Head of column to pass starting point - D. Coys H.Q. Mess- at 7.30.a.m. Coys and Transport will use road from Q.M. Stores past Bde H.Q. only, and will leave the road in front of Battn H.Q. clear.
Reveille: 4.30.a.m. Breakfast: 5.0.a.m. Sick parade on arrival in new billets. Dinners will be cooked en route.
All blankets to be tied and labelled in bundles of 10, and to be stacked at Q.M. Stores by 6.0.a.m. ready to load on motor lorry. One man per Section and Company to travel with lorry. Officer's valises to be loaded at Q.M. Stores by 6.0.a. Mess Cart to be loaded by 6.30.a.m.
Billeting party to meet 2/Lieut. SAMUELS at Orderly Room at 6.30.a.m. All Billets to be left scrupulously clean, and ready for inspection by 6.30.a.m. One Officer per Coy to attend.
All claims for damages will be settled before leaving.

(sd) J. CORBAN 2/Lt & Adjt.
10th Bn York & Lancaster Regt.

OPERATION ORDER No. 117.

By Lt-Col. J.H. RIDGWAY D.S.O.
Comdg 10th York & Lancs Regt.
5th April 1917.

The Battalion will march to-morrow to NOVELLETTE.
Coys will be formed up in column of route on the road due west of the B. in BEAUFORT by 8.15.a.m. in the following order:
H.Q. Drums, B.C.D.A. Lewis Guns and Transport.
Dress: Full Marching Order.
Reveille: 5.30.a.m. Breakfast: 6.0.a.m. Sick Parade on arrival in new billets. Dinners will be cooked en route.
All blankets to be tied and labelled in bundles of 10, and to be stacked in bundles of 10 at Q.M. Stores by 7.0.a.m. ready to load on motor lorry.
Officer's valises to be loaded at Q.M. Stores by 7.0.a.m. Mess Cart to be loaded by 7.00.a.m. Only one mess box per Coy to be loaded on Mess Cart.
Billeting Party to meet 2/Lieut. SAMUELS at H.Q. Mess at 7am
All billets to be left scrupulously clean, and ready for inspection by 7.30.a.m. One Officer per Coy to attend.

(sd) J. CORBAN 2/Lieut. & Adjt.
10th Batt: York & Lancaster Regt.

SECRET.
Appx............ 5

OPERATION ORDER No. 118.

By Lt-Col. J.H. RIDGWAY D.S.O.
Comdg. 10th York & Lancs Regt.
7th April 1917.

The Battalion will march to-morrow to DUISANS.
Companies will be formed up in close column on Football Ground at 8.30.a.m. in the following order:-
D., A., B., C., Lewis Guns. Transport will follow when Battn is clear. Right markers to parade at 8.20.a.m. Headquarters and Drums will form up on Right flank.
Dress: Full Marching Order.
Reveille: 5.30.a.m. Breakfast: 6.0.a.m. Sick Parade on arrival in new billets. Dinners will be cooked en route.
Blankets to be tied and labelled in bundles of 10 and stacked at Q.M. Stores by 7.0.a.m. ready to load on motor lorry. One man per Coy. to travel with motor lorry.
Officer's valises to be loaded at Q.M. Stores by 7.0.a.m. Mess Cart to be loaded by 7.40.a.m.
Billeting party to report to 2/Lieut. SAMUELS at Battalion Orderly Room at 6.45.a.m.
All billets to be left scrupulously clean, and ready for inspection by 7.30.a.m. One Officer per Coy to attend.

(sd) J. CORBAN 2/Lieut. & Adjt.
10th Bn York & Lancaster Regt..

SECRET.

OPERATION ORDER No. 119.

By Lt-Col. J.H. RIDGWAY D.S.O.
Comdg. 10th York & Lancs Regt.
8th April 1917.

The Battalion will parade to-morrow ready to move off at 6.0.a.m. in the following order:- D., B., (including Lewis Gunners and 10 men detailed as carrying party from C Coy) A., and C.
Dress: Fighting Order.
N.C.Os and Men remaining in Transport lines will parade at Q.M. Stores under Major WELSH.
Right Markers parade at 5.50.a.m. at Q.M. Stores.
Reveille: 4.30.a.m. Breakfast: 5.0.a.m.
Officer's valises, Mess Cart and M.Os Cart to be loaded by 5.30.a.m.
All billets to be left clean.

(sd) J. CORBAN 2/Lieut & Adjt
10th Bn York & Lancaster Regiment

Appx. 6

SECRET.

13th April 1917.

Battalion moved by March Route to AGNEZ-LES-DUISANS in early morning. No Operation Order was published owing to urgency of move.

---oooooooooo---

SECRET.

OPERATION ORDER No. 120.

By Lt-Col. J.H. RIDGWAY D.S.O.
Comdg. 10th York & Lancs Regt.
14th April 1917.

The Battalion will move to-morrow by March Route, to MANIN.
Reveille: 7.0.a.m. Breakfast: 7.30.a.m.
Dinners will be cooked en route.
All blankets to be tied in bundles of 10 and stacked where unloaded to-day, ready for motor lorry. One man per Coy to be left in charge.
Dress: Full Marching Order with Steel helmets.
Parade: 10.0.a.m.
Order of March: H.Q., D., A., B., and C. Transport will be brigaded and march under Bde Transport Officer. 10th Y and L following T.M.B. Head of Column to pass Starting point K 5 d 4.5 at 12 noon.
Billeting party will report to 2/Lieut. SAMUELS at 8.30.a.m. and to Town Major MANIN at 11.0.a.m.
Mess Cart to be loaded by 9.30.a.m.

(sd) J. CORBAN, 2/Lieut. & Adjt.
10th Bn York & Lancaster Regiment

Appx......7..........

SECRET

OPERATION ORDER No. 121.

By Lt-Col. J.H. RIDGWAY D.S.O.
Comdg. 10th York & Lancaster Regt.
18th April 1917.

The Battalion will march to-morrow to GOUVES.
Reveille: 6.30.a.m.   Breakfast: 7.30.a.m. Sick Parade 8am
Order of March: H.Q. A, B, C, and D.
Starting Point: Cross Roads near Battalion Orderly Room.
Head of Column to pass this point at 10.0.a.m.
Dress: Full Marching Order.
    All blankets to be tied in bundles of 10 and stacked at
Q.M. Stores ready to be loaded by 9.0.a.m. One man per Coy.
to be left in charge. Officer's valises to be loaded by
9.15.a.m.
    Billeting parties to report to 2/Lieut. SAMUELS at Orderly
Room at 9.15.a.m.
    Transport will march with Battalion.
    Mess Cart to be loaded by 9.15.a.m.
    Billets will be left scrupulously clean and ready for
inspection by 9.30.a.m. One Officer per Coy. to attend.
    The Quartermaster will arrange to have a guide at MANIN
Church at 2.0.p.m. to guide lorry for blankets.
    Major WELSH will inspect the billets and obtain a certified
from the Town Major that the billets were left clean.

                    (sd) J. CORBAN Lieut. & Adjt.
                    10th Bn York & Lancaster Regiment.

SECRET.

OPERATION ORDER No. 122.

By Lt-Col. J.H. RIDGWAY D.S.O.
Comdg. 10th York & Lancaster Rgt.
19th April 1917.

The Battalion will move to-morrow to take over the line.
Three lorries are allotted to each Coy for carriage of
blankets, packs and men unable to march. These will be loaded
by 8.30.a.m. One half lorry will be available for Q.M. Stores
and will be at GOUVES Church by 2.0.p.m. This lorry will be
shared with Middx Rgt.
    C. Coy is detailed for carrying party and will accompany
the Battalion to trenches. They will be called for by the
Staff Captain later.
    Reveille: 6.0.a.m. Breakfast: 6.30.a.m.
    Mess Cart to be loaded by 9.0.a.m. Officer's valises to
be loaded by 9.0.a.m.
    Battalion will parade at 9.45.a.m. Order of March: H.Q.
B, C., D., and A.
    Transport Officer will detail L/Cpl. RIPLEY to report to
Bde T.O. at Bde H.Q. at 9.0.a.m. He Must be mounted.
    Coy. Commanders will proceed with the lorries and will
reconnoitre the line.
    Quartermaster will detail one guide to meet lorries at
GOUVES Church at 8.0.a.m.

                    (sd) J. CORBAN Lieut. & Adjt.
                    10th York & Lancaster Regiment.

APPX 8.

10th. York & Lancaster Regiment Instructions No. 1.

Reference :
Sheet 51 C and 51 B 1/40,000.   April 4th 1917.

The VI Corps, to which the 3rd, 12th, 15th and 37th Divisions have been allotted, will, in co-operation with the Corps on either flank, assume the offensive, on a date to be notified later.

The object of the VI Corps operations is to capture the German third line system from FEUCHY CHAPEL to FEUCHY and the high ground about MONCHY LE PREUX.

The VI Corps will attack with the 3rd, 12th and 15th Divisions in the front and with 37th Division in Corps Reserve.
The Divisional boundaries of the three Divisions in front line and the four objectives of the VI Corps are shown on Map "A".

    1st objective - Black Line)
    2nd   "   - Blue Line) Objectives of three leading
    3rd   "   - Brown Line) Divisions.

    4th   "   Green "   Objective of 37th Division.

The following is the preliminary outlined plan for the attack:-

The artillery bombardment prior to the attack will last 4 days and will consist of counter-battery work and the bombardment of the German first and second systems of defence.

At Zero hour all troops in the Corps will move forward, and by Zero plus three hours, the 37th Division will be closed upon the line DAINVILLE - WAGNONLIEU - ST AUBIN ready to move forward.
During this period (Zero to Zero plus 3 hours) the leading Divisions will have secured the Black Line, and after a pause of one hour, will have attacked and captured the Blue line.

At about Zero plus 3 hours, when the capture of the Blue line has been definitely established, and the majority of the enemy's guns, which are in the valley between the Blue and Brown lines, have consequently been silenced, the 37th Division will again move forward.
In this advance, 112th Infantry Brigade with 143rd Field Coy R.E., will move by the following route to an area of assembly which is to be notified later.

63rd. Infantry Brigade. PORTE BAUDIMONT, thence as shown on map (copy at Brigade Hdqrs).

At about Zero plus 7 hours, the leading Divisions will attack the Brown line, and the 37th Division will move forward to form up immediately West of it for the attack on MONCHY LE PREUX the same day

It is the intention that the attack on MONCHY LE PREUX should be carried out with the 112th and 111th Infantry Bdes in front line, on the right and left respectively, and 63rd Infantry Brigade in Divisional Reserve.
No details as to the manner in which this attack will be carried out or the time at which it will be possible to launch it, are yet available.

Further instructions and details as to Artillery co-operation administrative arrangements, will be issued later.

A description of the terrain will also be issued.

(Sd) J. CORBAN, 2/Lieut & Adjt.
10th. York & Lancaster Regiment.

APPX. 9.

10th. York & Lancaster Regiment. Instructions No. 2.

Reference :
Sheet 51 C. and 51 B

1. It is still uncertain what part the Brigade may have to take in the Course of operations.
   It may be used for any of the following:-
   (a) To assist 15th and 12th Divisions to capture BROWN line.
   (b) To assist 111th or 112th Brigades in reaching their objectives.
   (c) To capture the GREEN Line and prolong the line of the 111th Brigade.

2. In the event of (a) a new bombardment would be necessary, consequently orders would be issued.
   (b) This would consist of Battalions being lent to other Brigades, who would issue orders.
   (c) If the battle goes to programme the following will be the lines on which the Brigade will work :-
   Units will leave assembly trenches in following order:-
   Brigade Headquarters, 8th Lincolnshire Regt., 1 Section 63rd Machine Gun Coy, 8th Somerset L.I., 4th Middlesex Regt., 10th York & Lancs Regt., 152 Co. R.E., proceeding behind 11th Inf. Brigade (alongside and south of Railway embankment) to the valley in H.20.d. H.26.b. and H.27.c. and form up, 8th Lincolns on left with 4th Middlesex Regt. in rear, and 8th Somerset L.I. on right with 10th York & Lancs in rear in H.27.c.
   8th Somerset L.I. will be first Battn. to advance echeloned in rear of 111th Brigade (10th Royal Fusiliers). This Battn will assist 111th Brigade, and if objective reached will prolong GREEN Line to left.
   8th Lincolns, echeloned in rear of 8th Somerset L.I. will make good the Sunken Road about H.29.b. and will eventually close gap on left of Somerset L.I.
   4th Middlesex will be in support, and will eventually take up a line between 63rd Brigade Strong points. These Strong points are being garrisoned by 4th Middlesex.
   10th York & Lancs will remain in Valley about H.27.c. in Brigade reserve. If either 111th or 112th Brigades want assistance 10th York & Lancs will be placed under their order.
   The Left being the dangerous flank, careful watch must be kept of the high ground North of River
   The Battalion will occupy assembly trenches as follows:-
   D. Coy left of Reserve trench, B. Coy centre of Reserve trench, Headquarters, right of Reserve trench. A. Coy left of duplicate reserve trench, 152 Field Co. R.E. centre and right of duplicate reserve trench.
   Coy Commanders will occupy positions on right flank of their Coys.
   Order of march on leaving Camp will be:- D., B., Hdqrs. (including Lewis Gunners and the 10 men detailed for carrying from C. Coy) A., C. The latter Coy will come under orders of Staff Captain on arrival at Brigade Dump, West of ARRAS.
   Battn will follow 8th Lincoln Regt. on "Z" day from Dump West of ARRAS. When going through ARRAS, if by day platoons will be at 25 yards interval: if by night the Batt will march closed up.
   In assembly trenches Battn Hdqrs will be in a dug-out in reserve line between ITALY LANE and INVERNESS LANE. Coys will report all in trenches by sending word "HOPEFUL".
   On leaving Assembly trenches Order of march will be as follows:-
   Hdqrs., B., D., A., and will be by platoons at 25 yards interval (if shelling permits)
   Instructions regarding Packs and Blankets will be issued later.

(Sd) J. CORBAN, 2/Lieut & Adjt.
10th. York & Lancaster Regiment.

Appx......10

Report on Operations covering period 9th to 12th April 1917.

This Battalion occupied about 1.0 pm, 9th inst., the Reserve and 2nd Reserve Trenches between Infantry and Inverness Communication Trenches.

About 3.40 pm your message B.M.13 dated 9th inst. arrived. The Battn. then followed in rear of 4th Bn. Middlesex Regt. and eventually reached Battery Valley where Battn occupied an old German Communication Trench on West side of Valley.

We remained there tull 3.0 am, when, under instructions received in your B.M. message dated 10th and timed 2.40 am. I moved over the top to the Railway and along this to Sunken Road in H.23.b., where two Coys dug in as per Map, the other Coy in support in Quarry at H.23.d.0.0 and Battn. H.Q. in H.23.b.4.2.

I gained touch here with mounted troops of the 9th Division in FAMPOUX on my left, and later on got in touch with the 4th Battalion Middlesex Regt., who were 1000 yards on my right rear

From here I sent out patrols to Railway bridge at H.24.a.5.7 and found nothing of the enemy, and the Bridge intact.

About 12.0 noon your B.M. 27 dated 10th inst. arrived.

I immediately prepared to follow 4th Middlesex Regt., after they had passed through me. My 2 leading Coys crossed the Sunken Road leading from H.23.b.8.2 to H.23.d.7½.7½., and on reaching the low ground about H.24.c.2.8. came under heavy M.G fire from the direction of Mount Pleasant Wood. My other Coy was still in Sunken Road H.23.b.8.2.

As the 4th Middlesex Regt. were just in front of me held up, I dug in, and waited for dark.

Your B.M. message 37 dated 10th and timed 4.55 p.m. arrived ordering me to Lone Copse Valley in support. I proceeded there about 8.0 pm and dug in along the bank with my right resting on Lone Copse. Here I was joined by 3 Coys 4th Bn. Middlesex Regt

From here I sent out patrols in the direction of MONCHY and REOUX.

I remained in Lone Copse Valley till I received your Message B.M. 49 dated 11th inst. timed 10.30 a.m.

At 11.15 am I moved Battn as advance guard to the Brigade in the direction of Bois des Aubepines. On reaching the top of the spur, the Battn came under heavy frontal and enfilade M.G. fire and had severe casualties in the leading Coy. I then trickled the remainder of the Battn. over the Danger Zone and got into and occupied the German practice trenches at H.36.d.7.6 These I consolidated.

Here I got in touch with those troops of the 15th Division who were entrenched about I.31.c.2.5. There were also the remnants of 2 Coys H.L.I. on my left in German practice trenches.

From here I made a personal reconnaissance and spoke to O.C. 13th R.B. who was entrenched about N.6.b.4.8. facing N.E.

9.0 pm. 9th April.	Occupied trench in Battery Valley on W. side
12.0 mn. 9/10th April.	do.
6.0 am. 10th April.	2 Coys dug in in Sunken Road H.23.d.5.8 wit 1 Coy at H.23.d.0.0 and Bn. H.Q. at H.23.b.4.2
12.0 noon 10th April	do.
6.0 pm 10th April.	2 Coys dug in at H.24.c.2.8. 1 Coy dug in at H.23.d.0.8. with Bn. H.Q. at H.24.c.0.9.
12.0 mn. 10/11th April.	Dug in in the Bank with my right resting on Lone Copse.
6.0 am. 11th April.	do.
6.0 pm 11th April.	Dug in in German practice trenches at H.36.d.7.6.
12th April.	do.

16th April 1917.

App. 11

OPERATION ORDERS, No. 124 (Provisional)
By Lt.Col. J.H. RIDGWAY, D.S.O.,
Comdg. 10th. York & Lancaster Regiment.
21st. April 1917.

The Division will attack in conjunction with the 51st Division on right, and 63rd Division on left

Objectives:-

BLACK LINE)
BLUE LINE) Maps will be issued later.
BROWN & RED LINE)

The 63rd. Brigade will be right Division with 111th Brigade on left and 112th Brigade in reserve

The dividing line between Battalions will be a line running through I 7 central - Cross roads (marked by left tree of a line of trees) inclusive to Right Battalion. Left of Battalion will be demolished house (known as t-he Inn)

The Battalion will assemble in HONEY TRENCH and a line of shell holes now occupied by the 4th Middlesex Regt.

This trench will be occupied as follows :- B.Coy, left, D.Coy, right, A.Coy, support. Battn.Hdqrs. will follow support Coy.

Coys will attack first in a Northeasterly direction on BLACK Line, then in an Easterly direction.

Coys will attack on a one platoon frontage each, with support Coy prepared to support either Coy.

B.Coy will take care to have Bombers on left to bomb up HUSSAR TRENCH if required.

The following will be ordered tomorrow from Bde Dump :-
Flares   1 per man (if available)
Bombs   1 "   " and 6 per bomber
Riflemen will be made up to 170 rounds per man
Picks and Shovels at the rate of 1 pick to 10 Shovels up to 75% of strength.

A.Coy will arrange to draw and carry up to Assembly trench tools for Battn. Hdqrs.

Plan of barrage and time of lifts will be issued as soon as received, also Zero hour and time of being in Assembly trenches.

It must be impressed on everybody the vital necessity of following up the barrage as closely as possible. If this is not done, the enemy have time to get their machine guns in action. Leading waves should keep within 50 yards of the barrage.

On reaching final objective - BROWN and RED LINE, Coys must immediately push forward Lewis Guns and covering troops whilst remainder dig in and consolidate before counter attack is delivered.

O.C. Coys will please report to Comdg. Officer at present Bn. Hdqrs. at 10.0 am tomorrow.

Major DRYNAN calling first at Bde H.Q. for their Operation Orders or any others they have to issue.

O.C. Carrying party to arrange to fill all mens water bottles before moving tomorrow night. Rations will also be served out.

Men are to be warned that it is uncertain when the next supply of water or rations will be available.

Flares will be sent up by leading troops when Aeroplane calls for signals.

Further orders will be issued on receipt of Brigade Orders.

(Sd) J. CORBAN, Lieut & Adjt.
10th. York & Lancaster Regiment.

APPX 12

OPERATION ORDERS. No. 125.
By Lieut R.M. WILKINSON,
Comdg. 10th. York & Lancaster Regt.
27th April 1917.

1. (a) The 37th Division will capture and consolidate the objective shewn by the BLACK LINE on the map issued.
   (b) The 112th Brigade will attack on the right, the 63rd. Infantry Bde in the centre and the 111th Brigade on the left.
2. The Dividing lines between Infantry Brigades and between 34th and 37th Divisions are shewn on the map issued.
   Smoke shells which in the dark look like golden rain rockets will be fired at the WINDMILL in I 14 b from Zero until Zero plus 45 minutes in order to assist in guiding the troops.
3. A line of posts will be stablished roughly along the BLACK LINE and these will be joined up to make a continuous line as soon as possible.
4. 153 Field Co. R.E. will construct a strong point at I 7 b.7.5. The remainder of Coy will assist in consolidating the BLACK LINE
   The O.C. 4th Middlesex will be prepared to garrison this with 1 platoon and 2 Lewis Guns.
5. On the morning of 28th April by Zero - 45 minutes assaulting Battalion will be formed up under cover of darkness on the following points :-
   (a) 63rd. Infantry Brigade CUBA TRENCH from left of 112th Brigade to BRICKSTACK (I.7.a.6.9.) (350 yards)
   (b) The Brigade will assemble in the area given as follows :-
   8th Somersets on right (in touch with 112th Brigade) 8th Lincolns on left (in touch with 111th Brigade) both in CUBA TRENCH. In support, 4th Middlesex on right 10th York & Lancasters on left in new trench West of CUBA TRENCH and in trench dug last night between latter and the road.
   (c) Immediately the 8th Lincolns leave CUBA TRENCH C. & D. Coys will move up to the part of CUBA TRENCH vacated by them (C. Coy on left) A. and B. Coys will remain in the support Trench (A. Coy on left)
6. 63rd. M.G. Coy will detail two guns to accompany 8th Somersets and 8th Lincolns each. The remaining 4 guns will follow the supporting Battalions and assist as the situation demands
7. All Battalions will attack on a 2 platoon front. The leading platoon of the two leading Battalions will mop up the German trenches in I.7.b. The two rear platoons of the leading Battalions will pass over this trench and go to BLACK LINE
8. From Zero hour a 'creeping' barrage will be placed 200 yards in front of trench of departure and a standing barrage on the enemy line I.8.c.3.2 - I.7.b.7.3 - I.1.a.7.0 - Cross roads I.2.d.
   Barrage 200 yards East of CUBA TRENCH stops 2 mins.
   "   lifts 50 yards at Zero plus 2 and stops 4 mins.
   "   "   50   "   "   "   "   6   "   "   4   "
   "   "   100   "   "   "   "   10   "   "   6   "
   "   "   100   "   "   "   "   18   "   "   7   "
   "   "   100   "   "   "   "   25   "   "   7   "
   it then lifts 100 yards every 5 minutes.
   Final barrage will be 300 yards beyond BLACK LINE.
9. Zero hour will be 4.25a.m. 28th April.
10. One contact Aeroplane will call for flares at 6.15 am April 28th.
11. Coys will be ready to move off from present trenches at 11.0 p.m. April 27th and will move to assembly trenches via HUDSON, HUSSAR and CHILI trenches.
    Battn. will move off in following order C, D, A, B, Hdqrs.
12. C. Coy will be prepared to fill any gap between 8th Lincolns and 111th Brigade.

(Sd) J. CORBAN, Lieut & Adjt.,
10th. York & Lancaster Regiment.

Appx .....13...

Report on operations covering period from 22nd to 29th
April 1917.

This Battalion moved up from EFFIE TRENCH about 11.15 pm night of 22/23rd April, and relieved 4th Bn.Middlesex Regt in HONEY TRENCH, and a line of shell holes in H.11.b. the relief being completed by about 1 am on the morning of the 23rd April.
Immediately the attack was launched on the morning of the morning 23rd April the Battn went steadily forward andmet with heavy frontal and enfilade M.G. fire from about H.6.c.
Very soon after the battle opened Units of the Brigade became mixed up, and no information reached me from Officers of the Battn. I sent out patrols to getin touch with the Coys but no reliableinformation was brought back. I got in touch with O.C. 8th Lincoln Regt about H.12.b.7.8. where I made my Headquarters and again sent out two patrols. These onlymet scattered parties which were collected and under orders of O.C. 8th Lincoln Regt. formed a support line in CHILI TRENCH. I remained there under orders of O.C. 8th Lincolns during the night of 23/24th with two Officers and 38 Other ranks dug in on right of 6th Bedfords and joining up with the left of 11th Royal Warwicks about I.7.a.6.7. We remained in this position during the 24th until ordered to withdraw to HUDSON TRENCH and SUNKEN ROAD about 9.45pm by your B.M. 39 dated 24th.
The Battn. remained in these positions until 11.30 pm night of 27/28th April when it movedto ASSEMBLY TRENCHES west of CUBA TRENCH under the command of Lieut R.M. Wilkinson and got into position about 3.55 am. Battn. H.Q. being established at H.12.b.7.6.
At 4.25 am. the attack was launched, the Battn being in support to 8th Lincolns.. By 5.30 am the Battalion had taken and occupied trenches about I 1.d.8.8. At 6.30 am. the Battn. together with parties of other Units had taken up position N. of road at I.2.b. central. Owing to being isolated and under heavy M.G. fire they retired to a line of trenches occupied by the 111th Bde about I.1.d.9.7. at about 11.0 am. They remained there until relieved on night of 29th April.
Under orders received verbally from 2/Lt. SIMPSON, Battn. H.Q. with a few stragglers withdraw from CHILI TRENCH and proceeded to Bde H.Q. at about 4.0 am on the 29th and thence proceeded to ARRAS where Battalion embussed for MANIN to Billets.

2/5/1917.

Vol 21

Confidential

War Diary

of the

10th (Service) Battalion

York and Lancaster

Regiment.

May 1917.

Twenty-first Volume.

Confidential

The 10th (S) Battalion

The York and Lancaster Regiment

War Diary

May 1917

Twenty first Volume

WAR DIARY

1/5 Batt. York and Lancaster Regt.

INTELLIGENCE SUMMARY

Army Form C. 2118.

Place	Date 1917	Hour	Summary of Events and Information	Remarks and references to Appendices
MANIN	1st		Battn. in billets at MANIN. Battalion training being carried out.	
	7th		3 Officers (Capt. E.L.S. Fairlie, Capt. E.H. Stewart, 2/Lt. W. Tansy) and 60 other ranks joined. Capt. R.A.R.L. Ainslie (on east R.L.) posted to take over duties of 2 in Command.	
	8th		Draft of 55 other ranks joined. 2nd Lieut. E.H. Sutcliffe (instructor) and Sunderland (Summary) joined.	
	9th		Draft of 11 other ranks joined.	
	12th		Draft of 3 other ranks joined.	
	13th		1 Other rank joined.	
	15th		2nd Lt. K.H. Hughes and 2/Lt. A.H. Jackson.	
	16th		Draft of 11 other ranks joined	
	17th		Draft of 6 other ranks joined	
SINENCOURT	18th		Bn. proceeded by route march to SINENCOURT	
ACHICOURT	19th		Bn. proceeded by route march to ACHICOURT	
	24th		Capt. R.A. Coxe (1st Northern Cyclist Bn.) & T.J. Cybis 2/Lt. A. Clarkman joined from England	
	25th		Draft of 5 other ranks joined	
TILLOY-LES-MOUFLAINES	28th		Bn. less A.M. Stores and Transport remaining at Achicourt) proceeded by route march to TILLOY-LES-MOUFLAINES relieving 1/5 Rifle Brigade in Brigade Support.	
ARRAS	31st		Bn. proceeded by route march & proceeded to reliable camp 6 SCHRAMM BARRACKS, ARRAS. Ribbentrop Coy (W. Yorks) (w. ...)	

A5834 Wt W4973/M637 750,000 8/16 D. D. & L. Ltd. Form/C.2118/13.

List of Appendices

1. Strength
2. Roll of Officers
3. Honours & Awards
4. O.O. 126
5. O.O. 127
6. O.O. 128
7. O.O. 129

Appendix No.

10th Bn York & Lancaster Regt.

Strength during month of MAY 1917

April 30th 1917 Fighting Strength: Offrs. — 9
                                   Other Ranks — 584

May 31st 1917 Fighting Strength: Offrs. — 24
                                 Other Ranks — 414

Increase

Officers

Capt. E.C.T. FAIRNIE. Joined from Hospital 1/5/1917.
Capt. C.F. ELLWOOD.   "   "   England 1/5/1917.
2/Lt. V.S. PARRY.   "   "   "   1/5/1917.
Capt. R.A.B.P. WATTS. Joined to take over
   (Som. L.I.)   duties of 2nd in Command. 4/5/1917.
Lieut. E.H. SUTCLIFFE. Joined from England 8/5/1917.
   (W.&C. Yeo).
2/Lt. A.H. JACKSON. Joined from England 15/5/1917.
  "   H.D. HUGHES.   "   "   "   15/5/1917.
Capt. J.C. BOSS. Joined from England 24/5/1917.
   (Northern Cy. Bn.)
2/Lt. T.P. SYKES.   "   "   "   24/5/1917.
  "   A.F. GLADMAN. "   "   "   24/5/1917.

Other Ranks

60 O.Rs. joined from Base Depot. 1/5/1917.
55   "   "   "   "   "   8/5/1917.
16   "   "   "   "   "   9/5/1917.
 3   "   "   "   "   "   12/5/1917.
 1   "   "   "   "   "   13/5/1917.
 4   "   "   "   "   "   16/5/1917.
 6   "   "   "   "   "   17/5/1917.
 5   "   "   "   "   "   20/5/1917.

Decrease

Officers

2/Lt. J.B. TAYLOR. To England Sick
Capt. S. LUCAS.   "   "   Wounded

Other Ranks

 1 Accidentally Killed.
10 Evacuated Sick.
 2 To Temp. Commissions
 3 To Establishment of Lines
 1 To R.E. (Transfer)

10th Bn. York & Lancaster Regiment
Nominal Roll of Officers on Fighting Strength

Rank &	Name		If detached
Lt. Col.	Simkins	E. E. F.	
Capt.	Watts	R. A. P. B.	
"	Ellwood	C. F.	
"	Airey	C. F.	34th I. B. D.
"	Fairnie	E. G. J.	
"	Elsworth	L. A.	
"	Boss	J. G.	
Lieut	Robinson	A. R.	Leave
"	Wilkinson	R. M.	
"	Sutcliffe	C. H.	
"	Corban	J.	Corps Depot.
"	Lamond	A. W.	
2/Lt.	Mitchell	R. J.	152. Coy. R. E.
"	Rockley	W. R.	
"	Ayres	T. J.	
"	Horsfall	J. R.	
"	Gaunt	B. W.	63. T. M. B.
"	Walne	H. A.	
"	Cameron	H.	
"	Williams	S.	
"	Kaplan	I.	Bde. School
"	Parry	W.	
"	Hughes	A. H.	
"	Jackson	H. A.	
"	Sykes	T. P.	
"	Gladman.	A. F.	
Lt & Q. M.	Jamieson	A	
Lt. (R.A.M.C)	Gullett	H. R.	

31/5/17.

10th Bn York Lancaster Regiment

Extracts from Battalion Orders: published May 1917.

188. Honours, Awards.

1. Extract from B.R.O. No. 544 dated 11th inst.

The G.O.C. wishes to congratulate the following N.C.Os. and men to whom the Corps Commander has awarded Military Medals and bar to Military Medal for acts of gallantry in the Field near ARRAS. April 9th to 13th.

19630	Pte	A. Bradbury	York Lancaster Regt	
32204	"	J. Boldy	do	
14720	L/C	C. McDermott	do	
4548	Pte	W. Currell	do (Bar to M.M.)	

2. Extract from B.R.O. No. 568 dated 31/5/17.

The G.O.C. congratulates the undermentioned N.C.Os. and men to whom the decorations as under have been awarded for gallantry in the Field during the period 23rd - 30th April 1917.

19824	Pte	Sloan E.	York Lancaster Regt.	M.M.
32365	"	Root A.S.	do	do
32358	"	Howell A.J.	do	do
8998	Corpl	Howard E.S.	do	do

OPERATION ORDERS No. 126   SECRET
By Lt. Col. E.E.F. SIMKINS
Comdg. 10th York & Lancaster Regiment
17th May 1917

Orderly Officer for tomorrow: 2/Lieut. H.D. HUGHES
Next for duty   : 2/Lieut. J.H. HORSFALL

Battalion Orderly Sergeant : Sgt. G.W. Massey "B" Coy.

Reveille 6 a.m.   Breakfast 7 a.m.   Sick Parade 7.30 a.m.

All Blankets to be dumped at Q.M. Stores labelled and securely tied in bundles of 10 by 7 a.m.

Mess Cart will be loaded by 9.15 a.m.

The Battalion will march to SIMENCOURT tomorrow and will be paraded ready to move off at 10 a.m. on road passing Battalion Canteen with head resting on road junction near Q.M. Stores.
Order of march Signallers, Drums, B.C.D.A. Transport.

Distance of 200 yards between Companies and Sections of Transport (9 Vehicles to one Section) will be maintained on the march

Billets will be clean and ready for inspection by 2nd in Command by 9 a.m.

O.C. Coys will render a nominal roll to the Adjutant by 8.30 a.m. of men who are unfit to keep up with Battalion. These men will be marched as a separate party under the Orderly Officer and will parade at 9.15 a.m. at Orderly Room.

Dinners will be cooked en route

Billeting party will parade under Lieut. WILKINSON at Orderly Room at 9 a.m.

Chin Straps.
The Divisional General wishes it to be impressed on all ranks that the Chin Straps of Steel Helmets are now to be worn <u>under</u> the chin.

(Sd) L.A. ELSWORTH Capt. & Adjt.
10th York & Lancaster Regiment.

AFTER ORDERS

All Mens' packs will be dumped at the same time as Blankets at Q.M. Stores and will be transported by Lorry. Men are advised not to leave private property in packs. Dress will therefore be Fighting Order. Box Respirators to be worn over the right shoulder and under the left arm.

OPERATION ORDERS No. 127 SECRET

By Lt. Col. E.E.F. SIMKINS
Cmdg. 10th York & Lancaster Regt.
18th May 1917

Orderly Officer for tomorrow:　　2/Lieut. J.H. HORSFALL
　Next for duty　　　　　　　:　2/Lieut. H. CAMERON

Battalion Orderly Sergeant　:　　Sgt MAIDEN "A"Coy

The Battalion will march tomorrow to ACHICOURT

Reveille 6.a.m.　　　Breakfast 7.a.m.　　Sick parade 7.30 a.m.

Order of march Signallers, Drums, C.D.B.A.Transport
Dress. Fighting Order

　　Companies will parade ready to move off at 10.45 a.m. in Camp
Transport to be at Road junction Q.10c 8.1. at 11.a.m.

　　Distance of 200 yards between Companies and Sections of
Transport (9 Vehicles to one Section) will be maintained on the march

　　Blankets will be tied in Bundles of 10, labelled and with packs
stacked at Q.M.Stores by 7.a.m. Officers valises at the same time

　　Mess Cart will be loaded by 10.15 a.m.

　　Dinners will be cooked en route

　　O.C.Coys will render a nominal roll to the Adjutant by 8.30 a.m.
of men who are unfit to keep up with Battalion. These men will be
marched as a separate party under the Orderly Officer and will
parade at 9.15 a.m. at Orderly Room.

　　Billeting party will parade at Orderly Room at 9.a.m.

　　Billets will be clean and ready for inspection by 2nd in
Command by 9.45 a.m.

WATER
　　All ranks are warned again that water found in the wells of
this country is not fit for drinking unless boiled or chlorinated
and that disciplinary action will be taken against anyone filling
water bottles at a well. Only the water in Watercarts which has
been medically treated can be considered pure.

　　　　　　　　　　　　　　　　　(Sd) L.A. ELSWORTH Capt. & Adjt
　　　　　　　　　　　　　　　　　10th York and Lancaster Regiment

OPERATION ORDERS   No. 128

By Lt. Col. R.E.P. Simkins,
Comdg 10th York & Lancaster Regt.
28th May 1917.

Secret
Ref. 51. b.
1/40,000

1. The 10th York & Lancaster Regiment less Q.M. Stores and Transport will move into TILLOY area tonight and relieve 13th R.F. in Trenches in N.2.

2. Order of march: Signallers, Drums, D, A, B, C
   Starting point ACHICOURT Church (G. 33. c)
   Head of column to pass starting point at 6.50 p.m.
   Dress: Full marching order.

3. Distances of 500 yards between Companies and 200 yards between Platoons will be observed.

4. Watercarts, cookers, and tool wagons will be taken up and left in the Area.

5. Officers valises to be handed into Q.M. Stores by 4 p.m. these may be taken up.
   Mess Cart will be loaded by 6. p.m.

6. Billets will be clean and ready for inspection by 2nd in Command by 5.45. p.m.

(Sd) L. A. Elsworth, Capt & Adjt
10th York & Lancaster Regiment.

OPERATION ORDERS No. 129

Map reference
51. 6. 1/40,000

By Lt. Col. E.F.F. SIMKINS
Comdg 10th Bn York & Lancaster Regt.
30th May 1917

1. 10th York & Lancaster Regiment will be relieved tomorrow by the 4th Royal Berks Regt. during the morning.

2. The Battalion will be billeted during the night 31 May and 1st June in Arras and on 1st June will move to BEAUFORT by bus where they will occupy billets.

3. On being relieved Companies will march independently to ARRAS. Relief complete being reported by B.A.B code. Distances of 200 yds between Platoons will be observed.

4. Billeting representatives will report under Lt. Wilkinson to the Asst. Town Major, 6th Corps Area, at Town Commandants Office, ARRAS by 11 a.m. tomorrow.

5. Transport lines and B.M. Stores will remain in their present position until 1st June.

6. Details at Brigade School will complete 1st Course before rejoining Battalion.

7. Transport Officer will send horses to take away Water Cart, Tool Cart, Cookers, and transport for Officers valises, Mess Kit and Lewis Guns which will be ready by 11 a.m. also Coy. Commanders Chargers.

8. Breakfast will be arranged to be kept back by O.C. "C" Coy for Burial party which if late in returning will march independently to ARRAS, and report to Battn. H. Qs. on arrival. Position of Battn. H. Qs. will be found by enquiry at Asst. Town Major's Office, 6th Corps Area at Town Commandants Office.

9. Receipts will be given and taken for all Bivouac covers and Trench shelters, this is most important. Bn. H. Qs. will be notified of numbers.

10. Drums will be prepared to rejoin Battn. tomorrow afternoon. Guide will be sent to Q.M. Stores for same.

(Sgd) R.A. Elsworth, Capt & Adjt
10th York & Lancaster Regiment.

SECRET 63/37 *Confidential*

Vol 2

War Diary of the 10th Battalion York & Lancaster Regiment

June 1917

Twenty second volume

Army Form C. 2118.

WAR DIARY of
10th Bn L'n'k or Lancaster Reg't
INTELLIGENCE SUMMARY.
(Erase heading not required.)

Instructions regarding War Diaries and Intelligence Summaries are contained in F. S. Regs. Part II. and the Staff Manual respectively. Title pages will be prepared in manuscript.

Place	Date Hour	Summary of Events and Information	Remarks and references to Appendices
BEAUFORT	JUNE 1917 1st	Battalion moved by bus from ARRAS to billets in BEAUFORT. Transport proceeded and marched independently by route march to same place	
	2nd	Reinforcements comprising 5 Officers and 40 other Ranks joined from Base Depot. Names of Officers:- 2nd Lieut HOLT, W.L., FORREST, R.A., REVILL, A., TEASDALE, S.B., and BYRNE, T.	
CROISETTE	5th	Battalion moved by bus to CROISETTE taking over billets. 34th Division now in First Army Area	
HEUCHIN	6th	Battalion moved by route march to HEUCHIN taking over billets	
FRUGES	4th [7th]	March continued. Battalion moved by route march to the 80th Training Area. Billets in FRUGES. Reorganization and Training of Battalion carried out.	
	9th	Reinforcements comprising 4 Officers and 187 other Ranks joined from Base Depot. Names of Officers:- Capt W.J. TARRARD, 2nd Lieuts KNIGHT, J.W., MARSHALL, J.W.H., SNOWDEN, H.	
	11th	Reinforcements comprising 69 O.R. joined from Base Depot. Lt. Col. A.B. LAYTON, South Lancs Regt joined to command a Battalion vice Lt. Col. E.E.F. SIMKINS to hospital sick the next day. Capt. H.S.C. RICHARDSON Rifle Brigade joined to be 2nd in command vice Capt. (Captain) R.A.B.C. WATTS South L.I. to hospital sick	
	14th	Reinforcements of 5 O.R. joined from Base Depot. 2 O.R. joined from Base Depot.	
	15th	Reinforcements of 3 Offrs joined from Base Depot.	
	14th [16th]	and LEA, W.G., WOODMANSEY, K.E., DAWSON, E.C.	

Army Form C. 2118.

WAR DIARY of 10th York & Lancaster Regt.
INTELLIGENCE SUMMARY.

(Erase heading not required.)

Place	Date Hour	Summary of Events and Information	Remarks and references to Appendices
FRUGES & WESTREHEM	JUNE 1917 20th 22nd	Reinforcements of 4 other Ranks joined from Base Depot. 39th Division commence march to Second Army.	
THIENNES CAESTRE	23rd 24th	Battalion moved by route march to WESTREHEM Billets occupied. Battalion moved by route march to THIENNES Billets occupied. Battalion moved by route march to CAESTRE Billeting Area Billets occupied.	
BRULOOZE	25th	Battalion moved by route march to the BRULOOZE Area. Camp at GARDEN FARM occupied.	
	26th	Reinforcements of 13 ORs joined from Base Depot. 39th Division relieve 36th (Ulster) Division in line in front of WYTSCHAETE. This Battalion relieved 9th R. Inniskilling Fus. of 109th Infy Bde. in Left Bde support.	
TRENCHES	26th		
	30th	Battn relieve 14th Royal Irish Rifles in front line, night sub-section, Left Bde Section, the 7th Middlesex Regt on left, the 13th K.R.R.C. on right.	

Wournhauth (?) Lt. Col.
Comdg 10th Yorks & Lancs R.

List of Appendices

1. Roll of Officers
2. Strength
3. Honour and Awards
4. Operation Orders 131
5. Operation Orders 132
6. Operation Orders 133
7. Operation Orders 134
8. Operation Orders 135
9. Operation Orders 136
10. Operation Orders 137
11. Operation Orders 138
12. Operation Orders 139
13. Operation Orders 140.

10th Battalion York and Lancaster Regt
Roll of Officers — June 1917

Rank	Name		Present employment
Lt. Col.	LAYTON	A. B.	Cmdg Officer
Major	RICHARDSON	H. S. C	2nd in Command
"	WATTS	R. A. B. P	Attd. Bde HQ
Capt	ELLWOOD	C. F.	Coy Comdr
"	FAIRNIE	E. G. J.	Coy Comdr
"	JARRARD	W. J.	Act/ Adjutant
"	ELSWORTH	L. A	Leave
"	BOSS	J. R.	Platoon Comdr
Lieut.	ROBINSON	A. R.	Coy Comdr
"	WILKINSON	R. M.	Bombg. Officer
"	SUTCLIFFE	E. H.	Course of Inst.
"	CORBAN	J.	Platoon Comdr
"	LAMOND	A. W.	Coy Comdr
"	AYRES	F.	L. G. O
2/Lieut	MITCHELL	R. J.	Attd 152 Co. R. E
"	ROCKLEY	W. L.	Intelligence Officer
"	HORSFALL	J. R	Offr i/c Wiring
"	GAUNT	B. W.	Attd T. M. B.
"	WALNE	H. A	Transport Officer
"	WOODMANSEY	K. G.	Platoon Comdr
"	CAMERON	H.	Platoon Comdr
"	WILLIAMS	S.	Instructor. Base Depot.
"	KAPLAN	I	Army Rest Camp
"	PARRY	W.	Platoon Comdr
"	HUGHES	H D.	Platoon Comdr
"	JACKSON	A. H.	Platoon Comdr
"	SYKES	T. P.	Course of Instr.
"	GLADMAN	A. F.	Platoon Comdr.
"	HOLT	W. L.	Platoon Comdr
"	TEASDALE	S B.	Platoon Comdr.
"	BYRNE	J. A	Platoon Comdr.
"	REVILL	A	Platoon Comdr.
"	FORREST	R A.	Bde School
"	SNOWDEN	H.	Platoon Comdr
"	TUNE	G. E.	Bde Salvage Offr.
"	MARSHALL	J. W. H.	Platoon Comdr
"	KNIGHT	J. W.	Platoon Comdr
"	DAWSON	G. C.	Course of Instr
"	LEA	W. G.	Platoon Comdr
Lt & Q. M.	JAMIESON	A	Quartermaster
Lieut (RAMC)	GRELLET	H. R.	Medical Officer
Capt (C.F.)	THOMAS	H. G.	Chaplain

10th Battn. York and Lancaster Regt.
STRENGTH — June 1917

Fighting Strength   May 30th 1917   Officers 27
                                                                 O.R.   718

Fighting Strength   June 30th 1917   Officers 40
                                                                  O.R.   1003

Increase
Officers
- 2/Lt. S.B. TEASDALE
- " J. BYRNE
- " A. REVILL   } Joined 2/6/1917
- " R.A. FORREST
- " W.L. HOLT

- Capt. W.J. JARRARD
- 2/Lt. J.W. KNIGHT   } Joined 9/6/17
- " J.W.H. MARSHALL
- " H. SNOWDEN
- " Q.E. TUNE   Joined 13/6/17
- Capt. H.S.C. RICHARDSON   " 14/6/17
- 2/Lt. K.R. WOODMANSEY
- " W.G. LEA   } " 17/6/17
- " G.C. DAWSON

Other Ranks

187	O.Rs Joined	9/6/17
69	" "	11/6/17
2	" "	14/6/17
5	" "	15/6/17
7	" "	20/6/17
13	" "	27/6/17
40	" "	2/6/17

Decrease

Officers
Capt. C. FAIREY to S.B.D. P.B.   30/5/17

Other Ranks

1	O.R. to Base Depot (deformed foot)	2/6/17
2	" evacuated sick	2/6/17
2	" " "	6/6/17
2	" " "	8/6/17
4	" " "	10/6/17
1	" " "	11/6/17
1	" " "	16/6/17
1	" Transferred to L.O.R.C. →	18/6/17
1	" To England for Temp Comm	26/6/17
11	" Evacuated sick	26/6/17
2	" Transferred to R Es	28/6/17
3	" Evacuated sick	28/6/17
4	" " wounded	30/6/17

Honours, Awards, Mention in Dispatches

Battalion Orders concerning above subject and published during June 1917 are republished.

256 Honours and Awards d. 6/6/1917

The undermentioned has been awarded a Military Medal for gallantry during period 23/30th April 1917

15308 Sgt. T. R. BEETON   10th York & Lancs Regt.

(Authy: Div R.O. No 2544 d. 4.6.17)

269 Kings Birthday Dispatch d. 8/6/1917

Mentions in Dispatches

The following extracts from the "London Gazette" of the list of "Mentions in Dispatches" is re-published.

YORK & LANCASTER REGT

2nd Lt. A. W. LAMOND
T/2nd Lt. F. AYRES

Additional List.

MAJOR (T/Lt. Col.) J. H. RIDGWAY. D.S.O.
York & Lancs (Killed)

295 Honours and Awards. d. 14/6/1917

Extract from 37th D.R.O. dated 13/6/17

The Field Marshal, Commanding-in-Chief has under Authority granted by his Majesty the King, awarded decorations to the Officers and Other Ranks shewn below for acts of gallantry during operations S of the River Scarpe 9/13th April

Distinguished Service Order

X   X   X   X   X   X

Capt. (T/Major). W. B. DRYNAN   York & Lancs Regt.

X   X   X   X   X   X

OPERATION ORDERS   No. 131   SECRET

By Lt. Col. E.E.F SIMKINS
Cmdg. 10th York & Lancaster Regt.
4th June 1917

1. Orderly Officer for tomorrow : 2/Lt. W. PARRY
   Next for duty : 2/Lt. J.R. HORSFALL
   Battalion Orderly Sergeant : Sgt. MASSEY B Coy
   Reveille : 4.30 am. Breakfast : 5.0 am. Sick parade on arrival
   Dinner will be supplied on arrival at destination

2. 10th York & Lancaster Regt. will move tomorrow by bus to CROISETTE and WAGNIACOURT and will parade at 7.30 am.
   Dress : Full marching order.

3. Transport will move by road under the Brigade T.O. and will pass Starting point - Road junction S.W. of S in AMBRINS at 8.50 am.
   Billeting representatives will report to Lt. WILKINSON at Orderly Room by 6.0 am (Coy QMS. will represent Coys) who will report with party to the MAIRIE by 9.0 am.

4. Baggage wagons will be loaded by 6.0 am.
   Officers valises and all mess kit except one small box will be at Q.M. Stores by 5.45 am.
   Maltese cart will be loaded by 6.0 am.
   The one small box retained will be conveyed by one Lorry which is at the disposal of this Battn and the 8th Lincs for this purpose and will be ready for loading by 7.0 am at Q.M. Stores

5. Billets will be ready for inspection by M.O and Orderly Officer an hour before Battn leaves - 6.30 am
   Coys will report condition of Billets taken over and No. of Stragglers within half an hour of arriving in Billets
   This latter will be a Standing Order.
   In future, distances of 500 yards will be maintained in each Battn etc. Distances of 200 yards will be maintained between Transport of Units
   The Battn will march on the 6th & 7th

(Sd) L.A ELSWORTH
                    Capt & Adjt.
10th York & Lancaster Regt.

OPERATION ORDERS   No. 132   SECRET
By Lt. Col. E.E.F. SIMKINS
Cmdg. 10th York & Lancaster Regt.
5th June 1917

Ref. Map.
Lens 11.

1. Orderly Officer for tomorrow: 2/Lt. J.R. HORSFALL
   Next for Duty: 2/Lt. H. CAMERON
   Battalion Orderly Sergeant. Sgt. E.S. HOWARD 'C' Coy
   Reveille: 4.30 a.m. Breakfast: 5.0 a.m. Sick Parade: 5.0 a.m.
   Dinners will be cooked en route

2. The 10th York & Lancaster Regt. will march tomorrow
   to HEUCHIN. Route: LIBESSART - FLEURY - ANVIN
   Order of march: Signallers, Drums, C.D.A.B, Transport
   Starting point: 'B' Coys Billet.
   Head of column to pass Starting point at 6.30 a.m
   Dress: Fighting order.

3. Officers valises and mess kit will be stacked at
   Coy Hdqr Mess by 5.15 am when they will be collected
   by Transport

4. Coy Commanders will submit to Orderly Room the
   names of men unfit to march with Battalion an hour
   before Battalion moves. These men will parade
   under 2/Lt. CAMERON at Battn. Orderly Room at
   5.45 am

5. Billeting representatives will report to Lt. WILKINSON
   at Orderly Room by 6.30 am

6. Billets will be clean and ready for inspection
   by 5.30 am by Orderly Officer and M.O.

7. Packs will be stacked at Q.M. Stores by 5.0 a.m.
   One man per Coy and Section will be detailed to
   look after and load packs. Three lorries will
   be supplied to this Battn. for carrying packs
   and stores and will arrive about 7.45 am.

8. The Regtl. Police under the Orderly Officer will
   march 100x in rear of last Coy to collect Stragglers
   The M.O. will also march with this party.
   A Roll will be made of all men who fell out
   and disciplinary action will be taken against
   those the M.O. considers fit to march. They will
   also receive instructions in marching from 6.0 to
   8.0 p.m. under the Provost Sgt.

(Sd) L.A. ELSWORTH,
Capt & Adjt.
10th York & Lancaster Regt.

OPERATION ORDERS   No. 133   SECRET

By Lt. Col. E.E.F SIMKINS
Cmdg. 10th York & Lancaster Regt.
6th June 1917

1. Reveille: 7.0 am. Breakfast 8.0 am. Sick parade 9.0 am. Dinners will be cooked en route.

2. The 10th Bn York and Lancaster Regt. will march tomorrow to FRUGES.
Battalion will parade in square outside Orderly Room at 11.15 am. Markers 11.0 am.
Order of march: Drums, B.C.D.A, Signallers, Transport.
Dress: Full marching order.

3. Officers valises and mess kit will be stacked at Coy Hdqrs Mess by 9.15 am when they will be collected by Transport.

4. Coy Commanders will submit to Orderly Room names of men unfit to march with Battn at 9.0 am. These men will parade under Lieut SUTCLIFFE at Battalion Orderly Room at 10.0 am.

5. Billeting representatives will report to Lt. WILKINSON at Orderly Room by 8.30 am.

6. Billets will be clean and ready for inspection by 10.0 am by Orderly Officer and M.O.

(Sd) L.A. ELSWORTH.
Capt & Adjt.
10th York & Lancaster Regt.

OPERATION ORDERS No 134

Night Operations 20th June 1917.

Ref Map.
Hazebrouck 5A.

GENERAL IDEA

The enemy (BLUE) consisting of a force of all arms has retired before a superior British Force (RED) Patrols report that they now occupy an entrenched position on the high ground E of SENLIS with their Left Flank on the River TRAXENE at about the G in FRUGES

SPECIAL IDEA

The 37th Division will occupy LURY. The 1001st Div. will be on the left and the 1100th Div. will be on the right.

The 63rd Bde will move due E on a front of 1000 yards with its right flank on FRUGES-LURY Road. The junction of the two front line Battns will be the N. side of the cemetery on FRUGES-SENLIS Road. The Battns in the front line will be 4th Middlesex Regt on right, 10th York & Lancaster Regt on the left. 8th Lincolns in Support. 8th Somerset L.I. in Brigade reserve.

The role of the 63rd Bde is to capture the two first lines of enemy trench.

Zero hour will be 12.0 p.m.

The Brigade will be in position at 11.30 p.m.

OPERATION ORDERS
By Lt Col. A.B. LAYTON
Cmdg. 10th York & Lancaster Regt
20th June 1917

The Battalion will assemble on the field N.E of the CEMETERY on the FRUGES-SENLIS Road

A and B Coys form the front line close under the bank on the E side of the field.

The Right flank of A Coy will rest on a point on the bank bearing 100° Magnetic from the first tree past the N. corner of the cemetery hedge where the latter touches the FRUGES-SENLIS Road.

B Coy will prolong the left.

Both Coys will send patrols to get touch with their Right and Left respectively.

The Coys will extend into 2 waves with moppers up for the 1st objective (see appendix VIII S.S.143) and lie down.

The first wave will go to the 2nd objective.
These Coys will move via the FRUGES-SENLIS Road
C and D Coys will move along the Sunken Road
immediately S.W. of the F in FRUGES and halt
with the right of C Coy on the N.E corner of the
Cemetery. D. Coy will prolong the left of C. Coy.
At 11.0 pm. C and D Coys extend in two waves with
moppers up on the E side of the Sunken Road and
await orders.
Companies will parade and move independently
to their positions
A. Coy will be in position at 10.0 pm.
B " will be in position at 10.30 pm
C & D Coys will be in position at 10.45 pm.
O.C. Coys will report to Bn. H.Q. by runner
directly they are in position. The runner will
be retained to guide a H.Q runner back to
the Coy.

(Sd) L.A. ELSWORTH,
Capt & Adjt.
10th York & Lancaster Regt.

OPERATION ORDERS.   No. 135   SECRET
By Lt. Col. A.B. LAYTON,
Cmdg 10th York & Lancaster Regt.
21st June 1917.

Ref 1/100,000 Map
HAZEBROUCK 5A
1/40,000   THEROUANNE
BERGUENEUSE

1. The 37th Divn will be transferred to the Second Army and will march on 22nd and 23rd. The move of the Division will be continued on the 24th and 25th inst.

2. The 63rd Infantry Brigade group will move on the 22nd inst.

3. The 10th Bn York and Lancaster Regt will billet the night of 22/23rd at WESTREHEM. The Battn is the last Unit to pass Brigade Starting point at Cross roads 20 c 3.1 and follows the 8th S.L.I. at a distance of 500 yards.

4. The Battalion will fall in in road outside Q.M. Stores ready to move off at 9.30 am. Markers to report to R.S.M at 9.15 am.
Order of march. Drums, C.D.A.B. Hdqrs Transport.
Route: LUGY - BEAUMETZ - LES - AIRE - FEBVIN - PALVART - A5 - WESTREHEM.
Dress: Full marching order, Steel Helmets and Box respirators will be worn.

5. Reveille: 6.30 am. Sick parade: 6.30 am.
Breakfast: 7.30 am. Dinners will be cooked en route.
Billets to be clean and ready for inspection by 8.30 am.

6. Officers valises will be ready for collection by transport at 8.0 am.
Mess kits ready for loading at 8.30 am. Only one box per mess can be carried by Mess cart. Remainder to be stacked at Q.M. Stores by 8.0 am.

7. All men unfit to march will be paraded under 2/Lt. W.G. LEA. outside Orderly Room at 7.30 am. They will be given Breakfast early. Nominal roll will accompany each party.

8. The Regtl. Police under 2/Lt. G.C. DAWSON will march in rear of Battn and collect all Stragglers. The M.O. will accompany his party.

9. Billeting party will report to Lieut. ROBINSON at Orderly Room at 8.0 am.

(Sd) L.A. ELSWORTH.
Capt & Adjt.
10th York & Lancaster Regt.

AFTER ORDER

Reference B.O. 135 para. 4

Dress: Fighting order with Steel Helmets, sun curtains and Box respirators

All packs will be dumped at Q.M. Stores by 8.0.am. 6 O.Rs will be detailed by M.O as loading party. This party will remain behind under Town Major, 2/Lt HORSFALL and will also clean up area after Battalion has marched away

This party will rejoin Battalion with last load on Motor Lorry used for conveying packs.

(Sd) L A ELSWORTH,
Capt & Adjt
10th York & Lancaster Regt

OPERATION ORDERS No. 136 SECRET

By Lt Col A.B LAYTON
Comdg. 10th York & Lancaster Regt
22nd June 1917

Ref 1/100,000 Map
HAZEBROUCK 5A

1. The Battn. will move to THIENNES passing Brigade Starting point at 7.30 am.

2. ROUTE via RELY - LINGHEM - LAMBRES - Road passing N. of A in AIRES - NEUFPRE.

3. The Battalion will parade in column of route facing N.E. Head of column at Orderly Room ready to move off at 6.20 am. Markers will report to R.S.M at 6.0 am.

4. Order of march: D, C, Drums, B, A, HQrs, Transport.

5. Dress: Full marching order (packs will not be carried on lorries)

6. Reveille: 3.30 am. Sick parade: 3.30 am. Breakfast 4.15 am. Dinners on arrival. Billets to be clean and ready for inspection by 5.30 am.

7. Officers valises will be ready for collection by Transport at 5.30 am. Mess kits ready for loading at 5.30 am. Surplus kit to be stacked at QM Stores by 5.30 am.

8. All men unfit to march will be paraded under 2/Lt. REVILL outside Orderly Room at 4.30 am. They will be given breakfast early. Nominal Roll will accompany each party.

9. The Regtl Police under 2/Lt. W G LEA will march in rear of Battn. and collect all stragglers. The M.O. will accompany this party.

10. Billeting party will report to 2/Lt. SNOWDEN at Orderly Room at 6.0 am and will meet Battalion at entrance of village at about 11.0 am

11. 2 men per Coy will be detailed to report to Lt CORBAN at 6.15 am at Orderly Room. This party will be responsible that all billets used by this Battn are left in a clean and sanitary condition. Certificates being rendered to Orderly Room immediately on arrival at THIENNES. They will march independently on completion of their duty.

(Sd) L A ELSWORTH
Capt & Adjt
10th York & Lancaster Regt

OPERATION ORDERS No. 137   SECRET

By Lt. Col. A B LAYTON
Cmdg. 10th Bn York & Lancaster Regt.
23rd June 1917

Reference:
1/100,000 Map HAZEBROUCK 5A.
1/20,000 Sheet 27 S.E.

1. The Battalion will move to "B" area CAESTRE passing Brigade Starting point (the road junction 1100 yds S.W. of M in MORBECQUE) at 6.22 am.

2. Route: via MORBECQUE – HAZEBROUCK – LA BREARDE

3. The Battalion will be situated in Billets as below:—

W. 7. a. 8.8.	MACKE	80	} HQ & Transport
W. 7. b. 0.9.	CALOU BORDANT	20	
W. 7. a. 4.4.	DEGUIST	150	
W. 1. c. 1.6.	FERM LEROY	150	
W. 1. a. 2.8.	FERM ~~MERCHIE~~	150	} Rendezvous for guide to meet Battn at 8.30 am. Road junction V. 12. b. 5.9.
P. 36. a. 6.3.	FERM PLANCKE	80	
P. 36. c. 7.7.	BALLOY	80	
P. 36. a. 8.2.	HUGBHE	60	
P. 36. b. 6.7.	COEWELL	60	
Q. 31. a. 2.9.	WEESTEEN	100	
Q. 31. b. 3.1	BELLANOIER	80	

4. Battalion will parade in column of route facing N.E. Head of column 700 yds N.N.E. of Battn. Orderly Room on THIENNES – HAZEBROUCK Road (opposite A Coys billet.) Move off 5.15 am.

5. Order of march as per margin

   C.B.
   Drums
   Hdqrs.
   D.A.
   Transport

6. Dress: Full marching order (Packs will not be carried on lorries.)

7. Reveille 3.0 am. Sick parade 3.0 am. Breakfast 3.30 am. Dinners on arrival. Billets to be clean and ready for inspection by 4.30 am.

8. Officers valises will be ready for collection by Transport at 4.15 am. Mess kits to be ready for loading at 4.15 am. Surplus kit to be stacked at Q.M. Stores at 4.15 am.

9. All men certified by the M.O. as unfit to march as published in todays Battn orders or found subsequently unfit to march will be paraded on the THIENNES – HAZEBROUCK Road opposite the billet in which the unfit men are quartered at 3.30 am. Coys will arrange that these men are given breakfast before they start. 2/Lt. DAWSON will be in charge of this party. A nominal roll will accompany the party from each Company.

10. The Regtl. Police under Lt CORBAN will march in rear of Battn. and collect all stragglers. The M.O. will accompany this party.

11. Billeting party will meet the Battn. on arrival at 8.30 am on Road junction V.12.b.5.9.

12. 2 men per Coy will be detailed to report to 2/Lt W.PARRY at 5.0 a.m. at the Orderly Room. This party will be responsible that all billets used by this Battn. are left in a clean and sanitary condition. Certificates being rendered to Orderly Room immediately on arrival. They will march independently on completion of their duty.

13. Refilling point at Crossroads 2 miles S.W. of CAESTRE ½ mile S. of C. in BRECQUE at 10.0 a.m.

(Sd) W.T.JARRARD, Capt &
Act/Adjt
10th York & Lancaster Regt.

OPERATION ORDERS. No 138   SECRET
By Lt Col A.B. LAYTON
Cmdg 10th York & Lancaster Regt.
24th June 1917

Reference:
1/100,000 Map HAZEBROUCK 5A
1/20,000 Sheet 27 S E 4
1/20,000 "   28 S W.

1. The Battalion will move to No 6 & 8 Areas near BRULOOZE. Brigade Starting point (Cross Road W.12.b) at 6.50 a.m.

2. Route via METEREN - SHAEXKEN - MONT NOIR - MONT ROUGE.

3. The Battalion will be situated in billets within half a mile radius of BRULOOZE (N.24.b.)

4. The Battalion will parade in column of route facing S E on the SYLVESTRE - CAESTRE - ELETRE Road ready to move off at 5.50 am. Head of column will be at Road junction W.3. & 8.2 Companies, Transport, H.Q. details and Drums will move off from their billets independently to their positions in the column.

B.C. Drums
O.A. Hagu's
Transport.

5. Order of march as per margin

6. Dress Full marching order (Packs will not be carried on lorries)

7. Reveille : 3.0 am   Sick parade : 3.0 am. Breakfast 3.30 am. Dinners on arrival. Billets to be clean and ready for inspection by 5.0 am

8. Officers valises, Mess kits and surplus Mess kit will be ready for ~~~ collection by Transport at the following times
    A. Coy   3.50 am
    D. "   4.5 am
    C. "   4.15 am
    B. "   4.30 am
    H.Q.   4.40 am

9. All men certified by the M.O as unfit to march as published in today's Battn. Orders or found subsequently unfit to march will be paraded at Q.M. Stores at 5.0 am

10. Slow marching party: The NCOs and men whose names were published in Battn Orders today as composing the Slow marching party will concentrate at Battn H.Q. ready to move off at 4.45 am
    An officer of the Brigade Staff will meet this party at CAESTRE Church to conduct it by special route to the new area.

O.C. Coys are responsible that these men are paraded and that each is provided with Haversack Rations. Nominal rolls will be handed by the NCO in charge to 2/Lt. JACKSON who will conduct the party.

2/Lt. JACKSON will hand a nominal roll of the whole party to 2/Lt ANDREA at CAESTRE Church before 5.30 am.

11. The Regtl Police under 2/Lt CAMERON will march in rear of Battn. and collect all stragglers. The M.O will accompany this party.

12. The Billeting party will proceed on bicycles to report to the Staff Captain at the Office of the AREA COMMANDANT VI Area BRULOOZE M.24.£.15. at 9.0 am.
Billeting representatives to meet Billeting Officer at H.Qs Billet at 6.30 am sharp.

13. 2 men per Coy will be detailed to report to 2/Lt. HUGHES at 5.0 am at the Orderly Room. This party will be responsible that all Billets used by this Battn. are in a clean and sanitary condition. Certificates being rendered to Orderly Room immediately on arrival. They will march independently on completion of their duty.

14. Refilling point is on road running N.E from LOCRE ¼ mile N of C in LOCRE

15. The Battalion will be inspected by the Army Commander on the march through METEREN

(Sd) H.S.C RICHARDSON, Major
for Capt & Act/Adjt.
10th York & Lancaster Regt.

OPERATION ORDERS No 139   SECRET

By Lt Col A.B.LAYTON
Cmdg. 10th York & Lancaster Regt.
28th June 1917

Ref Maps: 1/20,000 Sheet 28. SW (5A)
1/10,000 WYTSCHAETE 28 SW(2)(5A)

1. Battalion will relieve the 9th INNISKILLING FUS. in the support line tonight

2. The Battalion will parade in Full marching order at 8.15 pm in NUT Road facing N.E. Head of column near Orderly Room.
Order of march as per margin

A, B, C, D
H.Q. L.G.
Limbers

3. Route: NUT Road — KEMMEL — YORK ROAD — VIERSTRAAT Road to WOOD DUMP at NAGSNOSE O.18 b 0 8

4. The Battalion will move by Companies at 300 yds intervals to KEMMEL and forward of this by platoons at the same interval.

5. A guide for each Platoon will meet the Battalion at NAGS NOSE WOOD DUMP at 9.45 pm. Platoons will take over from corresponding platoons of 9th I.F.

6. The Battalion H.Q. will be at ONRAET FARM O.14 a 3.1

7. Transport will march independently to N.10 central. The Q.M. Stores will be at GODEZONNE FARM

8. One officer and 4 N.C.O's per Coy to be detailed by Coy Commanders will proceed independently to WOOD DUMP NAGS NOSE to arrive there at 2.45 pm. This party will take over all stores and information. A list of articles taken over will be forwarded to Battn. H.Q. by 9.0 am 29th inst.

9. The Quartermaster will visit GODEZONNE FARM during today the 28th inst. with a view to taking over. The Transport Officer will report at the same place at 9.0 pm the 28th inst. and will accompany the ration party of the Battalion being relieved in order to become acquainted with the track.

10. O.C. Companies will report "relief complete" by 2nd Army Code or runner to Battn. H.Q. immediately relief is finished

(Sd) W.J. JARRARD, Capt &
Actg Adjt
10th York & Lancaster Regt.

OPERATION ORDERS No 140   SECRET
By Lt Col. A. B. LAYTON
Cmdg. 10th York & Lancaster Regt.
29th June 1917

Ref. Map 1/10,000 Sheet 28 S.W.(2) (5A)

1. The Battalion will be relieved in the support line tonight by the 8th Somerset Light Infantry and will then relieve the 14th Royal Irish Rifles in the front line.

2. Order of relief of Support Line
   A. Coy Y & L will be relieved by A Coy 8th S.L.I
   B . . . . B . . . .
   C . . . . C . . . .
   D . . . . D . . . .

   One officer and 4 N.C.O's per Coy from the 8th S.L.I will form an advance party to take over from Coy during the afternoon. These will act as guides for their own Coys.

3. The Battalion will relieve the 14th Royal Irish Rifles ~~tonight~~ in the front line tonight

4. Order of relief:
   A. Coy will relieve A. Coy 14th R.I.R.
   B . . . . B . . . .
   C . . . . C . . . .
   D . . . . D . . . .

5. A. Coy will hold the right half sector in the front line. C Coy will hold the right half sector in the support line. B. Coy the left half sector in the support line.

A.D.B.C
Hdqrs

6. Order of march as per margin. The leading platoon will move off at 10 pm.
   Relief will take place by platoons moving at 300 yards interval. Care must be taken that platoons do not close up on one another.

7. Scouts from the 14th R.I.R. will guide each platoon from ONRAET FARM to the extreme point of LEG COPSE where track branches off at O.20.b.40.60 marked "to the right" and "left" Support Companies. One runner per Coy will report at Battn H.Q. at 9.0 pm to guide these scouts to Coy H.Q.
   Each platoon at point O.20.b.40.60 will meet a guide to guide them as far as Support H.Q. A & D Coys for the front line will be provided at the Support H.Qrs with 4 guides (one per platoon) to guide them from Support H.Qrs into the front line

8. RATIONS Rations for A and C Coys will be brought by limber to O.21 Central. Bn. H.Q. rations will be dumped at end of track O.20.d.1.7. Rations for B and D Coys will

be brought by limber to EVANS FARM O.14.b.3.3.
L/cpl PELL and 2 Regtl. Police will proceed to EVANS FARM to take over B and D Coys rations
Carrying parties of 60 strong per Coy will be detailed by the support Coys to carry rations for Coys in the front line.

10. Reliefs complete in code or by runner, will be reported to Bn. H.Q. immediately on conclusion
11. Box respirators will always be worn in the 'alert' position
12. Coy Commanders will send to Orderly Room a copy of the list of material which they take over
13. 2/Lt. HORSFALL and 20 men will form a permanent wiring party. Coys will detail 5 men to report to that Officer
14. The Aid Post is at O.20.b.1.4.
15. Attention is drawn to 37th Divnl. Trench Orders

(Sd.) W.J. JARRARD, Capt. & act/Adjt
10th Bn. York and Lancaster Regt.

CONFIDENTIAL

Vol 23

10th (SERVICE) BATTALION

YORK & LANCASTER REGIMENT

WAR DIARY

JULY 1917.

TWENTY THIRD VOLUME

Army Form C. 2

WAR DIARY of
10th Batt York & Lancaster Regiment
INTELLIGENCE SUMMARY.

(Erase heading not required.)

July 1917.

Instructions regarding War Diaries and Intelligence
Summaries are contained in F. S. Regs., Part II.
and the Staff Manual respectively. Title pages
will be prepared in manuscript.

Place	Date 1917	Hour	Summary of Events and Information	Remarks and references to Appendices
TRENCHES	1st		Battn occupying trenches in front of Wytschaete, methods of holding line 2 Coys in front line 2 in Coys support 4 middle on left 13 KRRC on right. Bn front held by 2 Bns	Appx 2
KEMMEL - DRANOUTRE Resting Area	NIGHT 2nd/3rd		Battn relieved in trenches by 10th Worcs Regt 19th Divn & proceeded by route march to camp in Kemmel – Dranoutre Resting Area	Appx 3
	3rd		Capt R.C. White joined Battn from Base Depot. 9 ORs joined from Base Depot.	Appx 4
TRENCHES	NIGHT 11th-12th		Battn relieved 6 S.L.I. in support line	
	NIGHT 13th-14th		Battn redistributed on line so as to be in depth with C.B.W.& A on stated order from front to rear. 6 S.L.I. on left B.n of Australian Army Corps on right	Appx 5
	NIGHT 17th-18th		A Coy relieved D Coy in front line. Lt J Barker killed	Appx 6
	19th-20th		Battn relieved by 112th Bde. 10 York & Lancs by 6th Berks. Bn proceeded by route march to camp previously occupied. 3 ORs joined from Base Depot.	Appx 7
CAMP	21st		2 Lt H.A.Burdwood joined Battn from Base Depot	
TRENCHES	NIGHT 25th-26th		63rd Bde relieves 112th Bde. Battn relieves 6th Berks in trenches, as previously held. 6 S.L.I. on left. Bn of Australian Corps on right. Battn proceeded to trenches this time with all fighting equipment preparatory to taking the offensive in conjunction with Battalion attached to the french	Appx 8
Camp	26-27		Offensive postponed owing to inclement weather. 63rd Bde with drawn from line. Battn relieved by 10th Royal Fusiliers 111th Bde & proceeded to camp as per Bus list	Appx 9
TRENCHES	29-30th 31st		63rd Bde relieves 111th Bde in line. Battn relieves 10th Royal Fusiliers previous by held trenches. Offensive commenced See appx indices	Appx 10

A 5834 Wt W4973/M687 750,000 8/16 D. D. & L. Ltd. Forms/C2118/13.

List of Appendices.

1. Roll of Officers Serving.
2. Summary of Operations July 1st to 31st 1917.
3. Operation Order no 141.
4. Operation Order no 142.
5. Operation Order no 143.
6. Operation Order no 144.
7. Operation Order no 145.
8. Operation Order no 146.
9. Operation Order no 148.
10. Operation Order no 149.
11. Operation Order no 147.
12. Strength Casualties etc.

Appx N° 1

10th Batt York & Lancaster Regt
Nominal Roll of Officers 31-7-17

Rank & Name		Remarks
Lt Col Layton	A.B.	Commanding Officer
Major Fairnie	E.G.J.	Sick
Capt Watts	R.A.B.P.	Attached Bde
" Boss	J.G.	Coy. Commander
" White	R.G.	Acting Qr. Mr.
" Ellwood	C.4.	Coy Commander
" Jarrard	W.J.	"
" Elsworth	L.R.	Adjutant
" Wilkinson	R.M.	Coy Commander
" Robinson	A.R.	Course of Instruction
Lt Sutcliffe	E.H.	Bde. Salvage Offr
" Ayres	4.	Acting Transport Offr
2nd Lt Rockley	W.L.	Intelligence Offr
" Walne	H.A	Leave
" Hughes	H.D	Signalling Offr
" Mitchell	R.J.	Attached 152 Coy RE
" Gaunt	B.W.	" 63rd T.M.B
" Cameron	H.	
" Parry	W.	
" Horsfall	J.R.	
" Byrne		
" Gladman	J.4.	
" Cleveland	H.B	
" Forrest	R.A.	
" Kaplan	J	Course of instruction
" Lea		" " "
" Holt	W.G	" " "
" Snowdon	W.L	" " "
" Woodmansey	H.G	Bde School Instructor
" Williams	S.	Instructor Base
" Marshall	J.W.H	Course of Instruction
" Jackson	A.H	
Lt & Q.M. Jamieson	A	Leave
Lt McConnell	W.G	M.O.

1.

10th York and Lancaster Regiment Appx No 2

Summary of Operations from 1st to 31st July 1917.

Ref maps { Sheet 28 S.W 2 edition 5A 1:10,000
{ " 28 S.W " 5A 1:20,000

JULY 1917

1st TRENCHES — Bn was occupying front line trenches E of Wytschaete in O16 - O22. The method of holding the line was 2 coys in front line & 2 coys in close support. The 4th Middx on the left and 13th KRRC on right with 8th S.L.I. in support.

During the night 2/Lt Byrne A coy took out a patrol of 12 O.R with the object of (1) retrieving the Lewis Gun lost on the patrol the previous evening (2) Obtaining an identification. The enemy were found to be exceedingly on the alert & in considerable strength with the result that the patrol met with no success.

During the night also, 2/Lt Knight took out a patrol of 10 O.R with the object of securing an identification. Although unsuccessful in the main effort, a good deal of useful information was obtained as to the strength of the garrison of buildings etc held by the enemy on our immediate front.

Night 2nd-3rd — Bn was relieved by 10th Worcester Regt 19th Div. The Bn then proceeded by route march to the Bde Support area in Kemmel - Dranoutre.

3rd-11th — During this period the Bn remained in Bde Support area, carrying out intensive training, special attention being paid to specialists and also the important work of patrolling

Night 11th-12th — Bn relieved 8 S.L.I. in support line S.E. of Wytschaete with H.Q at Lumm Fm. two coys in Ridge Defences & two in Reserve Line.

Night 13th-14th — Defensive scheme re-arranged. Bn now holding line in depth with C coy in front line (now known as Shell Hole Line) & B. D & A coys behind

8th S.L.I were rearranged in the same way on the left flank. The right flank was held by a Bn of the 9th Aust Bde. C Coy were allotted the task of connecting up the series of shell holes in order to form the Shell Hole Line

night 15th–16th
2nd Lt Cameron took out a patrol of 17 O.R from C Coy with the object of (1) Locating enemy posts
(2) Establishing post at O29.c.7.6
(3) Establishing an intermediate post at O29c 6.7
An enemy post was located at O29c 8.8, which appeared to be strongly garrisoned, very lights being fired as our patrol approached.
This patrol established two posts at O29c 55.60
O29c 70.50

night 16th–17th
2nd Lt Cameron again took out a patrol of C Coy with the object of ascertaining (1) the position of enemy posts if any (2) Strength of garrison (3) Condition of No Mans Land.
Our patrol could not find any enemy posts, but established one at O29c 55.40
The ground in No Mans Land was found to be much pitted with shell holes

night 17th–18th
A Coy relieved C Coy in Shell Hole Line.
2nd Lt Teasdale I/c of 7 O.R A Coy established a post at O29c 8.3

night 18th–19th
2nd Lt Teasdale again took out a patrol from A Coy, with the object of locating enemy post at about O29c 48.50 and ascertaining approx strength of its garrison. Although the patrol passed over the spot where the enemy post was supposed to be, no trace of it could be found The vicinity was searched but no enemy were discovered.

night 19th–20th
Bn relieved by 6th Beds & occupied previous camp

Night 25th 26th	Bn relieved 6th Beds in trenches as previously held. 8th S.L.I. on left and Bn of Australian Inf Bde on right.
Night 26th 27th	Bn relieved by 10th R.F.s owing to postponement of offensive as a result of inclement weather.
Night 29th 30th	Bn proceed to trenches with all fighting equipment, prepared to take offensive in conjunction with Bn. to the N. B & D coys occupied the shell hole line and shell holes in front under command of Capt WILKINSON. A & C coys occupied Reserve Line, ~~under the C.C.~~ the latter coy. moving up to Shell Hole Line on night Y/Z.
31st.	Offensive commenced in two phases, the Bn. being concerned only with the 2nd (ie ZERO + 4)

At this hour our creeping barrage commenced, one platoon following it up and establishing a post at O.29.a.55.20, thereby covering the advance of the 8th S.L.I. on our left.

At ZERO + 4½ a previously prepared tape was ran out and fixed on the new line from O.29.c.65.15 to O.29.a.60.20 in order to facilitate the task of digging in.

ZERO + 5 a covering party of 2 platoons went out and were followed immediately by the remaining 3 platoons. ~~On reaching the tape these 3 platoons~~ On reaching the tape these 3 platoons dug a series of rifle pits 4½ ft deep every 10 yds.

At noon on 31st a small party of the enemy were seen reconnoitring the ground along the course of the BLAUWEPOORT BEEKE. Fearing that a counter attack might be launched against this part of our front which was unconnected with the Australians, A coy was ordered to reinforce this flank, two platoons to the FRONT LINE, 2 platoons to the SHELL HOLE LINE.

C. coy were moved up to take over the SHELL HOLE LINE from GRASS FM to WAMBEEK at 8.15 pm. They then passed under orders of O.C. 8th S.L.I.

As soon as it was dark on the 31st wire was put out along ⅔ of the new front.

L.A. Elsworth Capt & Adj
for Lt Coln
Commdg 10th Batt York & Lancaster Regt

Appx No 3

OPERATION ORDER No 141
By Lt. Col. A.B. Rayston,
Comdg 10th York & Lancaster Regt
2nd July 1917.

Ref Map:-
France 1/20,000 Sheet 28 S.W. (5A)
Wytschaete 1/20,000 Sheet 28 S.W. 2 (5A)

1. The Battalion will be relieved in the front line tonight by the 10th Worcester Regt.

2. <u>Order of Relief</u>

The front line held by A and D Coys will be relieved by 3 platoons of A Coy 10th Worcesters.

The Close Support line held by A and D Coys will be relieved by C Coy 10th Worcesters plus 1 platoon of A Coy 10th Worcesters. The platoon from A Coy of the Worcesters being on the right.

B Coy will be relieved by D Coy of the Worcesters.

C Coy's position will not be occupied by the relieving unit.

Representatives from A, C, and D Coys of the Worcesters will form an advance party and visit Coys in the line today to discuss details of relieving and handing over.

All trench stores documents etc will be handed over to these officers and receipts obtained in duplicate. Receipts will be sent to this Office by 9.0 a.m on 3.7.17.

3. <u>Guides</u> as under will report to Bn H.Q. at 8 a.m when they will proceed under 2/Lt Rockley to the WOOD DUMP on the VIERSTRAAT-WYTSCHAETE Road near the NAG'S NOSE to meet incoming platoons at 9.30 pm.

From A Coy 3 Guides
" D " 5 "
" B " 4 "
" H.Q " 1 "

4. <u>Transport</u>

All Stores and Mess Kit from Bn H.Q, B and D Coys will be dumped at H.Q. Ration Dump at the end of Track O.20.d.1.y by 10.30 pm. Stores and Mess Kit from A and C Coys will be dumped at O.21 Central by 10.30 pm. Lewis Guns and ammunition will be carried by platoons when relieved to the H.Q. Ration Dump at the end of Track O.20.d.1.y where they will be met by Transport at 12 pm.

5. **Route** On completion of relief, platoons will move independently at 200 yds interval via H.Q. Ration Dump O.20.d.1.y. to quarters in KEMMEL DRANOUTRE AREA Guides will meet Coys at
Care will be taken to prevent platoons closing up
C. Coy will hand over to a representative of the 10th Worcesters and march off at 10pm The Dump Guards at EVAN'S FARM under L/Cpl PELL and the wiring party under 2/Lt HORSFALL will march with 'B' Coy.

6. Reliefs complete will be notified to this Office by code words as follows:—

        A – MAN
        B – WOMAN
        C – DOG
        D – CAT

7. All trenches and dug-outs will be handed over clean

8. The Quartermaster will arrange for a hot meal for men on arrival at their quarters.
    The usual Billeting party and in addition 1 N.C.O. and 5 men for tent pitching will proceed from the transport lines and report to Major Watts SOMERSET L.I. at the Cross Roads N.21.d Central at 10am The Transport Officer will arrange for a representative to report at the same time to take over Transport lines. It AYRES will also report at the same time and take charge of the whole party.
    Major Watts will allot a billeting Area and arrange for guides to meet Coys at

Platoons will close up at this point
The premises at present occupied by Q.M. Stores will be vacated by 8am July 3rd

                (Sd) W.J. JARRARD
                     Capt & Adjt
          10 York & Lancaster Regiment.

OPERATION ORDERS No. 142

by Lt A.B. Layton
Comdg 10th York & Lancaster Regt
10th July 1917

Ref. Maps. BELGIUM and FRANCE
Sheet 28 Scale 1:40,000
and enlargements.

1. The 63rd Brigade will relieve the 111th Brigade in the line on the 10/11th inst.

2. The 10th Bn York & Lancaster Regt less Transport and Q.M. Stores will relieve the 8th Somerset L.I. in right support. Bn H.Qrs at LUMM FARM O.26.d.1.4. on the night 11/12th.

H.Q. Sections
C Coy
B "
A "
D "

3. Battn starting point M.36.b.45.80. (on road) Order of march as in margin. An interval of 200 yds will be maintained between Coys as far as KEMMEL afterwards the Battn will move by platoons at 200 yds interval. Head of column will pass starting point at 8.45 pm.

4. Route: Cross Roads N.19.c - KEMMEL - O.19.c.50.40. - O.20.c.20.40 thence along MESSINES ROAD

5. Dress: Full Marching Order

6. Camp will be clean and ready for inspection by 7.45 pm

7. Coys will take over positions as reconnoitred by the respective Coy Commanders
1 Officer and 2 O.Rs. from each Coy will parade at Bn Orderly Room under 2/Lt ROCKLEY at 4 pm and take over stores etc of Coys they will relieve.
2/Lt ROCKLEY and Sgt Signaller will move up to H.Q at same time

8. Relief complete will be reported by code words as follows:—
"A" Coy HORSE "B" Coy COW "C" Coy DOG "D" Coy PIG

9. Trench stores, Defence schemes, maps, aeroplane photographs etc will be taken over and receipts given, copies will be sent to Battn H.Qs. as soon as possible after relief.

10. Officers valises will be dumped at Q.M. Stores by noon. Mess Cart to be loaded by 8.30 pm.

11. Lewis Gun wagons will accompany their Coys.
Rations will be dumped at Ration dump on MESSINES road O.26.d.40.40. at 12.30 am. Ration parties will report to Provost Sgt at dump quarter half an hour before

12. Q.M. Stores and Transport will move to N.34.a.1.4. in their own time

(Sd) L.A. ELSWORTH
Capt & Adjt
10th York & Lancs Regt

SECRET OPERATION ORDERS. NO. 143. Copy No. 1.
Appx No 5

By Lt. Col. A.B. LAYTON.
Comdg. 10th York & Lancaster Regt.
13/1/18.
Ref. MAP. Sheet 28. S.W. 1-10,000.

1. The defence of the present Brigade Sector is to be reorganized and will be held by four Battalions distributed in depth.

2. The 10th Battn. York & Lancaster Regt will relieve the 8th Somerset L.I. in the right half of the Battn. Sub. Sector now held by them, tonight.

3. The Northern Boundary will be a line joining 0.29.c.80.95
X roads 0.28.d.80.85 (inclusive to 8th S.L.I.)
Rd. junct. 0.27.d.40.05 (" " " ")
October Support. 0.26.c.85.30.
The Southern Boundary will be the BLAUWEPOORT-BEEK Stream.

4. The defence organization of the line is as follows:—
(a). Outpost line.
The following are the Map References of the positions of the outpost positions.
0.29.c.35.42.
35.60.
30.87.
(b). Front line (formerly outpost line) (0.29.c.05.05 –
0.28.d.90.40 – 0.28.d.85.40 – 0.28.d.65.85.
This is well sited and in course of completion.
(c). Support Line. YORK. TRENCH from 0.28.d.50.15 to 32.82.
(d). Reserve Line (or Y Line) from DESPAGNE. FM. (0.33.6.) to 0.27.d.45.65. N.B. X Line will not be occupied.
(e). Ridge Defences. from 0.32.c.15.65. to 0.26.d.45.35.

Bn. H.Q. at
0.88.a.90.80.
C. Coy/outposts
and front line.
0.28.c.60.80.
B. Coy. YORK
TRENCH. HQ. C.
0.27.c.90.00.
D. Coy. RIDGE
DEFENCES.
H.Q. remains
in present
position.
0.26.c.50.30.

5. The Battalion will be disposed as in margin when redistribution is complete positions to be reconnoitred by Coy. Commanders today. No movement will take place before 9.30.p.m tonight. Bn. Hdqrs will remain in present positions till 8th S.L.I. H.Q. is able to move, when all concerned will be notified.

6. Signallers will reconnoitre stations today and prepare future Bn. H.Q.

7. Coys will notify Bn. Hdqrs when move is completed by the following code words.
A. Coy. Apricot.   C. Coy. Cherry.
B. " Banana.   D. " Date.

8. Rations will continue to be dumped at present Bn. H.Qs. at 10.30 p.m. till the latter moves.

(SD). L. A. ELSWORTH.
Capt & Adjt.
10th York & Lancaster Regt.

Copy No.

AFTER ORDERS.
13/7/17.

Reference Operation Orders No. 143. paragraph. 5. Time given namely 9.30 p.m is amended hereby. Moves for Coys. will be as follows :-

C. Coy. Y&L. will relieve A. Coy. 8th S.L.I. at 12.15 a.m.
B " " will move to YORK TRENCH at 1.0 A.M.
D " " will move to Yor. Reserve Line at 1.0 A.M.
A " " will move to Ridge Defences R. Section 1.A.M

(SD). L. A. ELSWORTH.
Capt & Adjt.
10th York & Lancaster Regt.

Appx No 6

OPERATION ORDERS. No. 144.

By Lt. Col. A. B. LAYTON
Comdg 10th York & Lancaster Regt.
17th July 1917.

Ref. Map. Sheet. 28. S.W. 2. 1:10,000.
  " 28. S.W.   1:20,000.

1. "A" Coy will relieve "C" Coy in the front line and shell hole line to night. — "C" Coy will mann the Ridge Defences on Relief.
   "C" Coy will leave 2/Lts TEASDALE and MARSHALL who will remain in Front and Shell hole line. 2/Lt. LEA. will remain in Ridge Defences with "C" Coy.

2. Rations for "A" Coy will be sent up from Q. M. Stores to 8th S.L.1. Ration Dump with those from "B" and "D" Coys and will be carried up to "A" Coy by "D" Coy. "C" Coy Rations to H. Q. dump.

3. Relief complete will be reported by code word "BOTTLE".

(SD). L. A. ELSWORTH.
Capt & Adjt.
10th York & Lancaster Regt.

Appx. No 7

OPERATION ORDERS No. 145.

By Lt. Col. A. B. LAYTON
Comdg. 10th York & Lancaster Regt.
19th July. 1917.

Ref. Maps. Sheet. 28. S.W. 1: 20,000.

1. The 10th York & Lancaster Regt. will be relieved by the 6th Bedford Regiment to night (19/20th.)

2. (a). Details of relief have already been arranged by Coy. Commanders with 6th Bedford advance party.

"A" Coy. 6th Bedfords will relieve A Coy 10th York & Lancs in Shell Hole & front line.
"D" " " " " " " " B " " YORK TRENCH
"B" " " " " " " " C " " RIDGE DEFENCES.
"C" " " " " " " " D " " RESERVE LINE (or Y LINE.)

(b). One guide per platoon and one for H.Q. Details will be at PICK HOUSE at 9.15 p.m. and report to 2/Lt. HUGHES.

3. Signed receipts will be taken for all Stores handed over, copies of which will be sent to Bn. H.Qs. early on the 20th inst.

4. Relief complete will be reported by wire or runner to H.Qs. the following code words to be used.
"A" Coy. "AZALIA"   "C" Coy. "CARNATION"
"B" " "BLUEBELL"   "D" " "DAHLIA"

5. On relief platoons will march independently back to Camp last occupied by the Battalion. Route and intervals between platoons and H.Q. Sections as on the march to the line.

6. Capt Wilkinson will go forward as billeting officer and take over Camp reporting to Brigade H.Qs at 3 p.m to day. C.Q.M.S. will take over tents and bivouacs to be occupied by Coys. from Billeting Officer before Battalion arrives in Camp.

7. (a). 2/Lt. KAPLAN will be responsible that information with regard to area cleared of salvage is handed over to 6th Bedford Salvage Officer and that the Salvage at present on dump is loaded on Bn. Transport to night.

(b). 2/Lt. HORSFALL will be responsible that Stores on Battn. Dumps are properly cleared and handed over to 6th Bedford Dump Officer, that Water points are relieved and that Ration Dumps are properly cleared by Battn. Transport.

(c). All mess tins and Coy Stores that will not be handed over, will be at Ration Dumps by. 10 p.m and hand over to N.C.O/c Ration Dumps. Sgt. Franklin will be N.C.O/c H.Q. Ration Dump.

L/cpl. Pell. will be N.C.O/c. Bn. Ration Dump at 8th S.L.I. H.Q's
The above Officers will march their parties back to camp
independently on completion of above duties.

8.(a). Q.M. Stores and Transport will move in their own
time.
(b). Sufficient Transport will be sent up to remove above
mentioned salvage................ Mess Kits.
Mess Kits, Coy Stores and also H.Q. Stores (including Orderly
Room Boxes)
(c). Water will be brought up in Petrol tins in the
ordinary way unless arrangements are made otherwise
by Q.M. with Q.M: of Bedfords.

(SD). L.A. ELSWORTH.
                    Capt & Adjt.
16th York & Lancaster Regt.

Appx N° 8

OPERATION ORDERS. No 146.

By Lt. Col. A.B. LAYTON
Comdg. 10th York & Lancaster Regt.
25th July 1917.

Ref. Map. 28.S.W. 1: 20,000.

1. The 63rd. Infantry Brigade will relieve the 112th Infantry Brigade in the Trenches during the night 25/26th July.

2. The 10th York & Lancaster Regt will relieve the 6th Bedfords. Regt.

3. The line will be taken over exactly as held by the 6th Bedfords, any readjustment will be made after relief.

SHELL. HOLE. LINE.
RESERVE LINE

D Coy.
B "
C "
A "

4. The Coys will take over the line as in margin.

5. Coys will parade and march off same route with same intervals as in previous relief. Time of passing starting point 7.45 p.m.
Order of March as in Margin.
Dress: Fighting Order.
Coys and Sections will march with Box Respirators on for 1 mile immediately after leaving camp to night.

6. Q.M. Stores and Transport will move to same camp as before occupied, they will move in their own time.

7. All packs, spare Lewis Guns, Ammunition &c and Officers Valises will be stacked at Q.M Stores at once. Mess Carts will be loaded at 7.30 p.m.
Camp will be clean and ready for inspection by 6.15 p

8. Lewis Gun limbers will precede Coys to 150 yards S of PICK. HOUSE at which point teams will take over their guns and ammunition.
The Medical Cart will go independently to 8th Somerset. Dump. Ration parties will report to N.C.O in charge this dump at 11.15 p.m. The reserve line Coys will carry rations for the front line Coys for to night.

9. The Provost Sgt and one N.C.O per Coy will report to 2/Lt. HORSFALL at Orderly Room at 5 p.m to proceed in advance to take over Coy and Battn Trench Stores. Receipts for Defence Schemes Stores etc. will be given, copies of which will be forwarded to Battn H.Q. early on the 26th inst.

10. Relief complete will be reported by wire or Runner, the following code words being used.
   "A" Coy. RED.   C. BOY.
   B" ... CAT.   D. BLUE.

11. Officers and ORs to be left out of action will remain at Q.M. Stores under charge of Capt. WILKINSON.

12. 20 ORs of the 63rd. ~~Infantry~~ Machine Gun. Coy. to be attached to this Battalion will join Battn. at PECKHAM. DUMP. at 9.15 p.m. and follow Battn. behind H.Q. sections.

Rations for tomorrow will be taken with them. Rations for 27th onwards will be arranged between Q.M.S concerned.

(SD). L.A. ELSWORTH.
                Capt & Adjt.
10th York & Lancaster Regt.

Appx No 9

OPERATION ORDERS. No. 148

By Lt. Col. A.B. LAYTON.
Comdg. 10th York & Lancaster Regt.
26th July. 1917.

1. 63rd Infantry Brigade will be relieved by the 111th Infantry Brigade to night and will move into the Support Brigade area.

2. The 10th York & Lancaster Regiment will be relieved by the 10th Royal Fusiliers Regt.

3. Incoming troops will not cross the WYTSCHAETE MESSINES Ridge before 9.15 A.M. and outgoing troops must be west of this point by 11. A.M.
   All troops will move out as they are relieved by incoming units except 2 Officers and 100 ORs of C Coy. who will complete their carrying for 2/Lt. HORSFALL prior to leaving the line.

4. On relief, Battalion will move to the same camp as vacated before. Details for relief will be the same as when leaving the line recently, with the following exceptions. Only the dump near present Battn. H.Qs. will be used for dumping Mens Kits, Lewis Guns and Ammunition, and any Coy. Stores to be taken out of the line.

5. Stores and Defence schemes will be handed over as usual.

6. Transport for relief will be at the above mentioned dump at 12. midnight.

7. Transport, Q.M. Stores and party under Capt. WILKINSON will move in their own time. Huts and tentage in Camp will be taken over by QUARTERMASTER.

8. Table below gives details of relief of Coys and guides. Guides will report to 2/Lt. ROCKLEY. Battn. H.Qs. at 9.p.m. One guide will be provided from H.Qs.

R.F. Coy.	Will take & occupy.	Will relieve 10th Y&L. Coy.	1 Guide per platoon to H.Q. 9.A.M. from
A. Coy.	Shell Hole L	D. Coy.	D. Coy.
D. "	YORK. TRENCH.	B. "	B. "
B. "	RES. LINE	C. "	C. "
C. "	RIDGE DEFENCES	A. "	A. "

9. 20 ORs of 63. M.G. Coy attached to D Coy. will relieve with D Coy. and rejoin their unit to night.

(SD). L.A. ELSWORTH,
Capt & Adjt.
10th York & Lancaster Regt.

Appx. No 10

OPERATION ORDERS. No. 149
By Lt. Col. A.B. LAYTON
Comdg. 10th York & Lancaster Regt.
29th July 1917.

Ref. Map. 28. S.W. 1 - 20,000.

1. The 63rd. Infantry Brigade will relieve 111th Infantry Brigade in the front line to night.

2. The 10th York & Lancaster Regt will relieve 10th Royal Fusiliers in the right sub. sector.
   Coys will take over line as in margin.
   Two sections of the 63rd M.G. Coy will be attached to Coys in Shell-hole line. They will meet the Battalion at PECKHAM dump at 8.45 p.m. and will proceed up to the line under the orders of O.C. D. Coy. Rations for 30th inst will accompany them. Rations for 31st onwards will be arranged between Q.Ms. concerned. Troops will not cross the WYTSCHAETE MESSINES RIDGE before 9.15 p.m.

B & D Coys SHELL HOLE LINE, AND FRONT LINE.
A. Coy. RESERVE TRENCH.
C. RIDGE DEF.

3. Coys will march off same route with same intervals as in previous relief. Time of passing starting point 7.15 p.m.
   Order of march as in margin.
   Dress: Fighting Order.

D. Coy.
B. "
A. "
C. "
H.Qs.

4. Q.M. Stores and Transport will move to same camp as previously occupied. They will move in their own time.

5. All packs, Lewis Guns, Ammunition etc and Officers valises to be left behind will be stacked at Q.M. Stores by 3 p.m. Guard will be mounted over these by the Quartermaster from the personel to be left behind.
   Camp will be clean and ready for inspection by 6.15 p.m.

6. Arrangements for Transport of Lewis Guns and Rations, Medical Stores and Mess Kits will remain the same. Ration parties will report to N.C.O. i/c dump at 11.15 p.m.
   A. Coy will provide ration parties for all Coys, 25 ORs per Coy.
   C. Coy will provide 100 ORs as carrying party to 2/Lt. HORSFALL.
   OCs A Coy and C will ensure that sufficient Officers are provided with these parties and that all Rations and Material carried reach their destination.

7. All defences schemes and stores will be taken over, copies of receipts will be sent to Orderly Room early on the 30th inst.

8. Relief complete will be reported by wire or Runner, following code words being used:-
   A. Coy. PEARS.   C. Coy. COAL.
   B. "   CARBOLIC.   D. "   TAR.

9. B and D Coys will draw 45 Water Bottles and carriers each from Q.M. Stores.

10. All details to be left out of action will remain at Q.M. Stores under the Quartermaster.

(SD). L.A. ELSWORTH.
                    Capt & Adjt.
        10th York & Lancaster Regt.

SECRET   Appx No 11

OPERATION ORDER No 147 COPY No
By Lt.Col. A.B. Layton
Comdg. 10th York & Lancs Regt

Ref. Map.
WYTSCHAETE. 28.S.W.2.   29th July. 1917

1. On the night of the 29/30th July Battalion will relieve 10th Royal Fus. in the front line.

2. On Z. day the disposition of the Coys will be as follows:—
   B and D Coys Shell-hole line & shell holes in front under command of Capt WILKINSON
   A and C. Coys Reserve line under command of C.O. Coys in Shell hole line will provide their own covering party

3. Action on Y day. During the night of Y.day C. Coy will move from the RESERVE LINE to the SHELL-HOLE LINE
   The O.C. Shell-hole line will take over the post occupied by the 8th SOMERSETS. at O.29.A.25.10. which post will be moved forward on Z day as described in para. 4

4. O.C. Shell-Hole line will establish a post at O.29.a.55.20. immediately after the barrage moves forward.

5. Action on Z day. Battalions to the north will attack. Every opportunity will be taken to assist them by Rifle and Lewis Gun fire and cause loss to such of the enemy as expose themselves Special attention to be paid to the supposed enemy position running from O.29.d.3.5. northward which will be bombarded by T.M's and Field Guns. Care must be

2.

taken not to fire on the SOMERSET posts in BEEK FARM enclosure. One Coy in Shell-Hole line will be held in readiness to support the 8th SOMERSETS if required.

6. Digging. A trench will be dug from the left post at O.29.a.55.20. to the BLAUWEPOORT BEEK approximately 700 yds. A line to be selected by Capt WILKINSON close in front of the present SHELL HOLE line. This work will not be commenced until ZERO + 5.

7. Holding the line. The line when dug and the covering party has been withdrawn will be held by platoons with 3 double sentries in front at about 35 yds distance. These sentries will be relieved from the platoons and will withdraw to the trench at daylight.

8. Headquarters will be at CABIN HILL O.33.a.9.9.
Dressing Station near FANNYS FARM at O.27.B.9.1.

(Sd) L.A. ELSWORTH
Capt & Adjt for
O.C. Comdg. 10 York & Lancs Regt.

<u>Appx No. 12</u>

<u>10th Battalion York & Lancaster Regiment.</u>

<u>STRENGTH during month of JULY, 1917.</u>

June 30th 1917 : Fighting Strength : Officers 29.
              Other Ranks 819

July 31st 1917 : Fighting Strength : Officers 23.
              Other Ranks 694.

<u>INCREASE</u>

 <u>Officers:-</u>
  Capt. White R.C.   Joined from England   3-7-17
  Lt. McConnell W.G.   "   "   "   4-7-17
  2/Lt. Cleveland H.A.   "   "   "   21-7-17
 <u>Other Ranks:-</u>
  6 Other Ranks from 34th Inf Base Depot 2-7-17
  9   "   "   "   "   "   "   "   4-7-17
  3   "   "   "   "   "   "   "   21-7-17

<u>DECREASE.</u>

 <u>Officers:-</u>
  Major Richardson, H. To Command Bn. S.L.I. 15-7-17
    "   Fairnie, E.G.J. Hospital Sick   27-7-17
  Capt. Lamond, G.W. Sick to England 17-7-17
  Lt. Corban, J. Killed   17-7-17
  2/Lt. Revill, A. Wounded   13-7-17
    Dawson, W.G. do   30-7-17
    Knight, J.W. do   31-7-17
    Sykes, T.P. do   31-7-17
    June, G.E. Sick to Hospital 30-7-17
 <u>Other Ranks</u> Killed - - - - 16
        Wounded   90
        Sick Wastage 37   Total <u>143</u>

Confidential

War Diary

of the

10th York and Lancs.

August 1917.

Vol XXIV.

To. 37th Divl. H.Q.

Enclosed please find.

War Diary, 10th York & Lancs Reg. Vol XXIV for August 1917

A Rockley
2/Lt a/adjt.
10th Batt York & Lancaster Regt.

6/9/17.

Army Form C. 2118.

WAR DIARY of
10th Battn. York & Lancaster Regt.
INTELLIGENCE SUMMARY.

(Erase heading not required.)

Instructions regarding War Diaries and Intelligence Summaries are contained in F. S. Regs., Part II. and the Staff Manual respectively. Title pages will be prepared in manuscript.

Place	Date	Hour	Summary of Events and Information	Remarks and references to Appendices
DRANOUTRE	August 1st 1917		Battalion relieved in line near Wycheate by 13 Royl Fusiliers, and proceeded to camp near Dranoutre.	
LOCRE	2nd		Battalion moved by route march to Wlasfrick Huts near LOCRE.	
ROSSIGNOL	9th		Battalion moved by route march to Camp at Rossignol Wood.	
Trenches	15/8/16		Bttn. relieved 12th Regt in line. Bttn. relieve 11th Royl Warwick line near Wycheate.	
	16th		Capt F.C. Smith. N. Staff Regt joined Bn. from 10 R.F. to be 2nd in Command.	
	19th		5 Offr. joined Battn. from Base in France.	
ROSSIGNOL	24/20		Battn. relieved in line by 10th Royl York. Lanc. and proceeded by route march to camp towards of Rossignol Wood.	
KEMMEL	26th		Battn. moved with Reserve Bde area Bn. moved by route march to Kemmel shelters occupying Intrenchmts.	
TRENCHES	27th		Bttn. of Bde relieve 119th Bde in line near Wicheete. Bttn. relieve 17th K.R.R.C. in own support.	
	29/8/20		Battn. relieved in Bn support by 8th Lincolns R.I. and proceeded to line relieving 14th Sherbome Foresters.	

Comdg. 10th York Lancs Regt.

A 5834 Wt W 4973/M657 750,000 8/16 D. D. & L. Ltd. Forms/C. 2118/13.

10th Bn York & Lancaster Regt.

1. Fighting Strength on last day of Aug. 1917

Officers	O.R.	Details (included).	
		Officers	O.R.
37	800	12	79

2. Reinforcements received during Aug. 1917.

Rank & Name of Officer	No. of O.R.	Date of arrival.
	4	4 - 8 - 1917
	9	11 - 8 - 1917
	4	14 - 8 - 1917
Major F. C. AUSTIN. (N. Staffs Regt)		16 - 8 - 1917
Lieut. C. B. DIXON.		
" C. P. SANSOM.		
2/Lieut. A. HARDWICK.		19 - 8 - 1917
" F. J. W. LYONS.		
" T. P. McNALLY.		
	5	23 - 8 - 1917
	14	28 - 8 - 1917

3. Casualties during August 1917.

Rank & Name of Officer	No of O.R.	Nature of Casualty.
Lieut. G. E. TUNE		Wd (Gas)
" R. A. FORREST		Wd (Gas)
" S. WILLIAMS		Sick
" H. SNOWDEN		Sick
	11	Kd in A.
	12	Wd in A.
	1	Md in A.
	25	Evacuated Sick

10th York & Lancaster Regiment

Roll of Officers — August 31st 1917

RANK	NAME		REMARKS
Lt Col.	Layton	A.B.	Leave
Major	Austin	J.C.	2nd i/c 70B
"	Fairnie	E.J.	Sick
Capt	Watts	R.A.B.P.	Attd Bde Staff
"	Boss	J.C.	Coy Comdr
"	White	R.C.	"
"	Jarrark	D.J.	"
"	Elsworth	L.A.	Adjt
"	Robinson	A.R.	Coy Comdr
"	Wilkinson	R.M.	Army Rest Camp
Lieut	Ayres	F.	L.G.O.
"	Dixon	G.B.	Pln Comdr
"	Sanson	C.P.	do
2/Lt	Rockley	H.E.	Int. Off.
"	Walne	N.A.	I.O.
"	Gaunt	B.W.	Attd 63 T.M.B.
"	Horsfall	J.R.	Pln Comdr
"	Snowden	N	Sick
"	Cameron	N	Pln Comdr
"	Normanvey	M.G.	Bde School
"	Mitchell	R.J.	Attd 152 & RE
"	Sutcliffe	C.H.	Bde Salvage Off
"	Williams	S	Sick
"	Jackson	att	Pln Comdr
"	Parry	A	Course of Inst
"	Hughes	AN	do
"	Forrest	R.A.	Sick
"	Marshall	JWH	Course of Inst
"	June	G.E.	Sick
"	Kaplan	J	Pln Comdr
"	Byrne	J	Course of Inst
"	Leh	W.G.	Pln Comdr
"	Gledman	A.E.	do
"	Holt	W.E.	do
"	Hardwick	A	do
"	Lyon	J.J.N.	do
"	McNally	J.P.	Bde School
"	Jamieson	A	Q.M.
"	McConnell	W.G.	M.O.
"	Thomas	H.S.	Chaplain

Lt Colonel
Comdg 10th York & Lancaster Regt

DRANOUTRE	Aug. 2nd	Battn spent the day cleaning up after coming out of the line.
LOCRE	Aug. 3rd to Aug. 8th	Battn continued training, special attention being paid to Extended Order, Arm Drill and Box Respirator Drill.
ROSSIGNOL	Aug. 8th to Aug. 15th	Battn in Support, provided working parties day and night, for carrying and work up the line
SUPPORT TRENCHES	Aug. 15th to Aug. 21st	Battn. supplied working parties to the Front Line Battns.
ROSSIGNOL	Aug. 22nd to Aug. 25th	Battn supplied working parties up the line. Lecture to Officers and N.C.Os at Bde School on Patrolling, by an Officer from Army H.Qrs. Training also carried out.
KEMMEL	Aug. 26th to Aug. 28th	Battn. supplied working parties up the line. Also continued with training, special attention being paid to Specialist work, Lewis Gun, Bombing etc.
TRENCHES	Aug. 29/30th	On this night Battn went up into the front line. On the night of the 31st Aug. 2/Lt HARDWICK A. took out a patrol to ascertain if enemy had any posts out. He came across one on the road O.12.a.55.25. which was strongly held. He also heard enemy talking on road running E from HOLLEBEKE at a point about O.12.a.70.60

CONFIDENTIAL

10th Battn. York & Lancaster Regiment.

WAR DIARY

SEPTEMBER 1917.

XXV VOLUME

C O N F I D E N T I A L.

37th Division "Q"

    Herewith WAR DIARY of this Battalion for month of September 1917.

                                          Captain.
                                      for Lt-Col.
                          Comdg: 10th York & Lancs Regt.

3rd Oct: 1917

Army Form C. 2118.

WAR DIARY
10th York Lancaster Regiment
INTELLIGENCE SUMMARY.

(Erase heading not required.)

Instructions regarding War Diaries and Intelligence Summaries are contained in F.S. Regs., Part II. and the Staff Manual respectively. Title pages will be prepared in manuscript.

Place	Date Sept 1917	Hour	Summary of Events and Information	Remarks and references to Appendices
TRENCHES	1st		Battalion occupying front line trenches in vicinity of HOLLEBEKE, 4th Battalion Middlesex Regt. on right, Australians on left.	
BOIS CONFLUENT	Night 2/3rd		Battalion relieved in front line by 8th Somerset L.I. and proceeded to support area BOIS CONFLUENT	
KENNEL	7th		63rd Infy Bde relieved by 111th Infy Bde. 10th York & Lancs proceeded by route march to KENNEL Shelters. Huttments taken over.	
KOKEREELE Camp	10th		63rd Infy Bde proceeded by route march to the BOESCHEPE training area. 10th York & Lancs to camp at MONT KOKEREELE	
KENNEL	19th		63rd Infy Bde proceeded to Reserve Area, in support of 19th Division, taking part in active operations. 10th York & Lancs occupying Huttments at KENNEL Shelters.	
KOKEREELE Camp	21st		63rd Infy Bde proceeded by route march to the BOESCHEPE training area. 10th York & Lancs to Camp at MONT KOKEREELE.	
TRENCHES	29th		63rd Infy Bde relieve 118th Infy Bde, 39th Divn in line in vicinity of SHREWSBURY FOREST. 10th York & Lancs moved by bus, embussing at MONT KOKEREELE and debussing at BUS HOUSE, from thence proceeding to front line, relieving 4/5th Bn Royal Highlanders (Black Watch) in line in front of SHREWSBURY FOREST (just on right of YPRES – MENIN Road), having their by 19th Division on right and 4th Bn Middlesex Regt. on left.	
	30th.		Line advanced about 600 yards. Line never operations but enemy shell fire.	

Off. T.P. McNally killed

[signature] Capt for
Lt Col.
Comdg. 10th York Lancs Regt.

10th Bn. York & Lancaster Regiment.

Fighting Strength of last day of September 1917

Officers	O.Rs.	Details included	
		Officers	O.Rs.
31	711	10	71

Reinforcements received during September 1917

Rank and Name of Officers	No. of O.Rs.	Date of Arrival
	3	10/9/17
	4	12/9/17
	3	17/9/17
	1	21/9/17
	4	23/9/17

Casualties during September 1917

Rank and Name of Officers	No. of O.Rs.	Nature of Casualty
2nd Lt. A.H. Jackson		Wounded 30/9/17
2nd Lt. T.P. McNally		Killed in action 30/9/17
	10	Killed in Action
	19	Wounded in Action
	2	Missing in Action
	44	Evacuated Sick

10th Bn. York & Lancaster Regiment.
Roll of Officers serving with Battalion 30th September 1917

Rank and	Name		Present Employment
Lt. Col.	Layton	A.B.	C.O.
Major	Austin	F.C.	Sick
"	Boss	J.C.	Coy. Comdr.
Capt.	Watts	R.C.B.P.	Sick
"	White	R.C.	Pln. Comdr.
"	Jarrard	J.G.	Coy. Comdr.
"	Elsworth	L.A.	Sick
"	Robinson	A.R.	Coy. Comdr.
"	Wilkinson	R.M.	Coy. Comdr.
Lieut	Ayres	F.	C. of Instn.
"	Dixon	C.B.	do
"	Sansom	C.P.	do
"	Rockley	W.L.	Adjutant
2nd Lt.	Walne	H.A.	T.O.
"	Gaunt	B.W.	63rd T.M.B.
"	Horsfall	J.R.	Pln. Comdr.
"	Snowden	H.	Sick Leave
"	Cameron	H.	Pln. Comdr.
"	Woodmansey	K.G.	Bde. School.
"	Mitchell	R.J.	152 Co. R.E.
"	Sutcliffe	E.H.	Sick
"	Parry	W.	Leave
"	Hughes	H.D.	Sig. Offr.
"	Marshall	J.W.H.	Pln. Comdr.
"	Kaplan	I.	do
"	Byrne	J.	do
"	Lea	V.G.	do
"	Holt	W.L.	Sick
"	Hardwick	A.	C. of Instn.
"	Lyons	J.W.	Sick
Lt. & Q.M.	Jamieson	A.	Quartermaster
Capt.	McConnell	V.G.	M.O.
"	Thomas	H.G.	Chaplain.

CONFIDENTIAL-

WAR DIARY

OF

The 10th Battalion,

YORK and LANCASTER Regiment.

OCTOBER
1917

Twentysixth Volume.

Army Form C. 2118

WAR DIARY of
10th Bn York & Lancs Regt.
INTELLIGENCE SUMMARY
(Erase heading not required.)

Instructions regarding War Diaries and Intelligence Summaries are contained in F.S. Regs., Part II. and the Staff Manual respectively. Title Pages will be prepared in manuscript.

Place	Date Hour	Summary of Events and Information	Remarks and references to Appendices
TRENCHES	1917 OCT. 1st	Battalion reoccupying front line. Right sub-sector, Right Bde Sector of 37th Division. Sector immediately in front of the YPRES - MENIN Road. 4th Middlesex Regt. on left and chief of 49th Division on right.	
	Night 1/2nd	Battalion relieved in front line by 8th Som. L.I. and moved to close support previously occupied by 8th Som. L.I. after 1st Corp distributed as follows:- 3 Coys close support to 8th Som. L.I., 1 Coy close support to 8th Lincolns Regt.	
	Night 5/6th	63rd Inf Brigade relieved by 112th Inf Bde. Batts relieved in close support by 6th Batt Regt. and moved on relief. 2 Coys to support area SHREWSBURY FOREST and 2 Coys and H.Q. to Reserve Area East of MOUNT SORREL. Battn now in support to 112th Inf. Bde.	
VIERSTRAAT	8th	Battalion relieved in support and reserve area by 13th R.B. and proceeded by bus to the VIERSTRAAT Area, 1 Corps and H.Q. Training Details at BEAVER Camp and 3 Corps to WILLEBEKE Camp. Tanks occupied.	
TRENCHES	10th	63rd Inf Brigade relieve 112th Inf Brigade in line. Previously held by the Bde. Battalion relieve 11th Royal Warwick Regt. in support.	
MONT KOKEREELE	Night 14/15th	63rd Inf Brigade relieved by 116th Inf Brigade 39th Division. Battalion relieved by 13th Sussex Regt. and proceeded by Bus to MONT KOKEREELE Area. PARK CAMP taken overand Details occupied. Details proceeded from BEAVER CAMP to PARK CAMP by route march during afternoon 14th.	
HETEREN	21st	Battalion proceeded by route march to the HETEREN Area. Billets at MOOLENACKER occupied.	
	28th	The Battalion with detachments from the 4th Middlesex Regt. and 8th Louis R. form a working party of 500 O.R. and proceed by Bh. to Camp just NE of YPRES to work in the found area. Detail move by rail tomorrow to area of 4th Middlesex R., H.Q. at BELLE CROIX Farm on the HETEREN - OULTERSTEIN Road.	
	31st	As for 28th when all moves were carried out.	

M.H.Howarth Major
Comdg 10th York & Lancs Regt.

10th York & Lancaster Regiment.

NOMINAL ROLL OF OFFICERS -- OCTOBER 1917.

Rank & Name		Present employment.
Lt-Col. Layton	A.B.	Commanding Officer.
Major. Ostle	H.K.E.	Second in Command.
" Boss	J.G.	Coy Comdr.
Capt. White	R.C.	Platoon Comdr.
" Robinson	A.R.	Coy Comdr.
" Wilkinson	R.M.	Coy Comdr.
" Willis	C.H.S.	a/Adjutant.
Lieut. Ayres	F.	Course of Instruction.
" Dixon	C.B.	Platoon Comdr.
" Sansom	C.P.	Hospital Sick.
" Mitchell	R.J.	Attached 152 Co. R.E.
" Sutcliffe	E.H.	Hospital Sick.
2/Lt. Walne	H.A.	Transport Officer.
" Woodmansey	K.G.	Instructor 63rd Bde School.
" Horsfall	J.R.	Course of Instruction.
" Parry	W.	Coy. Comdr.
" Hughes	W.D.	Signalling Officer.
" Forrest	R.A.	Platoon Comdr.
" Marshall	J.W.M.	Platoon Comdr.
" Lea	W.G.	Platoon Comdr.
" Kaplan	I.	Platoon Comdr.
" Byrne	J.	Course of Instruction.
" Holt	W.L.	Platoon Comdr.
" Cameron	H.	Bombing Officer.
" Stops	T.S.	Platoon Comdr.
" Mansfield	H.	Platoon Comdr.
" Stears	S.C.	Platoon Comdr.
" Mills	H.	Platoon Comdr.
" Hastings	W.B.	Platoon Comdr.
" Moorhouse	G.H.	Platoon Comdr.
" Brierley	S.	Course of Instruction.
" Ranson	H.S.	Platoon Comdr.
" Darricott	W.H.	Platoon Comdr.
" Lyons	F.J.W.	Hospital Sick.
Lt. & Q.M. Jamieson	A.	Quartermaster.
Lieut. Scott (U.S.A., R.C.)	W.F.	Medical Officer.
Capt. Thomas	H.G.	Chaplain.

10th York & Lancaster Regiment.

Fighting Strength on last day of October 1917.

Officers	Other Ranks.	Details included.	
		Officers	Other Ranks.
34	619	7	103

Reinforcements received during October 1917.

Rank & Name of Offrs.	No. of O.R.	Date of arrival.
Major. Ostle. H.K.E.		11/10/17
Capt. Willis C.H.S.		20/10/17
2/Lt. Forrest R.A.		12/10/17
: Cameron H.		16/10/17
: Stears S.C.		16/10/17
: Moorhouse S.H.		17/10/17
: Stops T.S.		24/10/17
: Mansfield H.		do
: Mills H.		do
: Hastings W.B.		25/10/17
: Brierley S.		24/10/17
: Ranson H.		do
: Darricott W.H.		do
	26	4/10/17
	40	7/10/17
	8	9/10/17
	7	12/10/17
	3	19/10/17
	1	21/10/17
	8	24/10/17
	2	26/10/17
	1	28/10/17
	3	29/10/17

Casualties during October 1917.

Rank & Name of Officers	No. of O.R.	Nature of Casualty.
Lieut. W.L. Rockley		Killed 10/10/17
Capt. W.J. Jarrard		Wounded 11/10/17
2/Lt. H. Cameron		do 5/10/17
Capt. W.C. McCONNELL.		do 10/10/17
R.A.M.C.		Died of Wounds 13/10/17
	29	Killed in Action.
	59	Wounded in Action.
	1	Missing in Action.
	49	Evacuated Sick.

CONFIDENTIAL.

WAR DIARY OF THE

10th Battalion York & Lancaster Regiment.

NOVEMBER 1917.

TWENTYSEVENTH   WOLLUME.

Army Form C. 2118

WAR DIARY of
10th BN. YORK & or LANCASTER RET.
INTELLIGENCE SUMMARY
(Erase heading not required.)

Instructions regarding War Diaries and Intelligence Summaries are contained in F.S. Regs., Part II. and the Staff Manual respectively. Title Pages will be prepared in manuscript.

Place	Date Hour	Summary of Events and Information	Remarks and references to Appendices
ST. JEAN Area.	Nov. 1914 1st	Battalion together with detachments from 4th Middx Regt & 8th Line Regt forming Composite Battalion for work in ST. JEAN area under command of Major A.K.E. OSTLE. Accommodated in canvas. Detail of Bn. under command of Major J.C. BOSS billeted near HETEREN.	
HETEREN 6th		HQ at BELLE CROIX Farm on HETEREN-OUTERSTEEN Rd. Working party returned by bus to billets in HETEREN area as formerly occupied. Details rejoined same day.	
LOCRE. 9th		Battalion proceeded by march route to LOCRE. Accommodated at DONCASTER HUTS.	
BOIS. CONFLUENT 10th		Battalion proceeded by march route to BOIS CONFLUENT. Accommodated in dugouts and tents. Working parties provided while in this area for ethics in front line. Transport and QM Store accommodated at CAMBRIDGE CAMP near KEMMEL.	
DEXON CAMP 17th		Battalion proceeded by march route to DEXON Camp on the LOCRE — LA CLYTTE Road. Accommodated in huts. Transport and QM Store remain at CAMBRIDGE CAMP.	
TRENCHES 25th		Battalion proceed to front line relieving 13th R.F. in sector N. of YPRES canal near KLEIN ZILLEBEKE. Column near LA CLYTTE estaim, thence by march route to line. Battalion at SPOIL BANK. Transport and QM Store remain at CAMBRIDGE CAMP.	

D.L Wadsworth
Lt. Col.
Comdg 10th York Lancaster Regt.

10th York & Lancaster Regiment.

Fighting Strength at the end of November 1917.

Officers	Other Ranks	Details included.	
		Officers	Other Ranks
36	584	9	71

Reinforcements received during November 1917.

Rank & Name of Officers	No. of O.R.	Date of Arrival
Lieut. MAGEE J.F.		18/11/17
2/Lt. WRIGHT C.H.		do
: SEDGWICK L.E.S.		do
: NOLAN B.		do
	1	3/11/17
	2	4/11/17
	6	7/11/17
	3	16/11/17
	14	21/11/17
	2	26/11/17

Casualties during November 1917.

Rank & Name of Officers	No. of O.R.	Nature of Casualty
Lieut. SANSOM C.P.		To England Sick 6/11/17
: SUTCLIFFE E.H.		do do 18/11/17
	11	Wounded in Action.
	2	Killed in Action.
	41	Evacuated Sick.

In addition to above.

Lt-Col. LAYTON   A.B. — Left Battalion 1/11/17 to report to War Office. Command of Battalion taken over by Major H.K.E. OSTLE.

10th Battalion York & Lancaster Regiment.

NOMINAL ROLL OF OFFICERS -   NOVEMBER 1917.

Rank & Name.			Present Employment.
Major.	OSTLE	H.K.E.	Commanding Officer.
:	BOSS	J.G.	Brigade School.
Capt.	WHITE	R.C.	Coy Commander.
:	ROBINSON	A.R.	Coy Commander.
:	WILKINSON	R.M.	Hospital Sick.
c :	WILLIS	C.H.S.	Adjutant.
a/:	PARRY	W.	Coy Commander.
Lieut.	AYRES	F.	Coy Commander.
:	DIXON	C.B.	Course of Instruction.
:	MITCHELL	R.J.	Att: 152 Co. R.E.
:	MAGEE	J.F.	Platoon Commander.
2/Lt.	WALNE	H.A.	Transport Officer.
:	WOODMANSEY	K.G.	Brigade School.
:	HORSFALL	J.R.	Town Major. LA CLYTTE.
:	HUGHES	H.D.	Signalling Officer.
:	FORREST	R.A.	Intelligence Officer.
:	MARSHALL	J.W.H.	Platoon Commander.
:	LEA	W.G.	Platoon Commander.
:	KAPLAN	I.	Course of Instruction.
:	CAMERON	H.	Bombing Officer.
:	BYRNE	J.	Course of Instruction.
:	HOLT	W.L.	Leave to U.K.
:	LYONS	F.J.W.	Platoon Commander.
:	STOPS	T.S.	Platoon Commander.
:	MANSFIELD	H.	Course of Instruction.
:	STEARS	S.C.	Platoon Commander.
:	MOORHOUSE	S.H.	Course of Instruction.
:	MILLS	H.	Platoon Commander.
:	HASTINGS	W.B.	Course of Instruction.
:	BRIERLEY	S.	Platoon Commander.
:	RANSON	H.S.	Platoon Commander.
:	DARRICOTT	H.H.	Platoon Commander.
:	WRIGHT	C.H.	Employed, Forward Area.
:	NOLAN	B.	Platoon Commander.
:	SEDGWICK	L.E.S.	Platoon Commander.
Lt.&QM.	JAMIESON	A.	Quartermaster.
Lieut.	SCOTT (U.S.A., M.C.)	W.F.	Medical Officer.
Capt.	THOMAS	H.G.	Chaplain.

Confidential

10th Service Battalion

York & Lancaster Regiment

War Diary

31st December 1917

D.A.

XXVIII Volume

WAR DIARY
or
INTELLIGENCE SUMMARY.
(Erase heading not required.)

Army Form C.2118.

Instructions regarding War Diaries and Intelligence Summaries are contained in F.S. Regs, Part II. and the Staff Manual respectively. Title pages will be prepared in manuscript.

Place	Date	Hour	Summary of Events and Information	Remarks and references to Appendices
TRENCHES	1914 1/10/17		Battalion in front line HOLLEBEKE B Subsector (CANAL to POTSDAM FARM) Battalion H.Qurs in RAILWAY TRENCH. Two Companies in front line (group system) one Company in support in RAILWAY TRENCH. One Company in Reserve at SPOIL BANK	
SUPPORT	6/10/17		Battalion relieved by 8th EAST LANCS. Came out of line into hutments at RIDGE WOOD (Support Area) Were engaged on working parties in front line under R.E. and PIONEER Battalion.	
RESERVE	13/10/17		Battalion marched via CONFUSION - HALLEBAST CORNER and LA CLYTTE to DE ZON CAMP, SCHERPENBURG into Reserve Area.	
TRENCHES	21/10/17		Battalion relieved 13th ROYAL FUSILIERS in front line HOLLEBEKE Sector as previously held. Support and Reserve Companies and Battalion H.Qurs in RAILWAY TRENCH.	
SUPPORT			Battalion relieved by 8th EAST LANCS. Moved to Hutments as previously held in RIDGE WOOD (Support Area)	
			Throughout the month the Transport and Quartermaster Stores were accommodated in CAMBRIDGE CAMP, KEMMEL.	

M.Palin Cotts
Lt. Colonel
½ th York & Lancs Regt.
Comdg 10th York & Lancs Regt.

10th York & Lancaster Regiment
Nominal Roll of Officers 31.12.17

Rank & Name		Remarks
Lt. Col. Ostle H.K.E.	(M.C)	Comdg. Officer
Capt Willis		Adjutant
" Robinson A.R.		Coy Commander
" Wilkinson R.M.		On Leave
" White		On Leave
Major Boos		Attd Brigade School
Lieut. Scott W.S.		Medical Officer
" Jamieson A.		Quartermaster
" Magee J.E.		
" Kaye G.K.C.		Course of Instruction
" Dixon C.B.		Attd 152 Coy R.E.
" Mitchell R.J.		Sick
" Ayres F.		Coy. Commander
2Lt Walne H.A.	(M.C)	Leave
" Hughes H.A.		Signalling Officer
" Forrest R.A.		Intelligence Officer
" Marshall J.W.H.		Asst. Adjutant
" Lea W.G.		Leave
" Kaplan I.		
" Byrne J		Attd Brigade School
" Mansfield H.		
" Stops J.S.		
" Forster I		
" Goad A.E.		
" Hastings W.B.		To Corps School
" Hills A		
" Weld J		
" Hall A		
" Parry W.	(M.C)	Coy Commander
" Cameron K		Coy Commander
" Lyons J.Jr.		Course of Instruction
" Moorhouse S.A.		
" Brierley S.		
" Nolan B		Course of Instruction
" Dickinson C.G.		
" Barratt H.H.		Course of Instruction

Rank & Name	Remarks
2Lt Wright C.H.	Employed Forward Area
" Ranson H.S.	
" Pugh R.N.	Course of Instruction
" Kirrall E.	
" Whitehead M.J.	
" Woodmansey H.C.	Attd Brigade School
" Hanspall J.R.	Town Major, La Clytte
" Sedgwick C.E.S.	Transport Officer

10th Bn York & Lancaster Regt

Strength during month of Decr 1914

Novr 30th 1914   Fighting Strength :- Officers 36
                                      Other Ranks 582

Decr 31st 1914   Fighting Strength :- Officers 44
                                      Other Ranks 664

Increase

Officers :-
Lieut G.L.C. Kaye   Joined 6/12/14
2nd Lt J. Wild   "   9/12/14
  "   J. Forster   "   "
  "   A.R. Pugh   "   "
  "   C.C. Dickinson   "   "
  "   A.E. Goad   "   "
  "   E. Merrall   "   "
  "   H. J. Whitehead   "   11/12/14
  "   A Hall   "   "
Lieut Briggs   "   21/12/14

Other Ranks
   4 O.Rs.   Joined 4/12/14
   2 "   "   8/12/14
   1 "   "   10/12/14
  73 "   "   12/12/14
   4 "   "   13/12/14
  86 "   "   14/12/14
   1 "   "   20/12/14
  21 "   "   26/12/14
                          "   30/12/14

Decrease

Officers
2/Lt Shears   to T.M.B. 12/12/14
2/Lt Holt W.R.   Killed in Action 23/12/14

Other Ranks
   5 Killed in Action
   4 Wounded in Action
  12 Sick wastage
   6 to M.G.C.
   1 to Commission
   1 to T.M.B
   1 to 5t Infy Bde

63rd Brigade.
37th Division.

Battalion broken up in February 1918.

10th BATTALION

YORK & LANCASTER REGIMENT.

JANUARY 1 9 1 8

CONFIDENTIAL

10th BATTALION

YORK & LANCASTER REGIMENT

WAR DIARY
FOR
JANUARY 1918

10th Bn. YORK & LANCASTER REGIMENT.

NOMINAL ROLL OF OFFICERS   JANUARY 1918

Rank	Name		Present Employment
Lieut.Col	OSTLE. M.C.	H.K.E.	Commanding Officer
Major	HUNTER GRAY	G.T.	2nd in Command
"	BOSS	G.J.	Course of Instruction
"	WHITE	R.C.	Coy. Commander
Captain	ROBINSON	A.R.	"
"	WILKINSON	R.M.	"
"	AYRES	F.	
"	WILLIS	C.H.S.	Leave
Lieut.	DIXON	C.B	Attd. 152 Coy. R.E.
"	KAYE	G.H.C.	Pln. Commander
"	MITCHELL	R.J.	Hospital
"	BRIGGS	G.	Pln. Commander
"	MORRIS	H.	"
2/Lieut.	WALNE M.C.	H	Act. Adjutant
"	HORSFALL	R.J.	Pl. Commander
"	PARRY. M.C.	T.	Leave to U.K.
"	CAMERON	H	Leave to U.K.
"	WOODMANSEY	K.G.	Course of Instruction
"	HUGHES	H.D.	Course of Instruction
"	WHITEHEAD	H.J.	Pln. Commander
"	LYONS	F.J.E.	Course of Instruction
"	FORREST R.H.		Intelligence Officer
"	MARSHALL	J.T.L.	Asst. Adjutant
"	SEDGWICK	L.E.C.	Act. Transport Officer
"	LEE	W.G.	Pln. Commander
"	BYRNE	J.	Pln. Commander
"	MANSFIELD	R.	Pln. Commander
"	STOPS	T.S.	Pln. Commander
"	FORSTER	T.	Pln. Commander
"	GOAD	A.E.	Brigade Gas Officer
"	JACKSON	F.C.	Act. Signalling Officer
"	HASTINGS	W.B.	Pln. Commander
"	MILLS	H.	Pln. Commander
"	WILD	J.	Pln. Commander
"	HALL	A.	Course of Instruction
"	MOORHOUSE	S.A.	Pln. Commander
"	BRIERLEY	S.	Pln. Commander
"	NOLAN	B.	Pln. Commander
"	DICKINSON	C.G.	Hospital
"	DARRICOTT	H.H.	Pln. Commander
"	WRIGHT	G.H.	Pln. Commander
"	RANSON	H.S.	Pln. Commander
"	PUGH	H.R.	Pln. Commander
"	MERALL	H.	Course of Instruction
Lieut & Q.Mr.	JAMIESON	A.	Quartermaster
Lieut	SCOTT	R.F.	Medical Officer
Capt	THOMAS	H.G.	Chaplain

T.O.4
S.O.

10th York & Lancaster Regiment.

Fighting Strength at the end of January 1918.

Officers	Other Ranks	Details included Officers	Other Ranks
45	649	12	185

Reinforcements received during January 1918

Rank and Name of Officers	No. of Other Ranks	Date of arrival
Major HUNTER-GRAY G.F.		7.1.18
Lieut. MORRIS H.		23.1.18
2/Lt. JACKSON F.C.		23.1.18
	3	5.1.18
	8	8.1.18
	18	23.1.18
	21	21.1.18
	1	25.1.18

CASUALTIES DURING JANUARY 1918

Rank and Name of Officers	No. of O.Rs.	Nature of Casualty
- -	1	Accidentally Killed
	4	Wounded.
In addition to above		
Lieut Maggee J.T.		To Base "P.B."
2/Lt. Kaplan I.		Transferred to M.G.C. (H.B.)

Lieut. Colonel
Commanding 10th York & Lancaster Regt.

1.2.18

Army Form C. 2118

WAR DIARY
or
INTELLIGENCE SUMMARY
(Erase heading not required.)

Instructions regarding War Diaries and Intelligence Summaries are contained in F.S. Regs., Part II. and the Staff Manual respectively. Title Pages will be prepared in manuscript.

Place	Date	Hour	Summary of Events and Information	Remarks and references to Appendices
In the Field	1.1.18		The Battalion was in Support at RIDGE WOOD CAMP find Working Parties in the front Line	
	5.1.18		On the 5th January it moved into Reserve at DE ZON CAMP but still continued finding Working Parties which were conveyed to the front line by Light Railway.	
	11.1.18		On the 11th January the Battalion moved to DICKEBUSCH (billets and BURGOMASTER CAMP) and found large day and night parties for work on the Corps Reserve Line in front of ZILLEBEKE. MAIDA CAMP was occupied while still on this work, on the 16th.	
	21.1.18		The Brigade moved into the Corps Reserve on the 21st and the Battalion proceeded by train from DICKEBUSCH to EBBLINGHEM and thence by route march to billets in SERCUS. The Regimental Transport proceeded by road via STRAZEELE.	
	28.1.18		On the 28th January the Battalion was inspected by Major General H.B.WILLIAMS, C.B., D.S.O., who announced that the Battalion with others in the Division would shortly be broken up owing to the difficulties its Regimental District was finding in supporting so many Battalions. The General in expressing his regret referred to the very fine work that had been done by the Battalion since it had been formed, especially in the line, and congratulated it on its smart appearance on parade, stating that it was the best turnout of the Battalions he had ever seen.	

www.ingramcontent.com/pod-product-compliance
Lightning Source LLC
Chambersburg PA
CBHW082011220426
43670CB00014B/2598